THE CRUELTY IS THE POINT

THE CRUELTY IS THE POINT

THE PAST, PRESENT, AND FUTURE OF TRUMP'S AMERICA

ADAM SERWER

**ONE WORLD
NEW YORK**

Published in the United States by One World, an imprint of
Random House, a division of Penguin Random House LLC, New York.

ONE WORLD and colophon are registered trademarks of
Penguin Random House LLC.

Grateful acknowledgment is made to *The Atlantic* for permission to reprint
the following essays by Adam Serwer: "Is This the Second Redemption?"
(*The Atlantic,* November 10, 2016), © 2016 The Atlantic Monthly
Group LLC; "The Myth of the Kindly General Lee" (*The Atlantic,* June 4,
2017) and "The Nationalist's Delusion" (*The Atlantic,* November 20, 2017),
© 2017 The Atlantic Monthly Group LLC; "Why Tamika Mallory Won't
Condemn Farrakhan" (*The Atlantic,* March 11, 2018) and "The Cruelty Is
the Point" (*The Atlantic,* October 3, 2018), © 2018 The Atlantic Monthly
Group LLC; "White Nationalism's Deep American Roots" (*The Atlantic,*
April 2019), "What We Do Now Will Define Us Forever" (*The Atlantic,*
July 18, 2019), and "Civility Is Overrated" (*The Atlantic,* December 2019),
© 2019 The Atlantic Monthly Group LLC; "The Coronavirus Was an
Emergency Until Trump Found Out Who Was Dying" (*The Atlantic,* May 8,
2020) and "The New Reconstruction" (*The Atlantic,* October 2020), © 2020
The Atlantic Monthly Group LLC. Reprinted with permission of *The Atlantic.*

Hardback ISBN 978-0-593-23080-0
Ebook ISBN 978-0-593-23081-7

Printed in the United States of America on acid-free paper

oneworldlit.com
randomhousebooks.com

2 4 6 8 9 7 5 3 1

First Edition

Book design by Susan Turner

For my grandparents, Zachary and Blanche, Drew and Dorothea

The negro still hopes that some day the United States will become as great intellectually and morally as she is materially, to protect and honor all her citizens regardless of "race, color, or previous condition," and thus make her professions a living reality.

IDA B. WELLS, May 28, 1894

CONTENTS

A NOTE TO
THE READER

THROUGHOUT THIS BOOK, I USE LOWERCASE WHEN REFERRING TO racial terms such as "black" or "white." This is against the prevailing trend in letters, but I do it because I fear that capitalization reinforces the notion that race is a biological reality rather than a social reality. Racism and bigotry are very real, but race itself is a biological fiction.

PROMISES MADE, PROMISES KEPT

THE DAY DONALD TRUMP DESCENDED THE GOLDEN ESCALATOR IN Trump Tower in 2015 to announce his presidential campaign, he made a lot of promises. He said he was going to "rebuild our infrastructure, our bridges, our roadways, our airports." He insisted that he would "save Medicare, Medicaid, and Social Security without cuts." He would "reduce our eighteen trillion dollars in debt." The Affordable Care Act would be repealed and "replaced with something much better for everybody." He promised to be "the greatest jobs president that god ever created." America's politicians were "controlled fully by the lobbyists, by the donors, and by the special interests, fully." But Trump would not be controlled.

The media at the time covered the speech with headlines like THE TEN BEST LINES FROM DONALD TRUMP'S ANNOUNCE-MENT SPEECH and THE BEST MOMENTS FROM DONALD TRUMP'S ANNOUNCEMENT SPEECH. An article in *Politico* gushed that "it's hard to pick just ten." *The Huffington Post* announced it was relegating coverage of Trump to its entertainment section. After all, this was the birtherism spouting host of *The Apprentice*, a reality show star the sitting president had dismissed as a "carnival barker." There was no way that Trump's overt bigotry—his demonizing of Latino immigrants as violent criminals and Muslims as terrorists, his caustic misogyny toward any woman with the temerity to criticize him—would fly in a nation that had just elected a black president, no matter what he was promising.

A lot of very smart people treated Trump like the whole thing was a big joke. At the time, I was at the BuzzFeed News offices in New York City, standing around a television screen tuned to CNN with my colleagues. The grotesque tone of the Trump years was still new and hard to describe. Later, my colleague John Stanton, a tall, tattooed former bouncer who is as kind as he looks tough, said to me after attending a few of Trump's rallies, "I think he's going to be president."

I was doubtful at the time—remember, this was before Trump steamrolled a bunch of guys who generated a year's worth of magazine cover stories on the next Republican president—but what Stanton said stuck with me. Win or lose, the dust Trump was kicking up would linger in the lungs. I started poring over old texts about racism, immigration, and nativism, like John Higham's *Strangers in the Land*. I found disturbing echoes of Trump's rhetorical style in Hannah Arendt's description of Stalinist and Nazi apparatchiks in *The Origins of Totalitarianism* and had epiphanies about the fragility of American democracy reading W.E.B. Du Bois's *Black Reconstruction in America*. Over the course of his presidency, I would write dozens of essays that drew on that history for *The Atlantic*, essays in which I tried to show how the ideological currents of the past had shaped the present. The realization dawned that Trump, win or lose, was summoning to the fore the most treacherous forces in American history and conducting them with the ease of a grand maestro.

But could he win a Republican primary? For the previous eight years, the GOP had piously espoused their small-government fiscal conservatism in opposing Barack Obama, and here was a foul-mouthed, bombastic television personality who had a documented history of liberal policy positions on certain issues and no record of conservative achievement. Republican elites—elected officials, right-wing intellectuals, ambitious staffers—denied that this heretic preacher could captivate their supposed small-government flock with the gospel of white identity politics.

They were wrong. They were wrong because they misunderstood their own base and the potency of Trump's appeal to a theme that would emerge more distinctly later in his general election campaign, the "rigged system." Trump adviser Roger Stone urged Trump to espouse two simple claims: that "the system is rigged against the citizens" and that, unlike other politicians, he "cannot be bought." These themes were specific enough to be evocative but vague enough to be misinterpreted. The "rigged system" was one thing to Trump supporters and another to many of the reporters, analysts, and intellectuals tasked with understanding what it meant.

After Trump's unexpected victory, journalists attributed the win to his success in attacking an unfair economic system, which had served so many millions of Americans poorly. The slow, grueling comeback from the 2008 recession, the magnitude of the housing crisis, the absence of wage growth, the plague of the opioid epidemic—these struggles and politicians' failure to address them effectively left the door open for an outsider who promised to fix them. Trump spoke often of these troubles as a candidate, but his presidency would reveal his true priorities.

Five years later, the legacy of Trump's presidency and his promises can be addressed. There never was an infrastructure bill. Trump's budgets consistently proposed cuts to the social programs he vowed not to touch. He did little to combat the opioid epidemic he promised to end, with deaths rising by the end of his tenure. The national debt Trump promised to erase has ballooned by almost $7.8 trillion. Trump's failed effort to repeal the Affordable Care Act and replace it with nothing remains the nadir of his public approval, surpassing even the days following his incitement of an armed attack on the Capitol building in an effort to overturn his 2020 election loss. Trump has the worst jobs record of any president since 1939, with more than three million lost. He is, in fact, the worst jobs president "god ever created," despite inheriting an economy that had finally begun to boom in the later years of the Obama administration. The promises of better health-care didn't materialize, and the job and wage growth from the economy he inherited were crushed by the pandemic he refused to address. Those were not the promises Trump kept.

Yet Trump's grip on the Republican Party is ironclad. The majority of conservative voters are devoted to the for-mer president and echo both his intolerance for the slightest deviations from total obedience and his appetite for punishing dissenters—lifelong Republican politicians who chose their duties over upholding Trump's will instantly found themselves inundated with harassment and threats of violence. Trump's word is truth hewn in stone, even if it contradicts something he said the day before. That doctrine is then amplified by a conservative media committed to ensuring their audiences' fidelity to their leader at any cost, whether that means lying to them about a deadly pandemic or misleading them about the results of an election. Their gospel is as he tells it.

Trump broke many of his policy promises, particularly those that diverged from Republican economic orthodoxy. But those policy promises weren't the only ones he made, in that initial speech or elsewhere. His characterization of Mexican undocumented immigrants as "rapists" and "drug dealers," his vows to ban Muslim travel to the United States, his undisguised contempt for black Americans—these were also promises. They were promises to fight against a rigged system—not the one fixed in favor of the wealthy that Bernie Sanders railed against but a different rigged system, one that elevated the unworthy over the worthy.

This was a system that coddled undocumented Latino immigrants with benefits denied to citizens. A system that gave black Americans undeserved benefits white Americans did not receive. A system that welcomed Middle Eastern refugees who would inevitably turn into terrorists, while ignoring the people who, as the cliché goes, "worked hard and played by the rules." It was a system in which you couldn't even talk frankly about crime, or terrorism, or religion, without some mouthy liberal disagreeing or calling you racist.

That was the system Trump's most committed supporters were angry about. It didn't matter that most of these griev-ances were false or—like political disagreement—part of liv-ing in a free society. What mattered was the sense of loss that accompanied the perception that a certain kind of conserva-tive cultural and political hegemony was coming to an end. For millions whose identities became intertwined with Trump and his politics, that loss was embodied by the election of the first black president and the possibility that Hillary Clinton might be his successor. But others were driven to Trump by the rapidity of recent cultural change, such as the swift acceptance of same-sex marriage, the vicarious thrill of watching Trump put ambitious women in their place, the growing diversity of their cities and towns, or simply the fact that the things Donald Trump was saying—the things that made perfect sense to them—were greeted with outrage. Faced with the existential threat posed by their fellow citizens, anything Trump might do—no matter how lawless, destructive, or cruel—was justified. Trump didn't need to read William F. Buckley, Edmund Burke, or Russell Kirk to understand how to appeal to American conservatives. He just had to watch Fox News and study its success at finding new sources of rage and fear to sustain its audience's perpetual sense of being under siege.

Trump didn't interfere with the actual rigged system. His greatest legislative achievement was cutting his own taxes and those of his donors, the populist president signing a tax-cut bill even more regressive than that of the previous Republican president, who himself was the son of another president. The slow wage growth of the recovery from the Great Recession was wiped out by Trump's unwillingness to confront the coronavirus epidemic, which led to half a million American deaths as of this writing. Amid all the families shattered by the plague, Trump to this day regards himself as its greatest victim.

Yet his voters stood by him, because he kept the promises that mattered to them. He imposed harsh restrictions on immigration and especially asylum. He attempted to rig the census to enhance the political power of white voters at the expense of black and Latino voters. He encouraged police to abuse suspects, then cheered them as they crushed protests against brutality. He railed against liberal censorship, then

imposed speech restrictions on universities, federal agencies, and government contractors to silence talk of systemic
racism. He barred transgender people from serving in the
military and pushed to repeal anti-discrimination protections
for LGBT people elsewhere. He imposed new restrictions
on abortion and appointed judges and justices—now fully a
third of the Supreme Court—inclined to gut or overturn *Roe
v. Wade*. His Justice Department all but abandoned fighting
racial discrimination in voting, employment, and education.
In the twilight of his administration, he made a futile attempt
to further rig the system so that he would remain in power.

These were the promises that actually mattered to his
most committed supporters—the promises to use the power
of the state to wage war against the people many Trump voters hold responsible for the state of the world and their place
in it. These were the promises he kept.

This book is a catalog of how the Trump administration
kept those promises and why. It is also a guide to the social
and ideological impulses that brought Trump to the fore. The
ideological currents that swept Trump into the White House
are not some aberration—they are essential forces of political conflict in American history that have been concealed by
accidents of conservative sentimentality and liberal optimism.

For this book, I selected the essays I think most effectively
capture the connection between the present and the past, adding introductions written at the end of the Trump administration to contextualize them. Although the result is by no means
an exhaustive exploration of Trumpism—that would require
more than one book—I have chosen these pieces because I
felt they best filled the gaps in American public memory.

This book also includes new pieces on subjects I was
unable to publish during the Trump presidency, including the

myth of the legal immigrant from the turn of the century, the internal Jewish community divisions exacerbated by Trumpism, and how the local politics of police unions went national, and a concluding essay on the past and present of American authoritarianism. This book is a story of the America we turned out to be rather than the one many of us wished we were. It is also a warning that, despite Trump's defeat, the unfreedom promised by his rise may yet come to pass. Reporters are often taught that journalism is the first draft of history, but American journalism is afflicted by a presentism, a kind of goldfish memory that struggles to think outside the present or recent past. That makes a certain amount of sense—the old chestnut is that the "news" is what is "new"—but an old editor of mine, David Corn of *Mother Jones,* used to say that the news is also what people have forgotten. The reactions to Trump, whether the enthusiasm or apprehension on the right or the disbelief on the left, showed that Americans had forgotten quite a bit, and I have spent the last five years trying to help people remember.

1

THE CRUELTY OF
BACKLASH

MANY PEOPLE WOKE UP ON NOVEMBER 9, 2016, FEELING LIKE their country hated them.

Donald Trump had run a campaign that, from its inception, sought to blame those he defined as foreigners for the failures of modern society. He announced his campaign by declaring that Mexican immigrants were "rapists" "bringing drugs" and "crime." He called for "a total and complete shutdown of Muslims" entering the United States and regaled campaign audiences with apocryphal tales of how dipping bullets in pigs' blood had helped Americans suppress a Muslim insurgency in the Philippines. He decried the "war on police," calling for nationwide stop and frisk and comparing black American neighborhoods unfavorably to "war zones." Every one of these problems, Trump assured his supporters, could be solved with the ruthless application of state force: arrest, execution, exclusion, or expulsion. And then just short of a majority of 2016 voters, more than 60 million people, decided to put him in charge of the country.

If you were part of, or related to, one of the groups Trump

targeted so effectively, you woke up on November 9 with the knowledge that some, perhaps many, of your work colleagues, perhaps your friends and family members, chose a man who promised to use the violence of the state to keep people like you in your place.

My mother and uncle were born into the long shadow of Redemption, the white-supremacist backlash to Reconstruction, in Florida. During Reconstruction, Southern states like Florida briefly experimented with multiracial democracy, only to fall into the shadow of racial authoritarianism in the 1870s. In the 1940s, when my mother was born, Florida was a Jim Crow state. Black voters were disenfranchised by law, schools, public transportation, and restaurants were segregated, and interracial marriage was banned. All of these laws were backed by the threat of both state and vigilante violence, in a state where more than three hundred Americans would be lynched between 1877 and 1950.

Like many other black southerners in that era, my grandparents packed up and fled north, settling in New York State, where their children would not have to attend segregated schools. What they also brought with them was the memory of racial backlash—the knowledge that previously unimaginable progress like that of the South during Reconstruction could be attained and then quickly destroyed. If a black president seemed the stuff of fiction prior to Obama, the racial backlash that followed—the election of a president who rose to power on the slander that the first black president was not even an American citizen—was all too familiar.

I wrote "Is This the Second Redemption?" shortly after the 2016 election results, with the knowledge that this backlash would not be as complete as the one that followed Reconstruction. Unlike the backlash of the late 1870s, Trump had won because his support was ideally geographically distributed for the electoral college, not because he had commanded support from a majority of the electorate. Trumpism did not command anything close to the political consensus among white Americans that white supremacy did at the close of the nineteenth century.

Nevertheless, he had been elected to destroy Obama's legacy, and for those Americans who were not as familiar with this chapter in America's past, I felt that Redemption was a useful analytical frame for what the future might hold. These family legacies are obviously not necessary to understand American history. But in a country where the typical education consciously elides the dark currents of our past, or portrays them as long vanquished, the living memories of your flesh and blood provide a potent counternarrative.

Unfortunately, much—though not all—of what I described in this essay was prescient. The Civil Rights Division under Trump filed a single voting-rights case in four years, and his Commerce Department tried and almost succeeded in deliberately using the census to increase white voting power at minority voters' expense. The Trump Justice Department abandoned systemic oversight of police departments, while the president himself vocally encouraged police brutality to audiences of officers who responded with applause. Migrant youth were deliberately separated from their parents and placed in squalid camps, for the express purpose of torturing such families into giving up their hope for a better life in America. The conservative-controlled Supreme Court blessed Trump's travel ban targeting Muslim countries once the administration removed explicit language referencing religion. In doing so, the right-wing justices wrote the blueprint for Trump-era discrimination: Even when the president announces his bigoted intentions to the world, the Supreme Court will turn a blind eye as long as the lawyers can provide a neutral-sounding pretext and adequate legal paperwork. But Trump's bluster and cruelty were sometimes a disadvantage. Republicans' attempt to repeal the Affordable Care Act—which was responsible for ensuring coverage for tens of millions of people—failed by a single vote, that of Senator John McCain, Obama's 2008 rival and a frequent target of Trump's insults.

Trump's defeat in the 2020 election may take the country in a new direction, but his lingering grip on his party suggests Trumpism will endure. The former president's most recent campaign was notable for shifting his rhetorical focus from enemies abroad to enemies within, making other Americans internal foreigners with no legitimate claim to govern. This too is an old American strain of thought—in the ransacking of the Capitol in early January 2021, one can still see the echoes of Redemption, repeated as both tragedy and farce. It was the first time that a sitting president had encouraged a mob to attack the legislature in an attempt to overturn an election. But throughout the South in the late nineteenth century, scenes of insurrectionary political violence were common. As with the so-called Redeemers, defeat at the ballot box may inspire further violence in pursuit of political dominance.

IS THIS
THE SECOND
REDEMPTION?

NOVEMBER 10, 2016

BETWEEN 1870 AND 1901, THERE WERE TWENTY BLACK REPRE-
sentatives in Congress and two black United States senators.
Between 1901 and 1929, there were none.

Those simple numbers offer a small glimpse of the total-
ity of the Southern counterrevolution against Reconstruction after the Civil War and the subsequent bloody Southern
Redemption, after which the political power of black Southerners was effectively extinguished. The radical dream of
an interracial politics, with its attendant federal investment
and redistribution of resources toward the poor, had been
destroyed. The optimism of emancipation leading to racial
equality in the South was annihilated with a completeness
that is difficult to fathom.

Southern Redemption had been led by white Democrats
and their paramilitary allies, but crucial to their decisive victory was the willingness of the Republican Party to abandon

black Southerners to their fate. "Many Northern Republicans also hoped to use the crisis to jettison a Reconstruction policy they believed had failed," wrote historian Eric Foner in *Reconstruction*. "The freedmen, insisted former Ohio Gov. Jacob D. Cox, must moderate their 'new kindled ambition' for political influence and recognize that they lacked whites' 'hereditary faculty of self-government.' Ulysses S. Grant, who had sent federal troops into the South to suppress the Ku Klux Klan, privately concluded that the 15th Amendment, adopted to protect the freedmen's right to vote, had been a 'mistake.' "

House speaker Paul Ryan announced Wednesday that "this needs to be a time of redemption, not a time of recrimination." But however hopefully the speaker meant it, the idea that America needs to be redeemed, like the notion that it needs to be made great again, rests on the notion that something has gone horribly wrong.

The notion that Trump's victory and the perception that society must be "redeemed" have nothing to do with a racist backlash might be comforting, but they fly in the face of available statistical evidence.

A Reuters survey in June found Trump supporters were more likely than Clinton supporters to see blacks as "criminal," "unintelligent," "lazy," and "violent," though Clinton supporters were certainly not immune to those prejudices. Analysis by the RAND Corporation's Presidential Election Panel Survey found that "Trump performs best among Americans who express more resentment toward African Americans and immigrants and who tend to evaluate whites more favorably than minority groups." And even those Trump voters who did not approve of his remarks and policy proposals aimed at black people, Muslims, and Latinos did not find them disqualifying.

The election of Donald Trump and the complete dominance of the Republican Party both in the federal government and in the states may usher in a new era of Redemption, one that could see the seemingly astounding racial progress of having a black president relegated to little more than symbolism.

The federal government currently protects people's ability to find a home, to make a living, to cast a ballot, to worship freely, to drink clean water and breathe clean air. A Trump administration can leave these rights unprotected for the people most vulnerable to having them denied because of the color of their skin or their faith, without having to ask Congress for a single vote on legislation.

The conservative backlash against Obama limited much of his agenda after the first two years to things that could be achieved by the executive branch. Trump can easily reverse these steps, beginning, as Bloomberg reports, with Obama's extension of relief from deportation to undocumented immigrants. That will affect some 750,000 people. Trump can shift deportation priorities so that undocumented immigrants previously considered a low priority for deportation—mothers with U.S.-citizen children, for example—no longer will be. That proposed ban on Muslim immigration? He won't even need Congress.

The entire civil-rights enforcement apparatus of the federal government will be under the control of a candidate who campaigned on using the power of the state against religious and ethnic minorities, proposing to ban Muslim immigration, establish a "deportation force" to purge the country of America's largely Latino population of undocumented immigrants, and establish "national stop and frisk," a policy that has targeted black communities. The Obama administration's aggressive enforcement of anti-discrimination law in housing, employment, and voting is likely to suffer. The Obama era saw an unprecedented rise in the Justice Department's efforts to combat racial discrimination in local policing. Trump campaigned with the explicit support of unions representing law enforcement and on "giving power back to the police."

Will a Trump administration continue to enforce federal religious-freedom laws in cases where local jurisdictions attempt to prevent mosques from being built? Will it advocate for Muslim women who are told by their employers they are not allowed to cover their hair at work? Would a Trump Equal Opportunity Employment Commission continue Obama's aggressive interpretation of civil-rights law protecting LGBT workers? Should women who are sexually harassed by their bosses expect that a president who bragged about sexual assault will defend their rights? Will the strict rules on sexual assault on college campuses survive in the Trump Department of Education? In each of these cases, the Obama administration moved to use federal power to protect the rights of minorities; absent the same commitment, they will not enjoy similar protections under Trump.

The Obama administration promulgated strict rules under the Clean Air and Clean Water acts. Republicans have already indicated their intention to revoke them, consequences that will be borne by everyone but most explicitly by the poor and people of color.

With the Republican dominance of the federal government, however, even Obama's legislative accomplishments are in peril. Congressional Republicans have long sought to repeal the Affordable Care Act, which would not only allow health-insurance companies to discriminate on the basis of preexisting conditions but would strip health-care coverage from 15 million of the poorest Americans. The 2010 Wall

Street Reform Act, including the Consumer Financial Protection Bureau, the agency built specifically to prevent another 2008-style economic crisis, will be on the chopping block. The CFPB's attempts to prevent financial services from preying on poor and working-class Americans is in peril. The impact of repealing these laws will fall most harshly on people of color, but poor and working-class whites will be hurt as well.

The Democrats will resist—how strongly or effectively, we will soon see. But history suggests they will fail. And with a conservative majority on the Supreme Court, there would be little else standing in the Republicans' way.

As Foner wrote in *Reconstruction*, "1877 marked a decisive retreat from the idea, born during the Civil War, of a powerful national state protecting the fundamental rights of American citizens." But the consequences were also dire for the white poor, for the simple reason that they stood to benefit from an activist government as well. "While the region's new upper class of planters, merchants, and industrialists prospered," Foner writes, "the majority of Southerners of both races sank deeper and deeper into poverty." Similarly, Republican dominance of government across the nation will reverse the Obama-era expectation that the state should work to even the playing field between the haves and have-nots.

The broad economic devastation wrought by the Redeemers might have been seen by Republicans as a political opportunity to forge an interracial coalition. But it was not to be. "The failure to develop an effective long-term appeal to white voters made it increasingly difficult for Republicans to combat the racial politics of the Redeemers," Foner argued.

Democrats now face a renewed white-identity politics whose appeal will be immensely difficult to neutralize, and the notion that a more vigorous left-wing economics will return the white working class to the Democratic fold is likely a fantasy. The last Democrat to come close to winning the white vote was Bill Clinton, who combined his economic populism with promises to "end welfare as we know it" and advertised his willingness to use state violence against black Americans, turning the execution of Ricky Ray Rector to his political advantage.

The uncomfortable truth is that, whether you're Donald Trump or Bill Clinton, economic populism is most effective in American politics when it is paired with appeals to racism. Maybe the Democrats can and will find a way to do so without such appeals. By the time they do, it may simply be too late to stop what is coming.

The Republican Party of yesteryear championed amendments abolishing slavery and seeking to protect the rights of the freedmen. It still abandoned black Americans when the political cost of defending them became too high. Today's Democratic Party is perfectly capable of doing the same to elements of the diverse coalition that twice secured the presidency for Barack Obama.

So America stands at the precipice of a Second Redemption. Unlike the first, it was not achieved by violence and has not ended in the total disenfranchisement of people of color. Its immediate consequences may not be as total or as dire. Yet it has a democratic legitimacy that extends far beyond the American South. The erasure of the legacy of the first black president of the United States will be executed by a man who rose to power on the basis of his embrace of the slander that Obama was not born in America.

Early historians of Reconstruction depicted it not as the terrible demise of interracial government but as an era when corrupt Republicans violated the South's natural order by "forcing" self-government on primitive blacks who were unprepared for the responsibility. "To the bulk of the white South," Foner wrote, "it had become axiomatic that Reconstruction had been a time of 'savage tyranny'" that "accomplished not one useful result, and left behind it not one pleasant recollection." Prepare for the Obama era to be framed in similar terms.

It took another few decades of scholarship, and the civil-rights movement, to shift the public perception of the era toward the truth. The few dissenting voices, like W.E.B. Du Bois, were ignored at the time and vindicated by historians only after decades of hindsight.

Perhaps the Trump administration will diverge from what Trump himself has promised to achieve. Perhaps he will move to enact his campaign-trail promises and voters will repudiate his agenda. But it seems more likely that someday Americans will look back at the Obama era much as historians have now come to look at Reconstruction: as a tragic moment of lost promise, a failed opportunity to build a more just and equitable society.

2

THE CRUELTY OF
THE LOST CAUSE

THE POPULARITY OF "THE MYTH OF THE KINDLY GENERAL LEE" was an unhappy accident. During the spring and summer of 2017, a movement to remove statues honoring the Confederacy—which had begun in earnest years earlier, after the massacre of black churchgoers in Charleston by a white supremacist—had gathered momentum. In May, then–New Orleans mayor Mitch Landrieu had removed four such memorials, including three devoted to the Confederate military leaders Robert E. Lee, Jefferson Davis, and P.G.T. Beauregard and one devoted to the 1874 victory of the terrorist White League over New Orleans's outnumbered and outgunned integrated police force.

The Battle of Liberty Place, as it was known to its victors, represented the violent reimposition of white-supremacist rule in Louisiana. It was not officially a Confederate victory, but if you take the view of W.E.B. Du Bois that Reconstruction was but an extension of the Civil War, then it could hardly be anything else.

I wrote "The Myth of the Kindly General Lee" around

Memorial Day of that year, as the debate was heating up over retaining Confederate statues in places of honor. Memorial Day, itself a holiday first celebrated by black Union troops in 1865, seemed an appropriate moment to pen a reconsideration of Lee's legacy with all that we now knew about his life and beliefs. The argument that removing such statues would amount to an erasure of history was risible even to their defenders—this was clear in the sense that arguments for retaining them relied on erasing what these statues and memorials actually represented. The most prominent of these myths was that Lee was anti-slavery, a reluctant Confederate, a quiet believer in racial equality, and magnanimous in defeat. Lee was none of these things.

An uncomfortable impediment to this false recollection of Lee was a resurgent white-supremacist movement, empowered by their belief that the election of Donald Trump represented a rising white racial consciousness they could exploit. Seeking converts, they attached themselves to the anti-removal backlash among conservatives, who argued that getting rid of the statues amounted to misguided political correctness. The intervention of the so-called alt-right was inconvenient for such defenders, because the white supremacists' understanding of the memorials and what they represented was more accurate than that of the mainstream conservatives who defended them. What they wanted was to win converts from the mainstream right by exploiting their outrage over the PC left supposedly slandering American heroes.

But the Confederate statues were not simple memorials to the dead. They were erected not after the Civil War but to celebrate the disenfranchisement of black men and the restoration of the South's traditional racial hierarchy in the late nineteenth and early twentieth centuries, decades later.

A second resurgence occurred in the middle of the twentieth century, as the civil-rights movement began. They are monuments to white supremacy, built to remind black Americans of their rightful place in the nation's racial hierarchy: at the bottom.

The piece on Lee was popular in June, when it was first published. After all, so many Americans have grown up with the mythological Lee and not the Lee who really was. But the essay truly took off in August, after the Unite the Right white-supremacist rally in Charlottesville. By gathering in defense of the Lee statue there, the organizers hoped the protest would bring overt white-supremacist groups back into the political mainstream. Instead, the event turned into a Klan riot in which one of the attendees murdered an anti-racist counterprotester named Heather Heyer.

The violence, and particularly Heyer's death, helped discredit the individual personalities and groups associated with the rally. But they were not without their influential defenders and sympathizers. Trump, who insisted shortly after Heyer's death that there were "very fine people on both sides" of the rally, would defend both Lee and the protesters again two years later. "People were there protesting the taking down of the monument of Robert E. Lee," Trump said to reporters in 2019. "Everybody knows that."

Why they were protesting the Lee statue removal was left unsaid. When it comes to Lee, the truth often is.

THE MYTH OF THE KINDLY GENERAL LEE

JUNE 4, 2017

THE STRANGEST PART ABOUT THE CONTINUED PERSONALITY CULT of Robert E. Lee is how few of the qualities his admirers profess to see in him he actually possessed.

Memorial Day has the tendency to conjure up old arguments about the Civil War. That's understandable; it was created to mourn the dead of a war in which the Union was nearly destroyed, when half the country rose up in rebellion in defense of slavery. This year, the removal of Lee's statue in New Orleans has inspired a new round of commentary about Lee, not to mention protests on his behalf by white supremacists.

The myth of Lee goes something like this: He was a brilliant strategist and devoted Christian man who abhorred slavery and labored tirelessly after the war to bring the country back together.

There is little truth in this. Lee was a devout Christian,

and historians regard him as an accomplished tactician. But despite his ability to win individual battles, his decision to fight a conventional war against the more densely populated and industrialized North is considered by many historians to have been a fatal strategic error.

But even if one conceded Lee's military prowess, he would still be responsible for the deaths of hundreds of thousands of Americans in defense of the South's authority to own millions of human beings as property because they were black. Lee's elevation is a key part of a 150-year-old propaganda campaign designed to erase slavery as the cause of the war and whitewash the Confederate cause as a noble one. That ideology is known as the Lost Cause, and as the historian David Blight writes, it provided a "foundation on which Southerners built the Jim Crow system."

There are unwitting victims of this campaign—those who lack the knowledge to separate history from sentiment. Then there are those whose reverence for Lee relies on replacing the actual Lee with a mythical figure who never truly existed.

In the *Richmond Times-Dispatch*, R. David Cox wrote that "for white supremacist protesters to invoke his name violates Lee's most fundamental convictions." In the conservative publication *Townhall*, Jack Kerwick concluded that Lee was "among the finest human beings that has ever walked the Earth." John Daniel Davidson, in an essay for *The Federalist*, opposed the removal of the Lee statue in part on the grounds that Lee "arguably did more than anyone to unite the country after the war and bind up its wounds." Praise for Lee of this sort has flowed forth from past historians and presidents alike.

This is too divorced from Lee's actual life to even be classed as fan fiction; it is simply historical illiteracy.

White supremacy does not "violate" Lee's "most

fundamental convictions." White supremacy was one of Lee's most fundamental convictions.

Lee was a slave owner—his own views on slavery were explicated in an 1856 letter that is often misquoted to give the impression that Lee was some kind of abolitionist. In the letter, he describes slavery as "a moral & political evil," but goes on to explain that:

> I think it however a greater evil to the white man than to the black race, & while my feelings are strongly enlisted in behalf of the latter, my sympathies are more strong for the former. The blacks are immeasurably better off here than in Africa, morally, socially & physically. The painful discipline they are undergoing is necessary for their instruction as a race, & I hope will prepare & lead them to better things. How long their subjugation may be necessary is known & ordered by a wise Merciful Providence. Their emancipation will sooner result from the mild & melting influence of Christianity than the storms & tempests of fiery Controversy.

The argument here is that slavery is bad for white people, good for black people, and, most important, better than abolitionism; emancipation must wait for divine intervention. That black people might not want to be slaves does not enter into the equation; their opinion on the subject of their own bondage is not even an afterthought to Lee.

Lee's cruelty as a slave master was not confined to physical punishment. In *Reading the Man*, the historian Elizabeth Brown Pryor's portrait of Lee through his writings, Pryor writes that "Lee ruptured the Washington and Custis tradition of respecting slave families" by hiring them off to other plantations, and that "by 1860 he had broken up every family but one on the estate, some of whom had been together since Mount Vernon days." The separation of slave families was one of the most unfathomably devastating aspects of slavery, and Pryor wrote that Lee's slaves regarded him as "the worst man I ever see."

The trauma of rupturing families lasted lifetimes for the enslaved—it was, as my colleague Ta-Nehisi Coates described it, "a kind of murder." After the war, thousands of the emancipated searched desperately for kin lost to the market for human flesh, fruitlessly for most. In *Reconstruction*, the historian Eric Foner quotes a Freedmen's Bureau agent who notes of the emancipated, "In their eyes, the work of emancipation was incomplete until the families which had been dispersed by slavery were reunited."

Lee's heavy hand on the Arlington, Virginia, plantation, Pryor writes, nearly led to a slave revolt, in part because the enslaved had been expected to be freed upon their previous master's death, and Lee had engaged in a dubious legal interpretation of his will in order to keep them as his property, one that lasted until a Virginia court forced him to free them.

When two of his slaves escaped and were recaptured, Lee either beat them himself or ordered the overseer to "lay it on well." Wesley Norris, one of the slaves who was whipped, recalled that "not satisfied with simply lacerating our naked flesh, Gen. Lee then ordered the overseer to thoroughly wash our backs with brine, which was done."

Every state that seceded mentioned slavery as the cause in their declarations of secession. Lee's beloved Virginia was no different, accusing the federal government of "perverting" its powers "not only to the injury of the people of Virginia, but to the oppression of the Southern Slaveholding States." Lee's decision to fight for the South can only be described as a choice to fight for the continued existence of human bondage in America—even though for the Union, it was not at first a war for emancipation.

During his invasion of Pennsylvania, Lee's Army of Northern Virginia enslaved free black Americans and brought them back to the South as property. Pryor writes that "evidence links virtually every infantry and cavalry unit in Lee's army" to the abduction of free black Americans, "with the activity under the supervision of senior officers."

Soldiers under Lee's command at the Battle of the Crater in 1864 massacred black Union soldiers who tried to surrender. Then, in a spectacle hatched by Lee's senior corps commander, A. P. Hill, the Confederates paraded the Union survivors through the streets of Petersburg to the slurs and jeers of the Southern crowd. Lee never discouraged such behavior. As the historian Richard Slotkin wrote in *No Quarter: The Battle of the Crater*, "His silence was permissive."

The presence of black soldiers on the field of battle shattered every myth that the South's slave empire was built on: the happy docility of slaves, their intellectual inferiority, their cowardice, their inability to compete with white people. As Pryor writes, "Fighting against brave and competent African Americans challenged every underlying tenet of southern society." The Confederate response to this challenge was to visit every possible atrocity and cruelty upon black soldiers whenever possible, from enslavement to execution.

As the historian James McPherson recounts in *Battle Cry of Freedom*, in October of that same year, Lee proposed an exchange of prisoners with the Union general Ulysses S. Grant. "Grant agreed, on condition that black soldiers be exchanged 'the same as white soldiers.'" Lee's response was that "negroes belonging to our citizens are not considered subjects of exchange and were not included in my proposition." Because slavery was the cause for which Lee fought, he could hardly be expected to easily concede, even at the cost of the freedom of his own men, that black people should be treated as soldiers and not things. Grant refused the offer, telling Lee that "government is bound to secure to all persons received into her armies the rights due to soldiers." Despite its desperate need for soldiers, the Confederacy did not relent from this position until a few months before Lee's surrender.

After the war, Lee did advise defeated Southerners not to rise up against the North. Lee might have become a rebel once more and urged the South to resume fighting—as many of his former comrades wanted him to. But even in this task Grant, in 1866, regarded his former rival as falling short, saying that Lee was "setting an example of forced acquiescence so grudging and pernicious in its effects as to be hardly realized."

Nor did Lee's defeat lead to an embrace of racial egalitarianism. The war was not about slavery, Lee insisted later, but if it were about slavery, it was only out of Christian devotion that white Southerners fought to keep black people enslaved. Lee told a *New York Herald* reporter, in the midst of arguing in favor of somehow removing black people from the South ("disposed of," in his words), "that unless some humane course is adopted, based on wisdom and Christian principles, you do a gross wrong and injustice to the whole negro race in setting them free. And it is only this consideration that has led the wisdom, intelligence and Christianity of the South to support and defend the institution up to this time."

Lee had beaten or ordered his own slaves to be beaten for

the crime of wanting to be free; he fought for the preservation of slavery; his army kidnapped free black people at gun-
point and made them unfree—but all of this, he insisted, had
occurred only because of the great Christian love the South
held for black Americans. Here we truly understand Frederick Douglass's admonition that "between the Christianity of
this land and the Christianity of Christ, I recognize the widest
possible difference."

Privately, according to the correspondence collected
by his own family, Lee counseled others to hire white labor
instead of the freedmen, observing "that wherever you find
the negro, everything is going down around him, and wherever you find a white man, you see everything around him
improving."

In another letter, Lee wrote, "You will never prosper with
blacks, and it is abhorrent to a reflecting mind to be supporting and cherishing those who are plotting and working for
your injury, and all of whose sympathies and associations are
antagonistic to yours. I wish them no evil in the world—on
the contrary, will do them every good in my power, and know
that they are misled by those to whom they have given their
confidence; but our material, social, and political interests are
naturally with the whites."

Publicly, Lee argued against the enfranchisement of black
Americans and raged against Republican efforts to enforce
racial equality in the South. Lee told Congress that black
people lacked the intellectual capacity of white people and
"could not vote intelligently" and that granting them suffrage
would "excite unfriendly feelings between the two races." Lee
explained that "the negroes have neither the intelligence nor
the other qualifications which are necessary to make them
safe depositories of political power." To the extent that Lee

believed in reconciliation, it was among white people, and only on the precondition that black people would be denied political power and therefore the ability to shape their own fate.

Lee is not remembered as an educator, but his life as president of Washington College (later Washington and Lee) is tainted as well. According to Pryor, students at Washington formed their own chapter of the Ku Klux Klan and were known by the local Freedmen's Bureau to attempt to abduct and rape black schoolgirls from the nearby black schools.

There were at least two attempted lynchings by Washington students during Lee's tenure, and Pryor writes that "the number of accusations against Washington College boys indicates that he either punished the racial harassment more laxly than other misdemeanors, or turned a blind eye to it," adding that he "did not exercise the near imperial control he had at the school, as he did for more trivial matters, such as when the boys threatened to take unofficial Christmas holidays." In short, Lee was as indifferent to crimes of violence toward black people carried out by his students as he was when they were carried out by his soldiers.

Lee died in 1870, as Democrats and ex-Confederates were commencing a wave of terrorist violence that would ultimately reimpose their domination over the Southern states. The KKK was founded in 1866; there is no evidence Lee ever spoke up against it. On the contrary, he darkly intimated in his interview with the *Herald* that the South might be moved to violence again if peace did not proceed on its terms. That was prescient.

Lee is a pivotal figure in American history worthy of study. Neither the man who really existed nor the fictionalized tragic hero of the Lost Cause is worthy of a statue in a place of honor. As one Union veteran angrily put it in 1903 when Pennsylvania was considering placing a statue of Lee at Gettysburg, "If you want historical accuracy as your excuse, then place upon this field a statue of Lee holding in his hand the banner under which he fought, bearing the legend: 'We wage this war against a government conceived in liberty and dedicated to humanity.'" The most fitting monument to Lee is the national military cemetery the federal government placed on the grounds of his former home in Arlington.

To describe this man as an American hero requires ignoring the immense suffering for which he was personally responsible, both on and off the battlefield. It requires ignoring his participation in the industry of human bondage, his betrayal of his country in defense of that institution, the battlefields scattered with the lifeless bodies of men who followed his orders and those they killed, his hostility toward the rights of the freedmen and his indifference to his own students waging a campaign of terror against the newly emancipated. It requires reducing the sum of human virtue to a sense of decorum and the ability to convey gravitas in a gray uniform.

There are former Confederates who sought to redeem themselves—one thinks of James Longstreet, wrongly blamed by Lost Causers for Lee's disastrous defeat at Gettysburg, who went from fighting the Union army to leading New Orleans's integrated police force in battle against white-supremacist paramilitaries. But there are no statues of Longstreet in New Orleans. Lee was devoted to defending the principle of white supremacy; Longstreet was not. This, perhaps, is why Lee was placed atop the largest Confederate monument at Gettysburg in 1917, but the six-foot-two-inch Longstreet had to wait until 1998 to receive a smaller-scale statue hidden in the woods that makes him look like a hobbit riding a donkey. It's why

Lee is remembered as a hero, and Longstreet is remembered as a disgrace.

The white supremacists who have protested on Lee's behalf are not betraying his legacy. In fact, they have every reason to admire him. Lee, whose devotion to white supremacy outshone his loyalty to his country, is the embodiment of everything they stand for. Tribe and race over country is the core of white nationalism, and racists can embrace Lee in good conscience.

The question is why anyone else would.

3

THE CRUELTY OF
THE LIES WE
TELL OURSELVES

DURING THE 2016 ELECTION, I FELT AS THOUGH I WAS WATCHING history being whitewashed in real time. Despite the fact that Donald Trump's campaign was infused with sectarian and racist rhetoric, and that the man himself had risen to political prominence by endorsing the slander that the first black president was not born in America, many political journalists were going out of their way to avoid the implications of such a man being nominated.

The prevailing explanations put forth at the time involved euphemisms such as "political correctness" or "economic anxiety," phrases used to obscure rather than illuminate the ideological implications of Trump's rhetoric and worldview. Trump's appeal was not racism or bigotry, the prevailing consensus went, but lingering anger over issues of trade, wages, or deindustrialization. In fact, Trump's rival, Hillary Clinton, was the real racist—for describing some of his supporters as prejudiced.

This kind of analysis reflected the reality-distorting influence of a powerful demographic majority. Media outlets

feared alienating white audiences by suggesting that prejudice was the major factor in Trump's ascendancy. So they
landed on an alternative explanation, as though they were
mutually exclusive. Economic suffering did play a role in
Trump's rise, but embracing Trump's narrative explanation
for that suffering required accepting the ideological explanation Trump was offering. Contemporary media tried to avoid
coverage or commentary that placed too much emphasis on
that ideological frame, even as many journalists and activists
of color wrote and spoke with clarity about what was happening. They were frequently dismissed as biased or hysterical by
their colleagues.

At the time, I was searching for an explanation for how
the same country that elected Barack Obama could possibly
choose to make Donald Trump his successor. So I decided to
ask Trump voters themselves how they could reconcile their
own view that Trump was not a racist with his overtly discriminatory policies, which they supported even when they didn't
support his caustic remarks. That's how I discovered what I
refer to in this essay as the nationalist's delusion—the psychological mechanism that allowed Trump voters to pull the lever
for a racist candidate while denying that's what they were doing.

After Trump was victorious, the pressure to settle on the
economic explanation for his victory increased. The Trump
political coalition was ascendant, and that kind of victory
has an effect on the culture, particularly the culture of mainstream journalism, which tries to position itself as representing the interests of the average voter. When their perception
of who that voter is shifts, they shift with it. As shown in the
essay, even opinion journalists like me were encouraged to
accept benign explanations for Trump's victory, lest we alienate subscribers, viewers, or listeners—with power comes the

prerogative to take offense. Similarly, if Democrats wanted to have a chance at retaking political power, they would have to avoid language that would offend the conservative-leaning white voters whose geographic distribution made it possible for Trump to eke out a win in the electoral college while losing the popular vote.

I refused. My reporting told me what had happened and why. I took as both comfort and example the persistence of the black historian and social scientist W.E.B. Du Bois. In his seminal work of history, *Black Reconstruction in America*, Du Bois was going against the prevailing historical consensus of his day in arguing that Reconstruction after the American Civil War had been a flawed but admirable attempt at making real the promises of the Declaration of Independence.

The dominant trend in American history at that time was portraying Reconstruction as a terrible tragedy, a misguided and tyrannical effort to enforce an equality that black men were not prepared to accept, because of their cultural and biological inferiority. These historians, known as the Dunning School after their lead scholar, William Archibald Dunning, interpreted history through an explicitly white-supremacist lens. For them, enfranchising black men had been a mistake, and the violent overthrow of the Reconstruction state governments and the establishment of Jim Crow segregation had been a return to the natural order of things.

In his note to the reader at the introduction to *Black Reconstruction*, Du Bois writes:

If he believes that the Negro in America and in general is an average and ordinary human being, who under given environment develops like other human beings, then he will read this story and judge it by the facts adduced. If, however, he regards the Negro as a distinctly inferior creation, who can never successfully take part in modern civilization and whose emancipation and enfranchisement were gestures against nature, then he will need something more than the sort of facts that I have set down. But this latter person, I am not trying to convince.

This was inspiration in a dark moment. I did not set out to write this essay attempting to convince anyone of my point of view. I was simply laying down the facts as I saw them and attempting to get at the truth as best I could, so that, in a different time and place, one less deferential to Trump and Trumpism, someone would be able to access the truth.

It would take decades before historians would recognize that Du Bois's account of Reconstruction was more historically accurate than that of his white contemporaries. Recognizing the nature of Trumpism actually came much faster, in part because of the president's relative political weakness, and in part because Trump himself could not stop reminding the public at any given opportunity who he truly is. It was at Trump's own insistence that cultural and ideological explanations for Trump's appeal prevailed over the conveniently reductive economic ones offered early in his rise.

But it was also that, in contrast to Du Bois's era, there were enough journalists of color—people who came from the very communities Trump had savaged to win the presidency—who held positions of influence in mainstream institutions, who could prevent a new, Trumpist consensus on history from solidifying. And for all the talk of "identity politics" dooming the Democratic Party, it was ultimately black voters' choice of Joe Biden in the primary—itself an astute assessment of white identity politics—that helped lead to Democrats unseating Trump and assuming control of the government in 2021.

When it comes to who the president is and what he represents, there is something of a consensus between Trump and his harshest critics. The two don't really disagree about whether prejudice is an essential part of Trump's political appeal; they just disagree about whether to call it that. I don't regret my choice.

THE NATIONALIST'S DELUSION

NOVEMBER 20, 2017

THIRTY YEARS AGO, NEARLY HALF OF LOUISIANA VOTED FOR A Klansman, and the media struggled to explain why.

It was 1990 and David Duke, the former grand wizard of the Ku Klux Klan, astonished political observers when he came within striking distance of defeating incumbent Democratic U.S. senator J. Bennett Johnston, earning 43 percent of the vote. If Johnston's Republican rival hadn't dropped out of the race and endorsed him at the last minute, the outcome might have been different.

Was it economic anxiety? *The Washington Post* reported that the state had "a large working class that has suffered through a long recession." Was it a blow against the state's hated political establishment? An editorial from United Press International explained, "Louisianans showed the nation by voting for Duke that they were mad as hell and not going to take it anymore." Was it anti-Washington rage? A Loyola

University pollster argued, "There were the voters who liked Duke, those who hated J. Bennett Johnston, and those who just wanted to send a message to Washington."

What message would those voters have been trying to send by putting a Klansman into office?

"There's definitely a message bigger than Louisiana here," Susan Howell, then the director of the Survey Research Center at the University of New Orleans, told the *Los Angeles Times*. "There is a tremendous amount of anger and frustration among working-class whites, particularly where there is an economic downturn. These people feel left out; they feel government is not responsive to them."

Duke's strong showing, however, wasn't powered merely by poor or working-class whites—and the poorest demographic in the state, black voters, backed Johnston. Duke "clobbered Johnston in white working-class districts, ran even with him in predominantly white middle-class suburbs, and lost only because black Louisianans, representing one-quarter of the electorate, voted against him in overwhelming numbers," *The Washington Post* reported in 1990. Duke picked up nearly 60 percent of the white vote. Faced with Duke's popularity among whites of all income levels, the press framed his strong showing largely as the result of the economic suffering of the white working classes. Louisiana had "one of the least-educated electorates in the nation, and a large working class that has suffered through a long recession," the *Post* stated.

By accepting the economic theory of Duke's success, the media were buying into the candidate's own vision of himself as a savior of the working class. He had appealed to voters in economic terms: He tore into welfare and foreign aid, affirmative action and outsourcing, and attacked political-action committees for subverting the interests of the common man. He even tried to appeal to black voters, buying a thirty-minute ad in which he declared, "I'm not your enemy."

Duke's candidacy had initially seemed like a joke. The former Klan leader who had showed up to public events in a Nazi uniform and lied about having served in the Vietnam War, a cartoonishly vain supervillain whose belief in his own status as a genetic *Übermensch* was belied by his plastic surgeries. The joke soon soured, as many white Louisiana voters made clear that Duke's past didn't bother them.

Many of Duke's voters steadfastly denied that the former Klan leader was a racist. The *St. Petersburg Times* reported in 1990 that Duke supporters "are likely to blame the media for making him look like a racist." The paper quoted G. D. Miller, a "59-year-old oil-and-gas lease buyer," who said, "The way I understood the Klan, it's not anti-this or anti-that."

Duke's rejoinder to the ads framing him as a racist resonated with his supporters. "Remember," he told them at rallies, "when they smear me, they are really smearing you."

The economic explanation carried the day: Duke was a freak creature of the bayou who had managed to tap into the frustrations of a struggling sector of the Louisiana electorate with an abnormally high tolerance for racist messaging.

While the rest of the country gawked at Louisiana and the Duke fiasco, Walker Percy, a Louisiana author, gave a prophetic warning to *The New York Times*.

"Don't make the mistake of thinking David Duke is a unique phenomenon confined to Louisiana rednecks and yahoos. He's not," Percy said. "He's not just appealing to the old Klan constituency, he's appealing to the white middle class. And don't think that he or somebody like him won't appeal to the white middle class of Chicago or Queens."

A few days after Duke's strong showing, the Queens-born businessman Donald Trump appeared on CNN's *Larry King Live*.

"It's anger. I mean, that's an anger vote. People are angry about what's happened. People are angry about the jobs. If you look at Louisiana, they're really in deep trouble," Trump told King.

Trump later predicted that Duke, if he ran for president, would siphon most of his votes away from the incumbent, George H. W. Bush—in the process revealing his own understanding of the effectiveness of white-nationalist appeals to the GOP base.

"Whether that be good or bad, David Duke is going to get a lot of votes. Pat Buchanan—who really has many of the same theories, except it's in a better package—Pat Buchanan is going to take a lot of votes away from George Bush," Trump said. "So if you have these two guys running, or even one of them running, I think George Bush could be in big trouble." Little more than a year later, Buchanan embarrassed Bush by drawing 37 percent of the vote in New Hampshire's Republican primary.

In February 2016, Trump was asked by a different CNN host about the former Klan leader's endorsement of his Republican presidential bid.

"Well, just so you understand, I don't know anything about David Duke. Okay?" Trump said. "I don't know anything about what you're even talking about with white supremacy or white supremacists. So I don't know."

LESS THAN THREE WEEKS BEFORE the 2016 presidential election, Donald Trump declared himself "the least racist person you have ever met."

Even before Trump won, the United States was consumed by a debate over the nature of his appeal. Was racism
the driving force behind Trump's candidacy? If so, how could
Americans, the vast majority of whom said they opposed racism, back a racist candidate?

During the final few weeks of the campaign, I asked dozens of Trump supporters about their candidate's remarks
regarding Muslims and people of color. I wanted to understand how these average Republicans—those who would
never read the neo-Nazi website The Daily Stormer or go
to a Klan rally at a Confederate statue—had nevertheless
embraced someone who demonized religious and ethnic
minorities. What I found was that Trump embodied his supporters' most profound beliefs—combining an insistence that
discriminatory policies were necessary with vehement denials
that his policies would discriminate and absolute outrage that
the question would even be asked.

It was not just Trump's supporters who were in denial
about what they were voting for but Americans across the
political spectrum, who, as had been the case with those
who backed Duke, were searching desperately for any alternative explanation—outsourcing, anti-Washington anger,
economic anxiety—to the one staring them in the face. The
frequent postelection media expeditions to Trump country to
see whether the fever has broken or whether Trump's most
ardent supporters have changed their minds are a direct outgrowth of this mistake. These supporters will not change their
minds, because this is what they always wanted: a president
who embodies the rage they feel toward those they hate and
fear, while reassuring them that that rage is nothing to be
ashamed of.

"I believe that everybody has a right to be in the United States no matter what your color, no matter what your race, your religion, what sex you prefer to be with, so I'm not against that at all, but I think that some of us just say racial statements without even thinking about it," a customer-care worker named Pam—who, like several people I spoke with, declined to give her last name—told me at a rally in Pennsylvania. However, she also defended Trump's remarks on race and religion explicitly when I asked about them. "I think the other party likes to blow it out of proportion and kind of twist his words, but what he says is what he means, and it's what a lot of us are thinking."

Most Trump supporters I spoke with were not people who thought of themselves as racist. Rather, they saw themselves as anti-racist, as people who held no hostility toward religious and ethnic minorities whatsoever—a sentiment they projected onto their candidate.

"I don't feel like he's racist. I don't personally feel like anybody would have been able to do what he's been able to do with his personal business if he were a horrible person," Michelle, a stay-at-home mom in Virginia, told me.

Far more numerous and powerful than the extremists in Berkeley and Charlottesville who have drawn headlines since Trump's election, these Americans, who would never think of themselves as possessing racial animus, voted for a candidate whose ideal vision of America excludes millions of fellow citizens because of their race or religion.

The specific dissonance of Trumpism—advocacy for discriminatory, even cruel, policies combined with vehement denials that such policies are racially motivated—provides the emotional core of its appeal. It is the most recent manifestation of a contradiction as old as the United States, a society founded by slaveholders on the principle that all men are created equal.

While other factors also led to Trump's victory—the last-minute letter from former FBI director James Comey, the sexism that rationalized supporting Trump despite his confession of sexual assault, Hillary Clinton's neglect of the Midwest—had racism been toxic to the American electorate, Trump's candidacy would not have been viable.

Nearly a year into his presidency, Trump has reneged or faltered on many of his biggest campaign promises—on renegotiating NAFTA, punishing China, and replacing the Affordable Care Act with something that preserves all its popular provisions but with none of its drawbacks. But his commitment to endorsing state violence to remake the country into something resembling an idealized past has not wavered.

He made a farce of his populist campaign by putting bankers in charge of the economy and industry insiders at the head of the federal agencies established to regulate their businesses. But other campaign promises have been more faithfully enacted: his ban on travelers from Muslim-majority countries; the unleashing of immigration-enforcement agencies against anyone in the country illegally, regardless of whether they pose a danger; an attempt to cut legal immigration in half; and an abdication of the Justice Department's constitutional responsibility to protect black Americans from corrupt or abusive police, discriminatory financial practices, and voter suppression. In his own stumbling manner, Trump has pursued the race-based agenda promoted during his campaign. As the president continues to pursue a program that places the social and political hegemony of white Christians at its core, his supporters have shown few signs of abandoning him.

One hundred thirty-nine years since Reconstruction, and half a century since the tail end of the civil-rights movement, a majority of white voters backed a candidate who explicitly pledged to use the power of the state against people of color and religious minorities and stood by him as that pledge has been among the few to survive the first year of his presidency. Their support was enough to win the White House and has solidified a return to a politics of white identity that has been one of the most destructive forces in American history. This all occurred before the eyes of a disbelieving press and political class, who plunged into fierce denial about how and why this had happened. That is the story of the 2016 election.

ONE OF THE FIRST MENTIONS of Trump in *The New York Times* was in 1973, as a result of a federal discrimination lawsuit against his buildings over his company's refusal to rent to black tenants. In 1989, he took out a full-page newspaper ad suggesting that the Central Park Five—black and Latino youths accused of the assault and rape of a white jogger— should be put to death. They were later exonerated. His rise to prominence in Republican politics was initially fueled by his embrace of the conspiracy theory that the first black president of the United States was not an American citizen. "I have people that have been studying [Obama's birth certificate] and they cannot believe what they're finding," he said in 2011. "If he wasn't born in this country, which is a real possibility . . . then he has pulled one of the great cons in the history of politics."

Trump began his candidacy with a speech announcing that undocumented immigrants from Mexico were "bringing drugs. They're bringing crime. They're rapists." And "some," he said, were "good people." To keep them out, he proposed building a wall and humiliating Mexico for its citizens' transgressions by forcing their government to pay for it. He vowed to ban Muslims from entering the United States. Amid heightened attention to fatal police shootings of unarmed black people and a subsequent cry for accountability, Trump decried a "war on police" while telling black Americans they lived in "war zones," in communities that were in "the worst shape they've ever been in"—a remarkable claim to make in a country that once subjected black people to chattel slavery and Jim Crow. He promised to institute a national "stop and frisk" policy, a police tactic that turns black and Latino Americans into criminal suspects in their own neighborhoods, which had recently been struck down in his native New York as unconstitutional.

Trump expanded on this vision in his 2016 Republican National Convention speech, which gestured toward the suffering of nonwhites and painted a dark portrait of an America under assault by people of color through crime, immigration, and competition for jobs. Trump promised, "The crime and violence that today afflicts our nation will soon come to an end," citing "the president's hometown of Chicago." He warned that "180,000 illegal immigrants with criminal records, ordered deported from our country, are tonight roaming free to threaten peaceful citizens," and said that Clinton was "calling for a radical 550 percent increase in Syrian refugees on top of existing massive refugee flows coming into our country under President Obama."

A bleak vision, but one that any regular Fox News viewer would recognize.

The white-supremacist journal *American Renaissance* applauded Trump's message. "Each political party proposes an implicit racial vision," wrote one contributor. "A Trump Administration is a return to the America that won the West, landed on the moon, and built an economy and military that stunned the world. Nonwhites can participate in this, but only if they accept the traditional (which is to say, white) norms of American culture."

Most Trump supporters I spoke with denied that they endorsed this racial vision—even as they defended Trump's rhetoric.

"Anytime that you disagree with someone's point of view—if you say, 'I don't like Islam'—people say you're an Islamophobe, or if you don't like gay marriage, you're a homophobe, and you're hateful against the gays and Islam, or different things like that, where people are entitled to their opinion. But it doesn't mean that you're hateful or discriminatory," Scott Colvin, who identified himself as a Navy veteran, told me at a Trump rally in Virginia. "Seeing how women are treated in the Islamic religion, it's not very good, and he's bringing a lot of light to it—that there is a lot of drugs and crime coming across the border, and that Islam does not respect women, does not respect homosexuals—and so calling it out and raising awareness to that is pretty important.

"There's very little evidence of Trump being openly racist or sexist," Colvin insisted. "It wasn't until he started running for president that all these stories started coming out. I don't believe it. I've done the research."

The plain meaning of Trumpism exists in tandem with denials of its implications; supporters and opponents alike understand that the president's policies and rhetoric target religious and ethnic minorities and behave accordingly. But both supporters and opponents usually stop short of calling these policies racist. It is as if there were a pothole in the middle of the street that every driver studiously avoided but that most insisted did not exist even as they swerved around it.

That this shared understanding is seldom spoken aloud does not prevent people from acting according to its logic. It is the reason why, when Trump's Muslim ban was first implemented, immigration officials stopped American citizens with Arabic names; why agencies such as Immigration and Customs Enforcement and the border patrol have pursued fathers and mothers outside of schools and churches and deported them, as the administration has insisted that it is prioritizing the deportation of criminals; why Attorney General Jeff Sessions targets drug scofflaws with abandon and has dismantled even cooperative efforts at police accountability; why the president's voting commission has committed itself to policies that will disenfranchise voters of color; why both schoolchildren and adults know to invoke the president's name as a taunt against black people, Latinos, and Muslims; why white supremacists wear hats that say MAKE AMERICA GREAT AGAIN.

One measure of the allure of Trump's white identity politics is the extent to which it has overridden other concerns as his administration has faltered. The president's supporters have stood by him even as he has evinced every quality they described as a deal breaker under Obama. Conservatives attacked Obama's lack of faith; Trump is a thrice-married libertine who has never asked God for forgiveness. They accused Obama of being under malign foreign influence; Trump eagerly accepted the aid of a foreign adversary during the election. They accused Obama of genuflecting before Russian president Vladimir Putin; Trump has refused to even criticize Putin publicly. They attacked Obama for his ties to Tony Rezko, the crooked real-estate agent; Trump's ties to organized crime are too numerous to name. Conservatives said Obama was lazy; Trump "gets bored and likes to watch TV." They said Obama's golfing was excessive; as of August, Trump had spent nearly a fifth of his presidency golfing. They attributed Obama's intellectual prowess to his teleprompter; Trump seems unable to describe the basics of any of his own policies. They said Obama was a self-obsessed egomaniac; Trump is unable to broach topics of public concern without boasting. Conservatives said Obama quietly used the power of the state to attack his enemies; Trump has publicly attempted to use the power of the state to attack his enemies. Republicans said Obama was racially divisive; Trump has called Nazis "very fine people." Conservatives portrayed Obama as a vapid celebrity; Trump *is* a vapid celebrity.

There is virtually no personality defect that conservatives accused Obama of possessing that Trump himself does not actually possess. This, not some uncanny oracular talent, is the reason Trump's years-old tweets channeling conservative anger at Obama apply so perfectly to his own present conduct.

Trump's great political insight was that Obama's time in office inflicted a profound psychological wound upon many white Americans, one that he could remedy by adopting the false narrative that placed the first black president outside the bounds of American citizenship. He intuited that Obama's presence in the White House decreased the value of what W.E.B. Du Bois described as the "psychological wage" of whiteness across all classes of white Americans and that the path to their hearts lay in invoking a bygone era when this affront had not taken place, and could not take place.

That the legacy of the first black president could be erased by a birther, that the woman who could have been the first female president was foiled by a man who confessed to sexual assault on tape—these were not drawbacks to Trump's candidacy but central to understanding how he would wield power and on whose behalf.

Americans act with the understanding that Trump's nationalism promises to restore traditional boundaries of race, gender, and sexuality. The nature of that same nationalism is to deny its essence, the better to salve the conscience and spare the soul.

AMONG THE MOST POPULAR EXPLANATIONS for Trump's victory and the Trump phenomenon writ large is the Calamity Thesis: the belief that Trump's election was the direct result of some great, unacknowledged social catastrophe—the opioid crisis, free trade, a decline in white Americans' life expectancy—heretofore ignored by cloistered elites in their coastal bubbles. The irony is that the Calamity Thesis is by far the preferred "white-elite" explanation for Trumpism and is frequently invoked in arguments among elites as a way of accusing other elites of being out of touch.

Perhaps the most prominent data point for the Calamity Thesis is a pair of recent Brookings Institution studies by the professors Anne Case and Angus Deaton, which show that life expectancy has fallen among less-educated white Americans due to what they call "deaths of despair" from drugs, alcohol, and suicide. While the studies themselves make no mention of Trump or the election, the effects they describe are frequently invoked as explanations for the president's appeal: White people without college degrees are living in deprivation, and in their despair, they turned to a racist demagogue who promised to solve their problems.

This explanation appeals to whites across the political spectrum. On the right, it serves as an indictment of elitist liberals who used their power to assist religious and ethnic minorities rather than all Americans; on the left, it offers a glimmer of hope that such voters can be won over by a more left-wing or redistributionist economic policy. It also has the distinct advantage of conferring innocence upon what is often referred to as the "white working class." After all, it wasn't white working-class voters' fault. They were suffering; they had to do something.

The studies' methodology is sound, as is the researchers' recognition that many poor and white working-class Americans are struggling. But the research does not support the conclusions many have drawn from it—that economic or social desperation by itself drove white Americans to Donald Trump.

It's true that most Trump voters framed his appeal in economic terms. Kelly, a health-care worker in North Carolina, echoed other Trump supporters when she told me that, to her, "Make America great again" meant "people being able to get jobs, people being able to come off food stamps, welfare, and that sort of thing." But a closer look at the demographics of the 2016 electorate shows something more complex than a working-class revolt sparked by prolonged suffering.

Clinton defeated Trump handily among Americans making less than $50,000 a year. Among voters making more than that, the two candidates ran roughly even. The electorate, however, skews wealthier than the general population. Voters making less than $50,000, whom Clinton won by a proportion of 53 to 41, accounted for only 36 percent of the votes cast, while those making more than $50,000—whom Trump won by a single point—made up 64 percent. The most economically vulnerable Americans voted for Clinton overwhelmingly; the usual presumption is exactly the opposite.

If you look at white voters alone, a different picture emerges. Trump defeated Clinton among white voters in every income category, winning by a margin of 57 to 34 among whites making less than $30,000; 56 to 37 among those making between $30,000 and $50,000; 61 to 33 for those making $50,000 to $100,000; 56 to 39 among those making $100,000 to $200,000; 50 to 45 among those making $200,000 to $250,000; and 48 to 43 among those making more than $250,000. In other words, Trump won white voters at every level of class and income. He won workers, he won managers, he won owners, he won robber barons. This is not a working-class coalition; it is a nationalist one.

But Trump's greater appeal among low-income white voters doesn't vindicate the Calamity Thesis. White working-class Americans dealing directly with factors that lead to a death of despair were actually less likely to support Trump, and those struggling economically were not any more likely to support him. As a 2017 study by the Public Religion Research Institute and *The Atlantic* found, "White working-class voters who reported that someone in their household was dealing with a health issue—such as drug addiction, alcohol abuse, or depression—were actually less likely to express support for Trump's candidacy," while white working-class voters who had "experienced a loss of social and economic standing were not any more likely to favor Trump than those whose status remained the same or improved."

Trump's support among whites decreases the higher you go on the scales of income and education. But the controlling factor seems to be not economic distress but an inclination to see nonwhites as the cause of economic problems. The poorest voters were somewhat less likely to vote for Trump than those a rung or two above them on the economic ladder. The highest-income voters actually supported Trump less than they did Mitt Romney, who in 2012 won 54 percent of voters making more than $100,000—several points more than Trump secured, although he still fared better than Clinton. It was among voters in the middle, those whose economic circumstances were precarious but not bleak, that the benefits of Du Bois's psychic wage appeared most in danger of being devalued and Trump's message resonated most strongly. They surged toward the Republican column.

Yet when social scientists control for white voters' racial attitudes—that is, whether those voters hold "racially resentful" views about black people and immigrants—even the educational divide disappears. In other words, the relevant factor in support for Trump among white voters was not education or even income but the ideological frame with which they understood their challenges and misfortunes. It is also why voters of color—who suffered a genuine economic calamity in the decade before Trump's election—were almost entirely immune to those same appeals.

During the aftermath of the Great Recession, the meager wealth of black and Latino families declined significantly compared with the wealth of white families. According to the Federal Reserve, "Median net worth fell about 30 percent for all groups during the Great Recession. However, for black and Hispanic families, net worth continued to fall an additional 20 percent in the 2010–13 period, while white families' net worth was essentially unchanged." The predatory financial practices that fueled the housing bubble also targeted people of color—modernized versions of the very same racist plunder that caused the wealth gaps to begin with. But there was no corresponding radicalization of the black and Latino population, no mass election to Congress of ethno-nationalist demagogues promising vengeance on the perpetrators.

Those numbers also reveal a much more complicated story than a Trump base made up of struggling working-class Americans turning to Trump as a result of their personal financial difficulties, not their ideological convictions. An avalanche of stories poured forth from mainstream-media outlets, all with the same basic thesis: Trump's appeal was less about racism than it was about hardship—or, in the euphemism turned running joke, "economic anxiety." Worse still, euphemisms such as "regular Americans," typically employed by politicians to refer to white people, were now adopted by political reporters and writers wholesale: To be a regular or working-class American was to be white.

One early use of economic anxiety as an explanation for the Trump phenomenon came from NBC News's Chuck Todd, in July 2015. "Trump and Sanders supporters are disenchanted with what they see as a broken system, fed up with political correctness and Washington dysfunction," Todd said. "Economic anxiety is fueling both campaigns, but that's where the similarities end."

The idea that economic suffering could lead people to support either Trump or Sanders, two candidates with little in common, illustrates the salience of an ideological frame. Suffering alone doesn't impel such choices; what does is how the causes of such hardship are understood.

Some Trump voters I spoke with were convinced, for example, that undocumented immigrants had access to a generous welfare state that was denied to everyone else. "You look at all these illegal immigrants coming in who are getting services that most Americans aren't getting as far as insurance, welfare, Medicaid, all that jazz," Richard Jenkins, a landscaper in North Carolina, told me. Steve, a Trump supporter who runs a floor-covering business in Virginia's Tidewater area, told me that it "seems like people coming to this country, whether it's illegally or through a legal system of immigration, are being treated better than American veterans." If you believe that other people are getting the assistance you deserve, you are likely to oppose that assistance. But first you have to believe this.

The economic-anxiety argument retains a great deal of currency. As Mark Lilla, a Columbia professor, put it while defending the thesis of his book *The Once and Future Liberal: After Identity Politics* in an interview with *Slate*, "Marxists are much more on-point here. Their argument has always been that people become racist—and there are lots of reasons why they do, but the people who might be on the edge are drawn to racist rhetoric and anti-immigrant rhetoric because they've been economically disenfranchised, and so they look for a scapegoat, and so the real problems are economic. I think they're closer to the truth right now than to think that somehow just some racist demon is directing everything in this country. It's just not where the country is."

Lilla's argument falls apart at the slightest scrutiny: Wealth does not insulate one from racism, or the entire slaveholding planter class of the South could not have existed. Rather, racism and nationalism form an ideological lens through which to view suffering and misfortune. It is perhaps too much to expect that people who hope to use Marxist theory to absolve voters of racism cite those Marxist historians whose body of work engages precisely this topic.

In *Black Reconstruction in America,* W.E.B. Du Bois examined not only the acquiescence of Northern capital to Southern racial hegemony after the Civil War but also white labor's decision that preserving a privileged spot in the racial hierarchy was more attractive than standing in solidarity with black workers.

"North and South agreed that laborers must produce profit; the poor white and the Negro wanted to get the profit arising from the laborers' toil and not to divide it with the employers and landowners," Du Bois wrote. "When Northern and Southern employers agreed that profit was most important and the method of getting it second, the path to understanding was clear. When white laborers were convinced that the degradation of Negro labor was more fundamental than the uplift of white labor, the end was in sight." In exchange, white laborers, "while they received a low wage, were compensated in part by a sort of public and psychological wage." For centuries, capital's most potent wedge against labor in America has been the belief that it is better to be poor than to be equal to niggers.

Overall, poor and working-class Americans did not support Trump; it was white Americans on all levels of the income spectrum who secured his victory. Clinton was only competitive with Trump among white people making more than $100,000, but the fact that their shares of the vote was nearly identical drives the point home: Economic suffering alone does not explain the rise of Trump. Nor does the Calamity Thesis explain why comparably situated black Americans, who are considerably more vulnerable than their white counterparts, remained so immune to Trump's appeal. The answer cannot be that black Americans were suffering less than the white working class or the poor; rather, Trump's solutions did not appeal to people of color because they were premised on a national vision that excluded them as full citizens.

When you look at Trump's strength among white Americans of all income categories but his weakness among Americans struggling with poverty, the story of Trump looks less like a story of working-class revolt than a story of white backlash. And the stories of struggling white Trump supporters look less like the whole truth than a convenient narrative—one that obscures the racist nature of that backlash, instead casting it as a rebellion against an unfeeling establishment that somehow includes working-class and poor people who happen not to be white.

The nature of racism in America is that when the rich exploit everyone else, there is always an easier and more vulnerable target to punish. The Irish immigrants who in 1863 ignited a pogrom against black Americans in New York City to protest the draft resented a policy that offered the rich the chance to buy their way out; their response was nevertheless to purge black people from the city for a generation.

IN 2006, DURING A TELEVISED fundraiser for victims of Hurricane Katrina, Kanye West said President George W. Bush didn't care about black people. NBC News's Matt Lauer later asked Bush, "You say you told Laura at the time it was the worst moment of your presidency?"

"Yes," Bush replied. "My record was strong, I felt, when it came to race relations and giving people a chance. And it was a disgusting moment."

Bush singling out West's criticism as the worst moment of his presidency may seem strange. But his visceral reaction to the implication that he was racist reflects a peculiarly white

American cognitive dissonance—that most worry far more about being seen as racist than about the consequences of racism for their fellow citizens. That dissonance spans the ideological spectrum, resulting in blanket explanations for Trump that ignore the plainly obvious.

The explanation that Trump's victory wasn't an expression of support for racism because he got fewer votes than Romney, or because Clinton failed to generate sufficient Democratic enthusiasm, ignores the fact that Trump was a viable—even victorious—candidate while running racist primary- and general-election campaigns. Had his racism been disqualifying, his candidacy would have died in the primaries. Equally strange is the notion that because some white voters defected from Obama to Trump, racism could not have been a factor in the election; many of these voters did, in fact, hold racist views. Particularly during the 2008 campaign, Obama emphasized his uniqueness as an African American—his upbringing by his white grandparents, his elite pedigree, his public scoldings of black Americans for their cultural shortcomings. It takes little imagination at all to see how someone could hold racist views about black people in general and still have warm feelings toward Obama.

Perhaps the CNN pundit Chris Cillizza best encapsulated the mainstream-media consensus when he declared shortly after Election Day that there "is nothing more maddening—and counterproductive—to me than saying that Trump's 59 million votes were all racist. Ridiculous." Millions of people of color in the United States live a reality that many white Americans find unfathomable; the unfathomable is not the impossible.

Even before Election Day, that consensus was reflected in the reaction to Clinton's most controversial remarks of the campaign. "You know, to just be grossly generalistic," she said, "you could put half of Trump's supporters into what I call the basket of deplorables. Right? The racist, sexist, homophobic, xenophobic, Islamophobic—you name it."

Rolling Stone's Tim Dickinson, in a since-deleted tweet, observed, "Clinton is talking about Trump supporters the way Trump talks about Mexicans," whom Trump derided as rapists and criminals. Bloomberg's John Heilemann said, "This comment kind of gets very close to the dictionary definition of 'bigoted.'" The leftist writer Barbara Ehrenreich posted on Facebook that Clinton was "an elitist snob who writes off about a quarter of the American electorate as pond scum." As *New York* magazine's Jesse Singal put it, "Not to be too cute but I have racist relatives. I'd like to think they aren't 'deplorable' humans."

These reactions mirrored those of Trump voters. In Lancaster, Pennsylvania, a Trump supporter who gave his name as George acknowledged that "sometimes he says stuff he's probably better off not saying, because the media's gonna take everything he says and run with it." He added, "Hillary can say the same thing, like 'deplorable,' and they won't talk about that much."

Another Trump supporter in Lancaster, Beatrice, felt similarly about the "deplorables" remark. "Let's face facts, calling half of your voter base 'deplorables'—eh, that's okay," Beatrice said. "Trump says something and we have to hear about it again and again and again, and it's complete bias."

The defenses of Trump voters against Clinton's charge share an aversion to acknowledging an unpleasant truth. They are not so much arguments against a proposition as arguments that the proposition is offensive—or, if you prefer, politically incorrect. The same is true of the rejoinder that

Democrats cannot hope to win the votes of people they have condemned as racist. This is not a refutation of the point but an argument against stating it so plainly.

The argument for the innocence of Trump's backers finds purchase across ideological lines: white Democrats looking for votes from working-class whites, white Republicans who want to tar Democrats as elitists, white leftists who fear that identity politics stifles working-class solidarity, and white Trumpists seeking to weaponize white grievances. But the impetus here is not just ideological but personal and commercial. No one wants to think of his family, friends, lovers, or colleagues as racist. And no one wants to alienate potential subscribers, listeners, viewers, or fans either.

Yet nowhere did Clinton vow to use the power of the state to punish the constituencies voting for Trump, whose threats made his own rhetorical gestures toward pluralism risible. Clinton's arrogance in referring to Trump supporters as "irredeemable" is the truly indefensible part of her statement—in the 2008 Democratic primary, Clinton herself ran as the candidate of "hardworking Americans, white Americans" against Obama, earning her the "exceedingly strange new respect" of conservatives, who noted that she was running the "classic Republican race against her opponent." Eight years later, she lost to an opponent whose mastery of those forces was simply greater than hers.

The reason many equated Clinton's "deplorables" remark with Trump's agenda of discriminatory state violence seems to be the widespread perception that racism is primarily an interpersonal matter—that is, it's about name-calling or rudeness rather than institutional and political power. This is a belief hardly limited to the president's supporters but crucial to their understanding of Trump as lacking personal prejudice. "One thing I like about Trump is he isn't afraid to tell people what the problems in this country are," said Ron Whitekettle from Lancaster. "Everything he says is true, but sometimes he doesn't say it the way it should be said."

"Political correctness" is a vague term, perhaps best defined by the conservative scholar Samuel Goldman: "What Trump and others seem to mean by political correctness is an extremely dramatic and rapidly changing set of discursive and social laws that, virtually overnight, people are expected to understand, to which they are expected to adhere."

From a different vantage point, what Trump's supporters refer to as political correctness is largely the result of marginalized communities gaining sufficient political power to project their prerogatives onto society at large. What a society finds offensive is not a function of fact or truth but of power. It is why unpunished murders of black Americans by agents of the state draw less outrage than black football players kneeling for the national anthem in protest against them. It is no coincidence that Trump himself frequently uses the term to belittle what he sees as unnecessary restrictions on state force.

But even as once-acceptable forms of bigotry have become unacceptable to express overtly, white Americans remain politically dominant enough to shape media coverage in a manner that minimizes obvious manifestations of prejudice, such as backing a racist candidate, as something else entirely. The most transgressive political statement of the 2016 election, the one that violated strict societal norms by stating an inconvenient fact that few wanted to acknowledge, the most politically incorrect, was made by the candidate who lost.

•　•　•

EVEN BEFORE TRUMP, THE REPUBLICAN Party was moving toward an exclusivist nationalism that defined American identity in racial and religious terms, despite some efforts from its leadership to steer it in another direction. George W. Bush signed the 2006 reauthorization of the Voting Rights Act, attempted to bring Latino voters into the party, and spoke in defense of American Muslims' place in the national fabric. These efforts led to caustic backlashes from the Republican rank and file, who defeated his 2006 immigration-reform legislation, which might have shifted the demographics of the Republican Party for a generation or more. In the aftermath of their 2012 loss, Republican leaders tried again, only to meet with the same anti-immigrant backlash—one that would find an avatar in the person of the next Republican president.

In 2015, the political scientists Marisa Abrajano and Zoltan L. Hajnal published *White Backlash,* a study of political trends, and found that "whites who hold more negative views of immigrants have a greater tendency to support Republican candidates at the presidential, congressional, and gubernatorial levels, even after controlling for party identification and other major factors purported to drive the vote."

While that finding may seem obvious, it isn't simply a description of existing Republicans but of the trends driving some white Democrats into the Republican Party. Using data from the American National Election Survey, Abrajano and Hajnal conclude that "changes in individual attitudes toward immigrants precede shifts in partisanship" and that "immigration really is driving individual defections from the Democratic to Republican Party."

Cautioning that there are limits to social science, Abrajano told me, "All other things being equal, we see that immigration has a strong and consistent effect in moving whites toward the Republican Party. I think having the first African American president elected into the office . . . You can't disentangle immigration without talking about race as well, so that dynamic brought to the forefront immigration and racial politics more broadly, and the kind of fear and anxiety that many voters had about the changing demographics and characteristics of the U.S. population." The *Slate* writer Jamelle Bouie made a similar observation in an insightful essay in March 2016.

Half a century after Senator Barry Goldwater of Arizona rose to prominence by opposing civil-rights legislation designed to dismantle Jim Crow, the Republican Party's shift toward nativism foreclosed another path, not just to ethnic diversity but to the moderation and tolerance that sharing power with those unlike you requires.

In the meantime, more than a decade of war nationalism directed at jihadist groups has shaped Republican attitudes toward Muslims—from seeing them as potential Republican voters in the late 1990s to viewing them as internal enemies currently. War nationalism always turns itself inward, but in the past, wars ended. Anti-Irish violence fell following the service of Irish American soldiers in the Civil War; Germans were integrated back into the body politic after World War II; and the Italians, Jews, and Eastern Europeans who were targeted by the early twentieth century's great immigration scare would find themselves part of a state-sponsored project of assimilation by the war's end. But the War on Terror is without end, and so that national consolidation has never occurred. Again, Trump is a manifestation of this trend rather than its impetus, a manifestation that began to rise not long after Obama's candidacy.

"Birtherism was the beginning. It was a way of tying

together his foreignness and his name, in an effort to delegiti-mize him, from the get-go," says James Zogby, a Democrat whose Arab American Institute has spent years tracking pub-lic opinion about Muslim and Arab Americans. By 2012, the very idea of Muslims in public service "had become an issue in presidential politics, with five of the Republican candidates saying they wouldn't hire a Muslim or appoint one without special loyalty oaths."

Obama, as the target and inspiration of this resurgent wave of Republican anti-Muslim hostility, was ill-equipped to stem the tide. "The problem was that when situations would occur, and people would say, 'Why can't [Obama] speak out more forcefully,' I would say that the people he needs to speak to see him as the problem," Zogby argues. "It was the responsibility of Republicans to speak out, and they didn't. George Bush was forceful on the issue in the White House, even though he supported policies that fed it. . . . There were no compelling voices on the Republican side to stop it, and so it just festered."

That anti-Muslim surge on the right also provided a way for some conservatives to rationalize hostility toward Barack Obama, by displacing feelings about his race in favor of the belief that he was secretly Muslim—a group about which conservatives felt much more comfortable expressing outright animus.

"In 2004 there's very little relationship between how you felt about the parties and how you felt about Muslims," Michael Tesler, a political scientist, told me. But "Obama really activates anti-Muslim attitudes along party lines."

In 2012, according to Tesler's numbers, only 13 percent of voters who believed Obama was Muslim said they would not vote for Obama because of his race. But 60 percent of those voters said they wouldn't vote for him because of his religion—a frank admission of prejudice inseparable from their perception of Obama's racial identity.

The scorched-earth Republican politics of the Obama era also helped block the path toward a more diverse, and therefore more tolerant, GOP. In his 2016 book, *Post-Racial or Most-Racial?*, Tesler found that Obama racialized white opinions about everything from health-care policy to Portuguese water dogs to his closest white associates, such as Joe Biden and Hillary Clinton. Tesler argued, "Barack Obama consistently widened racial divides, despite his best efforts to neutralize the political impact of race," despite having "discussed race less in his first term than any other Democratic president since Franklin Roosevelt" and having "regularly downplayed accusations of race-based opposition to his presidency" during that time.

"Even after controlling for economic conservatism, moral traditionalism, religious beliefs and activity, and military support, racial attitudes became significantly stronger predictors of white partisanship in the Age of Obama," Tesler wrote. The "spillover of racialization into mass assessments of public figures will probably make racial attitudes a more powerful determinant of Americans' 2016 vote choices than they were in pre-Obama presidential elections."

That was not a foregone conclusion. In other instances, whites' fears that black political figures would give preferential treatment to black Americans had subsided as those black leaders took action in office. Despite Obama being "the least liberal president since World War II and the biggest moderate in the White House since Dwight Eisenhower," however, the nature of the Republican opposition—attacking health-care reform as a "civil-rights bill" and Obama as a foreign-born, terrorist-sympathizing interloper and freedom-destroying socialist—substantiated "any race-based anxieties about an Obama presidency destroying the country" and prevented consciousness of Obama's moderation from filtering to white voters, Tesler argued.

Instead, white voters became convinced that they had elected Huey Newton. There was effectively no opportunity for Obama to escape the racist caricature that had been painted of him, even though his challenge to America's racial hierarchy was more symbolic than substantive. An agenda that included record deportations and targeted killings in Muslim countries abroad did little to stem the conspiracy theories.

"I think you can draw a straight line between Obama and heightened racialization and the emergence of Trump," Tesler told me. "Birtherism, the idea that Obama's a Muslim, anti-Muslim sentiments—these are very strong components of Trump's rise and really what makes him popular with this crew in the first place."

It's not that Republicans would have been less opposed to Clinton had she become president or that conservatives are inherently racist. The nature of the partisan opposition to Obama altered white Republicans' perceptions of themselves and their country, of their social position, and of the religious and ethnic minorities whose growing political power led to Obama's election.

Birtherism is rightly remembered as a racist conspiracy theory, born of an inability to accept the legitimacy of the first black president. But it is more than that, and the insistence that it was a fringe belief undersells the fact that it was one of the most important political developments of the past decade.

Birtherism is a synthesis of the prejudice toward black people, immigrants, and Muslims that swelled on the right during the Obama era: Obama was not merely black but also a foreigner, not just black and foreign but also a secret Muslim. Birtherism was not simply racism but nationalism—a statement of values and a definition of who belongs in America. By embracing the conspiracy theory of Obama's faith and foreign birth, Trump was also endorsing a definition of being American that excluded the first black president. Birtherism and then Trumpism united all three rising strains of prejudice on the right in opposition to the man who had become the sum of their fears.

In this sense only, the Calamity Thesis is correct. The great cataclysm in white America that led to Donald Trump was the election of Barack Obama.

HISTORY HAS A WAY OF altering villains so that we can no longer see ourselves in them.

As the vice president of the Confederacy, Alexander Stephens, in his 1861 "Cornerstone Speech," articulated that the principle on which the Confederate states had been founded was the "great truth that the negro is not equal to the white man; that slavery, subordination to the superior race, is his natural and normal condition." That principle was echoed by the declarations of secession from almost all of the Southern states.

Sitting in his cell at Fort Warren years later, the rebels defeated and the Confederacy vanquished, Stephens had second thoughts. He insisted in his diary, "The reporter's notes, which were very imperfect, were hastily corrected by me; and were published without further revision and with several glaring errors." In fact, Stephens wrote, he didn't like slavery at all.

"My own opinion of slavery, as often expressed, was that if the institution was not the best, or could not be made the best, for both races, looking to the advancement and progress of both, physically and morally, it ought to be abolished," Stephens wrote. "Great improvements were, however, going on in the condition of blacks in the South. . . . Much greater would have been made, I verily believe, but for outside agitation."

Stephens had become first in line to the presidency of the Confederacy, an entity founded to defend white people's right to own black people as chattel. But that didn't mean he possessed any hostility toward black people, for whom he truly wanted only the best. The real problem was the crooked media, which had taken him out of context.

The same was true of the rest of the South, he wrote, which had no love for the institution of slavery. "They were ready to sacrifice property, life, everything, for the Cause, which was then simply the right of self-government," Stephens insisted. "The slavery question had but little influence with the masses." Again, the problem, as he saw it, was a media that deliberately lied about the cause of disunion. He singled out Horace Greeley, the founder of the *New-York Tribune*, saying that Greeley's description of the South as seeking to overthrow the Constitution in order to establish a "slave oligarchy" was "utterly unfounded."

Stephens's rewriting of his own views on race and slavery, the causes of the Civil War, and the founding principles of the Confederacy laid a different cornerstone. It served as a crucial text in the emerging alternate history of the Lost Cause, the mythology that the South had fought a principled battle for its own liberty and sovereignty and not, in President Ulysses S. Grant's words, an ideal that was among "the worst for which a people ever fought." The Lost Cause provided white Southerners—and white Americans in general—with a misunderstanding of the Civil War that allowed them to spare themselves the shame of their own history.

Stephens's denial of what the Confederacy fought for—a purpose he himself had articulated for the eternity of human memory—is a manifestation of a delusion essential to nationalism in almost all of its American permutations: American history as glorious idealism unpolluted by base tribalism. If a man who helped lead a nation founded to preserve the right to own black people as slaves could believe this lie, it is folly to think that anyone who has done anything short of that would have difficulty doing the same.

James Baldwin wrote about this peculiar American delusion in 1964, arguing that the founders of the United States had a "fatal flaw": that "they could recognize a man when they saw one." Because "they had already decided that they came here to establish a free country, the only way to justify the role this chattel was playing in one's life was to say that he was not a man. For if he wasn't a man, then no crime had been committed. That lie is the basis of our present trouble. It is an extremely complex lie."

Most important, the overgrown branches of that complex lie have become manifest during nearly every surge in American nationalism, enabling its proponents to act with what they believe is a clear conscience. Just as Stephens implausibly denied that his dream of a society with African servitude as its cornerstone held malice toward black people, so too the Lost Cause myth allowed Northerners to look the other way as

Southerners scuttled Reconstruction's brief experiment with multiracial democracy and replaced it with a society rooted in white supremacy.

That Southern society, like the planter aristocracy that preceded it, impoverished most black and white people alike, while concentrating wealth and power in the hands of a white elite. It lasted for decades, through both violence and the acquiescence of those who might have been expected to rise up against it.

Americans tend to portray defenders of Jim Crow in cartoonish, Disney-villain terms. This creates a certain amount of distance, obscuring the reality that segregation enjoyed broad support among white people. As the historian Jason Sokol recounts in his book *There Goes My Everything*, white Southerners fighting integration imagined themselves not as adhering to an oppressive ideology but as resisting one. "A certain notion of freedom crystallized among white southerners— and it had little to do with fascism overseas or equal rights. Many began to picture the American government as the fascist, and the white southerner as the victim," Sokol writes.

One letter (out of many) cited by Sokol, from a World War II veteran in 1964, provides an illustrative example. "Six brothers in my family including myself fought in World War II for our rights and freedom," a veteran from Charlotte, North Carolina, wrote to his representative. "Then why . . . am I being forced to use the same wash-room and restrooms with Negroes. I highly resent this. . . . I'd be willing to fight and die for my rights, but can't say this anymore for this country."

Nor did many white Southerners accept that Jim Crow segregation was a fundamentally unjust arrangement. Sokol recalls Harris Wofford's 1952 description of his time in Dallas

County, Alabama, which a woman who ran the county's chamber of commerce described as "a nigger heaven."

"The niggers know their place and seem to keep in their place. They're the friendly sort around here," she explained. "If they are hungry, they will come and tell you, and there is not a person who wouldn't feed and clothe a nigger."

The formulation is surely familiar: She attested to her intimate and friendly interpersonal relationships with black people as a defense of a violent, kleptocratic system that denied them the same fundamental rights that she enjoyed. In fact, it was the subordinate position of black people that made peaceful relations possible.

Like Stephens, the most-ardent defenders of Jim Crow later denied that the system they defended had been rooted in any kind of malice or injustice.

Four-time Alabama Democratic governor George Wallace lost his first gubernatorial race when he ran as an economic populist against a candidate with a segregationist platform and famously vowed never to be "outniggered again"—and he never was. He declared, "Segregation now, segregation forever!" as he took the oath of office in 1963. He stood in a schoolhouse's door in Tuscaloosa to prevent black students from integrating it. He was responsible for the vicious beating of voting-rights activists in Selma.

By 1984, however, Wallace's memory of his own actions, like Stephens's, had changed. "It was not an antagonism towards black people, and that's what some people can't understand," Wallace explained to a reporter from PBS for the documentary *Eyes on the Prize*. "White Southerners did not believe it was discrimination. They thought it was in the best interest of both the races.

"I love black people. I love white people. I love yellow people," Wallace said. "I'm a Christian and, therefore, I don't have any ill feeling toward anybody because of the race, 'cause our black people are some of our finest citizens."

In remarkable symmetry with Stephens's defense of treason in defense of slavery, Wallace recalled his defense of racial apartheid as resistance to tyranny.

"I spoke vehemently against the federal government, not against people. I talked about the, the government of the, the United States and the Supreme Court. I never expressed in any language that would upset anyone about a person's race. I talked about the Supreme Court usurpation of power. I talked about the big central government," Wallace said. "Isn't that what everybody talks about now? Isn't that what Reagan got elected on? Isn't that what all the legislators, electors, members of Congress, and the Senate and House both say?"

TRUMPISM EMERGED FROM A HAZE of delusion, denial, pride, and cruelty—not as a historical anomaly but as a profoundly American phenomenon. This explains both how tens of millions of white Americans could pull the lever for a candidate running on a racist platform and justify doing so and why a predominantly white political class would search so desperately for an alternative explanation for what it had just seen. To acknowledge the centrality of racial inequality to American democracy is to question its legitimacy—so it must be denied.

I don't mean to suggest that Trump's nationalism is impervious to politics. It is not invincible. Its earlier iterations have been defeated before and can be defeated now. Abraham Lincoln began the Civil War believing that former slaves would have to be transported to West Africa. Lyndon Johnson began his political career as a segregationist. Both came to realize that the question of black rights in America is not mere identity politics—not a peripheral matter but the central, existential question of the republic. Nothing is inevitable; people can change. No one is irredeemable. But recognition precedes enlightenment.

Nevertheless, a majority of white voters backed a candidate who assured them that they will never have to share this country with people of color as equals. That is the reality that all Americans will have to deal with and one that most of the country has yet to confront.

Yet at its core, white nationalism has and always will be a hustle, a con, a fraud that cannot deliver the broad-based prosperity it promises, not even to most white people. Perhaps the most persuasive argument against Trumpist nationalism is not one its opponents can make in a way that his supporters will believe. But the failure of Trump's promises to white America may yet show that both the fruit and the tree are poison.

4

THE CRUELTY OF RECONCILIATION

JOE BIDEN'S 2020 PRESIDENTIAL CAMPAIGN LEANED HEAVILY ON many different kinds of nostalgia. Nostalgia for the Obama era, in which he served as vice president, nostalgia for when Americans did not risk succumbing to a deadly pandemic simply by leaving their homes. But for Biden himself, the strongest sense of nostalgia was reserved for the time of his early Senate career, before the era of modern political polarization took hold, when cross-ideological legislation still seemed possible.

When I wrote this piece in the winter of 2019, I was trying to convey how "civility" had been weaponized to silence protest of the Trump administration and explain why Americans should not pine for the false comity of years past, which was rooted in the exclusion of black Americans from the polity. Multiracial democracy is hard and messy and sometimes rude, but it is preferable to the alternatives.

Nevertheless, Biden's victory suggests this appeal to nostalgia was a successful one, at least as far as campaign themes go. But as a political theory it remains erroneous in conception.

Big, cross-ideological legislation is still possible, as long as a Republican is in the White House. Congress spent more than five trillion dollars responding to the coronavirus pandemic in 2020, in aid bills that combined subsidies for businesses with stimulus checks and expanded unemployment insurance. The aid bills did not prevent massive job losses, but they did prevent the economy from cratering, and poverty temporarily fell as a result. The relative strength of the economy almost kept Trump in office.

In 2008, Democrats needed a near filibuster-proof majority to pass a stimulus half the size, in the midst of the worst recession since the Great Depression. With a Democratic president, Republicans calculated that prolonging economic pain was in their political best interest, and they were right. They swept both the House and state legislatures in the 2010 midterm backlash. Republicans didn't suddenly abandon their ideological predilections with Trump in the White House, but they were willing to legislate. Despite holding the House, Democrats were unwilling to make the calculation that Republicans made in 2010—to prolong economic catastrophe to secure political advantage. Trump supporters and Trump opponents alike benefited from the Democratic Party's refusal to make the passage of federal aid contingent on the presence of a president from their own party. After Trump's defeat, Republicans revived their 2010 playbook, unanimously opposing President Biden's popular coronavirus aid bill. With a Democrat back in the White House, alleviating public misery was no longer in their political interest.

The relative ideological diversity of each party's coalition helps explain the discrepancy—although liberals are the largest ideological group, conservatives and moderates together comprise the majority of the Democratic coalition.

As an institution, the Democratic Party is forced to practice coalition-building between diverse groups in order to hold power, and so they cannot express the kind of casual contempt for rival constituencies Republican federal lawmakers can. That also helps explain both the effectiveness of Biden's appeal to "civility" for Democrats and its one-sided conception among Republicans. In 2018, Senate majority leader Mitch McConnell, perhaps Trump's most important political ally, declared that "the American people know that the fact-free politics of hate, fear, and intimidation are not how we actually govern in our democratic republic."

"Hate, fear, and intimidation" are a concise summary of the politics of a candidate who not only ran on promises of mass deportations, Muslim bans, and birtherism but those of a president who used his authority to coerce others to intervene in elections on his behalf. While Biden was appealing to civility, Trump was attempting to coerce the leader of Ukraine to implicate Biden in a nonexistent crime. As Biden was promising to govern on behalf of all Americans regardless of party affiliation, Trump was attempting to intimidate Republican state legislatures into overturning their election results. When Biden and his transition team were pleading with the Trump administration for cooperation, the president was sending a mob to sack the Capitol building in an effort to keep him in power.

McConnell's 2018 remarks were responding to a statement from Hillary Clinton, Trump's Democratic rival from 2016, who had told CNN that Democrats "cannot be civil with a political party that wants to destroy what you stand for, what you care about. That's why I believe, if we are fortunate enough to win back the House and/or the Senate, that's when civility can start again."

Clinton's assessment was slightly more realistic than Biden's. Democracy, after all, is a set of rules the people agree upon for negotiating conflicts nonviolently. When you cannot simply overpower your political opposition, you have to find other ways of achieving your goals. That reality can produce the mutual respect necessary for civility to mean something more than deference to power—as long as there isn't a greater advantage to be gained from stalemate.

Yet the Democratic victories in 2018 and 2020 were not great enough to alter the dynamic I've described. Republicans can wield power with a minority of the vote, and both the electoral college and the Senate amplify the political influence of the most right-leaning segments of the country.

The initial 2020 election results suggested Republicans had not paid a dear price for their embrace of Trumpism, their mishandling of the coronavirus pandemic, and the economic crisis that followed. Democrats had barely kept the House, and polls before the election had overestimated Democrats' chances of taking the Senate.

After the January 2021 Senate runoff elections in Georgia, the final verdict looked far more grim for Republicans. Kelly Loeffler, wealthy former CEO, lost her election race against Raphael Warnock, the pastor of Martin Luther King Jr.'s Ebenezer Baptist Church in Atlanta, after falsely accusing him of child abuse and calling him a radical Marxist. Loeffler's attacks on Warnock drove massive turnout among black voters, who saw Loeffler as denigrating the Black Church. In the second Georgia Senate runoff, the increase in turnout was sufficient to drag Jon Ossoff, the other Democratic Senate candidate, across the finish line against Republican incumbent David Perdue, who had run ads exaggerating the size of Ossoff's nose. Ossoff is Jewish.

The loss of the House, Senate, and presidency may have restored a small but meaningful level of deterrence against the Republican embrace of Trumpist politics. But Democrats still face immense political pressure to appeal to Republican-leaning constituencies if they want to hold power. Biden's politics of civility, then, are not simply the nostalgia of an aging senator who remembers a better time but a rational political strategy for a party that faces tremendous structural disadvantages. What principles and which coalitions Democrats may be willing to sacrifice in the process, we shall see.

CIVILITY IS OVERRATED

DECEMBER 2019

JOE BIDEN HAS FOND MEMORIES OF NEGOTIATING WITH JAMES Eastland, the senator from Mississippi who once declared, "I am of the opinion that we should have segregation in all the states of the United States by law. What the people of this country must realize is that the white race is a superior race, and the Negro race is an inferior race."

Recalling in June 2019 his debates with segregationists like Eastland, Biden lamented, "At least there was some civility," compared with today. "We got things done. We didn't agree on much of anything. We got things done. We got it finished. But today, you look at the other side and you're the enemy. Not the opposition; the enemy. We don't talk to each other anymore."

Biden later apologized for his wistfulness. But yearning for an ostensibly more genteel era of American politics wasn't a gaffe. Such nostalgia is central to Biden's appeal as an antidote to the vitriol that has marked the presidency of Donald Trump.

Nor is Biden alone in selling the idea that rancor threatens the American republic. This September, Supreme Court justice Neil Gorsuch—who owes his seat to Senate Republicans depriving a Democratic president of his authority to fill a vacancy on the high court—published a book that argued, "In a very real way, self-governance turns on our treating each other as equals—as persons, with the courtesy and respect each person deserves—even when we vigorously disagree."

Trump himself, a man whose rallies regularly descend into ritual denunciations of his enemies, declared in October 2018, as Americans were preparing to vote in the midterm elections, that "everyone will benefit if we can end the politics of personal destruction." The president helpfully explained exactly what he meant: "Constant unfair coverage, deep hostility, and negative attacks . . . only serve to drive people apart and to undermine healthy debate." Civility, in other words, is treating Trump how Trump wants to be treated, while he treats you however he pleases. It was a more honest description of how the concept of civility is applied today than either Biden or Gorsuch offered.

There are two definitions of civility. The first is not being an asshole. The second is "I can do what I want and you can shut up." The latter definition currently dominates American political discourse.

The country is indeed divided today, and there is nothing wrong with wishing that Americans could all get along. But while nonviolence is essential to democracy, civility is optional, and today's preoccupation with politesse both exaggerates the country's divisions and papers over the fundamental issues that are causing the divisions in the first place. The idea that we're currently experiencing something like the nadir of American civility ignores the turmoil that has traditionally characterized the nation's politics and the comparatively low level of political violence today despite the animosity of the moment.

Paeans to a more civil past also ignore the price of that civility. It's not an unfortunate coincidence that the men Joe Biden worked with so amicably were segregationists. The civility he longs for was the result of excluding historically marginalized groups from the polity, which allowed men like James Eastland to wield tremendous power in Congress without regard for the rights or dignity of their disenfranchised constituents.

The true cause of American political discord is the lingering resistance of those who have traditionally held power to sharing it with those who until recently have only experienced its serrated edge. And the resistance does linger. Just this fall, a current Democratic senator from Delaware, Chris Coons, told a panel at the University of Notre Dame Law School that he hoped "a more diverse Senate that includes women's voices, and voices of people of color, and voices of people who were not professionals but, you know, who grew up working-class" would not produce "irreconcilable discord."

In his "Letter from Birmingham Jail," Martin Luther King Jr. famously lamented the "white moderate" who "prefers a negative peace which is the absence of tension to a positive peace which is the presence of justice." He also acknowledged the importance of tension to achieving justice. "I have earnestly opposed violent tension," King wrote, "but there is a type of constructive, nonviolent tension which is necessary for growth." Americans should not fear that form of tension. They should fear its absence.

• • •

AT THEIR MOST FRENZIED, CALLS for civility stoke the fear that the United States might be on the precipice of armed conflict. Once confined to right-wing fever swamps, where radicals wrote fan fiction about taking up arms in response to "liberal tyranny," the notion has gained currency in conservative media in the Trump era. In response to calls for gun-buyback programs, Tucker Carlson said on Fox News, "What you are calling for is civil war." The president himself has warned that removing him from office, through the constitutionally provided-for mechanism of impeachment, might lead to civil war.

Civil war is not an imminent prospect. The impulse to conjure its specter overlooks how bitter and fierce American politics has often been. In the early days of the republic, as Richard Hofstadter and Michael Wallace wrote in their 1970 book, *American Violence,* the country witnessed Election Day riots, in which "one faction often tried violently to prevent another from voting." In the 1850s, the nativist Know-Nothings fielded gangs to intimidate immigrant voters. Abolitionists urged defiance of the Fugitive Slave Act and lived by their words, running slave catchers out of town and breaking captured black people out of custody. Frederick Douglass said that the best way to make the act a "dead letter" was "to make half a dozen or more dead kidnappers."

During the Gilded Age, state militias turned guns on striking workers. From 1882 to 1968, nearly five thousand people, mostly black Americans, were lynched nationwide. From January 1969 to April 1970, more than four thousand bombings occurred across the country, according to a Senate investigation. As Hofstadter wrote, "Violence has been used repeatedly in our past, often quite purposefully, and a full reckoning with the fact is a necessary ingredient in any realistic national self-image."

The absence of this realistic national self-image has contributed to the sense of despair that characterizes American politics today. The reality, however, is that political violence is less common in the present than it has been at many points in American history, despite the ancient plague of white supremacy, the lingering scourge of jihadism, and the influence of a president who revels in winking justifications of violence against his political opponents and immigrants. Many Americans can't stand one another right now. But apart from a few deranged fanatics, they do not want to slaughter one another en masse.

THE MORE PERTINENT HISTORICAL ANALOGUE is not the fractious antebellum period that right-wing partisans seem so eager to relive but the tragic failures of Reconstruction, when the comforts of comity were privileged over the difficult work of building a multiracial democracy. The danger of our own political moment is not that Americans will again descend into a bloody conflagration. It is that the fundamental rights of marginalized people will again become bargaining chips political leaders trade for an empty reconciliation.

The Reconstruction amendments to the Constitution should have settled once and for all the question of whether America was a white man's country or a nation for all its citizens. The Thirteenth Amendment abolished slavery, the Fourteenth Amendment established that anyone could be a citizen regardless of race, and the Fifteenth Amendment barred racial discrimination in voting. But by 1876, Republicans had paid a high political price for their advocacy of rights for black people, losing control of the House and nearly losing the presidency to the party associated with a violent rebellion in defense of slavery. Democrats agreed to hand Rutherford B. Hayes the presidency in exchange for the withdrawal of federal troops in the South, effectively ending the region's brief experiment in multiracial governance. Witnessing the first stirrings of reunion, Douglass, the great abolitionist, wondered aloud, "In what position will this stupendous reconciliation leave the colored people?" He was right to worry.

One state government after another fell to campaigns of murder and terror carried out by Democratic paramilitaries. With its black constituency in the South disempowered, the Republican Party grew reliant on its corporate patrons and adjusted its approach to maximize support from white voters. As for those emancipated after a devastating war, the party of abolition abandoned them to the despotism of their former masters. Writing in 1902, the political scientist and white supremacist John W. Burgess observed, "The white men of the South need now have no further fear that the Republican party, or Republican Administrations, will ever again give themselves over to the vain imagination of the political equality of man."

The capitulation of Republicans restored civility between the major parties, but the political truce masked a horrendous spike in violence against freedmen. "While the parties clearly move back from confrontation with each other, you have the unleashing of massive white-supremacist violence in the South against African Americans and a systematic campaign to disenfranchise, a systematic campaign of racial terror in the South," Manisha Sinha, a history professor at the University of Connecticut and the author of *The Slave's Cause: A History of Abolition*, told me. "This is an era when white supremacy becomes virtually a national ideology."

This was the fruit of prizing reconciliation over justice, order over equality, civility over truth. Republicans' acquiescence laid the foundation for the reimposition of forced labor on the emancipated, the establishment of the Jim Crow system, and the state and extrajudicial terror that preserved white supremacy in the South for another century.

THE DAY WILLIAM HOWARD TAFT was inaugurated, in March 1909, was frigid—a storm dropped more than half a foot of snow on Washington, D.C. But Taft's inaugural address was filled with warm feeling, particularly about the reconciliation of North and South and the full and just resolution of what was then known as the "Negro problem."

"I look forward," the party of Lincoln's latest president said, "to an increased feeling on the part of all the people in the South that this Government is their Government, and that its officers in their states are their officers." He assured Americans, "I have not the slightest race prejudice or feeling, and recognition of its existence only awakens in my heart a deeper sympathy for those who have to bear it or suffer from it, and I question the wisdom of a policy which is likely to increase it."

To that end, he explained, black people should abandon their ambitions toward enfranchisement. In fact, Taft praised the various measures white Southerners had devised to exclude poor white and black Americans—"an ignorant, irresponsible element"—from the polity.

Writing in *The Crisis* two years later, W.E.B. Du Bois bitterly described Taft's betrayal of black Americans. "In the face of a record of murder, lynching and burning in this country which has appalled the civilized world and loosened the tongue of many a man long since dumb on the race problem, in spite of this, Mr. Taft has blandly informed a deputation of colored men that any action on his part is quite outside his power, if not his interest."

The first volume of David Levering Lewis's biography of Du Bois shows him in particular anguish over what he called the "Taft Doctrine" of acquiescence to Jim Crow, which, in Lewis's words, "had virtually nullified what remained of Republican Party interest in civil rights." Taft's Republican successors generally followed suit, culminating with Herbert Hoover, who in 1928 "accelerated the policy of whitening the GOP below the Mason-Dixon Line in order to bring about a major political realignment," as Lewis put it in the second volume of his Du Bois biography. Taft, who was now the chief justice of the Supreme Court, described the strategy as an attempt "to break up the solid South and to drive the Negroes out of Republican politics."

Taft couldn't have predicted exactly how this realignment would take place, but he was right about the result. Despite the best efforts of Southern Democrats to segregate the benefits of the New Deal, the policies devised by Franklin D. Roosevelt to lift America out of the Great Depression alleviated black poverty, reinvigorating black participation in politics and helping transform the Democratic Party. "Government became immediate, its impact tangible, its activities relevant," wrote the historian Nancy Weiss Malkiel in her 1983 book, *Farewell to the Party of Lincoln.* "As a result, blacks, like other Americans, found themselves drawn into the political process."

The New Deal's modest, albeit inadvertent, erosion of racial apartheid turned Southern Democrats against it. Thus began a period of ideological heterodoxy within the parties born of the unresolved race question. Whatever their other differences, significant factions in both parties could agree on the imperative to further marginalize black Americans.

Some of the worst violence in American history occurred during the period of low partisan polarization stretching from the late Progressive era to the late 1970s—the moment for which Joe Biden waxed nostalgic. In Ivy League debate rooms and the Senate cloakroom, white men could discuss the most divisive issues of the day with all the politeness befitting what was for them a low-stakes conflict. Outside, the people whose rights were actually at stake were fighting and dying to have those rights recognized.

In 1955, the lynching of Emmett Till—and the sight of his mutilated body in his casket—helped spark the modern civil-rights movement. Lionized today for their disciplined, nonviolent protest, civil-rights demonstrators were seen by American political elites as unruly and impolite. In April 1965, about a month after police attacked civil-rights marchers in Selma, Alabama, with billy clubs and tear gas, *National Review* published a cover story opposing the Voting Rights Act. Titled "Must We Repeal the Constitution to Give the Negro the Vote?," the article, written by James Jackson Kilpatrick, began by lamenting the uncompromising meanness of the law's supporters. Opposing the enfranchisement of black people, Kilpatrick complained, meant being dismissed as "a bigot, a racist, a violator of the rights of man, a mute accomplice to the murder of a mother-of-five."

The fact that *National Review*'s founder, William F. Buckley Jr., had editorialized that "the White community in the South is entitled to take such measures as are necessary to prevail, politically and culturally, in areas in which it does not predominate numerically" went unmentioned by Kilpatrick.

Both civility and democracy were marred by the inclusion of black people in politics because, in the view of Kilpatrick, Buckley, and many of their contemporaries, black people had no business participating in the first place.

SINCE THE 1970S, AMERICAN POLITICS has grown more polarized, as the realignment Taft foresaw moved toward its conclusion and the parties became more ideologically distinct. In recent years, the differences between Republicans and Democrats have come to be defined as much by identity as by ideology. If you are white and Christian, you are very likely to be a Republican; if you are not, you are more likely to be a Democrat. At the same time, Americans have now sorted themselves geographically and socially such that they rarely encounter people who hold opposing views.

It's a recipe for acrimony. As the parties become more homogeneous and more alien to each other, "we are more capable of dehumanizing the other side or distancing ourselves from them on a moral basis," Lilliana Mason, a political scientist and the author of *Uncivil Agreement*, told me. "So it becomes easier for us to say things like, 'People on the other side are not just wrong, they're evil,' or 'People on the other side, they should be treated like animals.'"

Ideological and demographic uniformity has not been realized equally in both parties, however. The Democratic Party remains a heterogeneous entity, full of believers and atheists, nurses and college professors, black people and white people. This has made the party more hospitable to multiracial democracy.

The Republican Party, by contrast, has grown more racially and religiously homogeneous and its politics more dependent on manufacturing threats to the status of white Christians. This is why Trump frequently and falsely implies that Americans were afraid to say "Merry Christmas" before he was elected, and why Tucker Carlson and Laura Ingraham warn Fox News viewers that nonwhite immigrants are stealing America. For both the Republican Party and conservative media, wielding power and influence depends on making white Americans feel threatened by the growing political influence of those who are different from them.

In stoking such fears, anger is a powerful weapon. In his book, *Anger and Racial Politics,* the University of Maryland professor Antoine J. Banks argues that "anger is the dominant emotional underpinning of contemporary racism." Anger and racism are so linked, in fact, that politicians need not use overtly racist language to provoke racial resentment. Anger alone, Banks writes, can activate prejudiced views, even when a given issue would seem to have little to do with race: "Anger operates as a switch that amplifies (or turns on) racist thinking—exacerbating America's racial problem. It pushes prejudiced whites to oppose policies and candidates perceived as alleviating racial inequality." This is true for politicians on both sides of the political divide—but the right has far more to gain from sowing discord than from mending fences.

Trumpists lamenting civility's decline do not fear fractiousness; on the contrary, they happily practice it to their own ends. What they really fear are the cultural, political, and economic shifts that occur when historically marginalized groups begin to exert power in a system that was once defined by their exclusion. Social mores that had been acceptable become offensive; attitudes that had been widely held are condemned.

Societies are constantly renegotiating the boundaries of

respect and decency. This process can be disorienting; to the once-dominant group, it can even feel like oppression. (It is not.) Many of the same people who extol the sanctity of civility when their prerogatives are questioned are prone to convulsions over the possibility of respecting those they consider beneath them, a form of civility they deride as "political correctness."

In a different political system, the tide would pull the Republican Party toward the center. But the GOP's structural advantage in the electoral college and the Senate and its success in gerrymandering congressional and state legislative districts all over the country allow it to wield power while continuing to appeal solely to a diminishing conservative minority encouraged to regard its fellow Americans as an existential threat.

The Trump administration's attempt to use the census to enhance the power of white voters was foiled by a single vote on the Supreme Court on the basis of a technicality; it will not be the last time this incarnation of the Republican Party seeks to rig democracy to its advantage on racial terms. Even before Trump, the party was focused not only on maximizing the influence of white voters but on disenfranchising minority voters, barely bothering to update its rationale since Taft praised Jim Crow–era voting restrictions for banishing the "ignorant" from the polity.

The end of polarization in America matters less than the terms on which it ends. It is possible that, in the aftermath of a Trump defeat in 2020, Republicans will move to the political center. But it is also possible that Trump will win a second term, and the devastation of the defeat will lead the Democrats to court conservative white people, whose geographic distribution grants them a disproportionate influence over

American politics. Like the Republicans during Reconstruction, the Democrats may bargain away the rights of their other constituencies in the process.

The true threat to America is not an excess of vitriol but that elites will come together in a consensus that cripples democracy and acquiesces to the dictatorship of a shrinking number of Americans who treat this nation as their exclusive birthright because of their race and religion. This is the false peace of dominance, not the true peace of justice. Until Americans' current dispute over the nature of our republic is settled in favor of the latter, the dispute must continue.

In the aftermath of a terrible war, Americans once purchased an illusion of reconciliation, peace, and civility through a restoration of white rule. They should never again make such a bargain.

5

THE CRUELTY OF
THE MOB

THIS IS ONE OF THOSE PIECES THAT BASICALLY WRITE THEM-
selves. The phenomenon it describes had been apparent from
the start of the Trump campaign, but I had lacked the words
to describe it, until the night in 2018 when I saw the president
of the United States use a woman who had come forward
with an allegation of sexual assault as a laugh line.

It did take me a minute to wrap my head around what I
had seen. I took a walk down the street in San Antonio, trying
to put it together. I thought back to the Trump rallies I had
covered in 2016 and how much fun the people there were
having. They enjoyed the insults, the mean jokes, the apocryphal stories about killing Muslims with bullets dipped in pigs'
blood or humiliating Mexico by forcing them to pay for a wall
on the southern border. Even if they didn't believe the wall
or the Muslim ban would happen—and many of the people
I spoke to didn't—they enjoyed Trump's gleeful expression of
their hatreds.

This is probably the most-read piece I've ever written, and
it shares its title with this book. I never expected the response

it got, but I think the reason it resonated was that it articulated something many of us implicitly felt but struggled to put into words: that the president enjoyed hurting people in ways large and small, and that many of his supporters enjoyed it when he hurt people. The more anguish you felt, the more fun it was for them. This is not simply an ethos but a policy approach.

On a smaller level, communities are forged through disdain every day. When people in an office share juicy gossip about a colleague who annoys them; when jazz enthusiasts roll their eyes at the lack of sophistication in today's popular music; when Red Sox fans bond over how much they hate the Yankees. It's not just the satisfaction of finding someone who hates the same people or things that you do—it's the sense of acceptance that comes from knowing you are not alone, the high of feeling like you belong. Many of us have experienced a friendship that began with the discovery of something or someone neither of you could stand. What distinguishes Trumpism from the personal indulgences of our own individual pettiness or cruelty is the way that its adherents collectively savor attacks on the vulnerable and, through the alchemy of politics, turn them into public policy.

Trump weaponized this feeling, taking advantage of a politics increasingly polarized not just along party lines but along lines of religion, race, and culture. The homogeneity of the Republican Party meant there was little price to pay for dehumanizing groups perceived to be outside its coalition— black people, Muslims, Latinos, trans people—groups reliant on diverse coalitions to wield political power. This insight applies just as much to the smaller communities I mentioned above—a racist joke in a workplace with only white people plays differently than one in which someone targeted by the joke is present. I speak from personal experience, as one of the few black people who end up in a room where these jokes get told.

These moments, however, are often private. They take place in whispers, in group texts, through phone conversations, over email and on Facebook. One of the reasons white supremacist groups latched on to Trump was their belief that, by taking these moments public, he was helping to resurrect a culture in which casual bigotry did not result in social sanction. By saying, in the words of many of the Trump supporters I spoke to, what "we were all thinking," he was making it okay for them to say such things too. This not only made them feel free; it made them feel protected by the others around them seeking the exhilaration of saying what they wanted to say without being judged. At a Trump rally, there are no scolds to spoil the fun—and no one who could remind you of the humanity of those being attacked.

The flip side is that culture can change rapidly when the community is expanded. When I was a teenager, it was extraordinarily common to hear words like "gay" and "fag" as pejoratives. But as more Americans came out of the closet—and more Americans realized people they loved were part of the LGBT community—public opinion changed rapidly. In 2004, overt anti-gay politics were seen as effective and popular; today, Republicans with statewide or national aspirations try to couch such politics in euphemism. For most people, enjoying cruelty requires a healthy distance from the target.

That said, sometimes when the community expands, that merely means redrawing certain lines so that new members can enjoy the privilege of looking down on and exploiting others. The cruelty isn't necessarily the point then, but it is a sign that you've finally made it. That feels pretty good too.

THE CRUELTY
IS THE POINT

OCTOBER 3, 2018

THE MUSEUM OF AFRICAN AMERICAN HISTORY AND CULTURE IS IN part a catalog of cruelty. Amid all the stories of perseverance, tragedy, and unlikely triumph are the artifacts of inhumanity and barbarism: the child-size slave shackles, the bright-red robes of the wizards of the Ku Klux Klan, the recordings of civil-rights protesters being brutalized by police.

The artifacts that persist in my memory, the way a bright flash does when you close your eyes, are the photographs of lynchings. But it's not the burned, mutilated bodies that stick with me. It's the faces of the white men in the crowd. There's the photo of the lynching of Thomas Shipp and Abram Smith in Indiana in 1930, in which a white man can be seen grinning at the camera as he tenderly holds the hand of his wife or girlfriend. There's the undated photo from Duluth, Minnesota, in which grinning white men stand next to the mutilated, half-naked bodies of two men lashed to a post in the street—one of the white men is straining to get into the picture, his smile cutting from ear to ear. There's the photo of a crowd of white men huddled behind the smoldering corpse of a man burned to death; one of them is wearing a smart suit, a fedora hat, and a bright smile.

Their names have mostly been lost to time. But these grinning men were someone's brother, son, husband, father. They were human beings, people who took immense pleasure in the utter cruelty of torturing others to death—and were so proud of doing so that they posed for photographs with their handiwork, jostling to ensure they caught the eye of the lens, so that the world would know they'd been there. Their cruelty made them feel good, it made them feel proud, it made them feel happy. And it made them feel closer to one another.

The Trump era is such a whirlwind of cruelty that it can be hard to keep track. This week alone, the news broke that the Trump administration was seeking to ethnically cleanse more than 193,000 American children of immigrants whose temporary protected status had been revoked by the administration, that the Department of Homeland Security had lied about creating a database of children that would make it possible to unite them with the families the Trump administration had arbitrarily destroyed, that the White House was considering a blanket ban on visas for Chinese students, and that it would deny visas to the same-sex partners of foreign officials. At a rally in Mississippi, a crowd of Trump supporters cheered as the president mocked Christine Blasey Ford, the psychology professor who has said that Brett Kavanaugh, whom Trump has nominated to a lifetime appointment on the Supreme Court, attempted to rape her when she was a teenager. "Lock her up!" they shouted.

Ford testified to the Senate, utilizing her professional

expertise to describe the encounter, that one of the parts of the incident she remembered most was Kavanaugh and his friend Mark Judge laughing at her as Kavanaugh fumbled at her clothing. "Indelible in the hippocampus is the laughter," Ford said, referring to the part of the brain that processes emotion and memory, "the uproarious laughter between the two, and their having fun at my expense." And then at Tuesday's rally, the president made his supporters laugh at her.

Even those who believe that Ford fabricated her account or was mistaken in its details can see that the president's mocking of her testimony renders all sexual-assault survivors collateral damage. Anyone afraid of coming forward, afraid that she would not be believed, can now look to the president to see her fears realized. Once malice is embraced as a virtue, it is impossible to contain.

The cruelty of the Trump administration's policies and the ritual rhetorical flaying of his targets before his supporters are intimately connected. As Lili Loofbourow wrote of the Kavanaugh incident in *Slate*, adolescent male cruelty toward women is a bonding mechanism, a vehicle for intimacy through contempt. The white men in the lynching photos are smiling not merely because of what they have done but because they have done it together.

We can hear the spectacle of cruel laughter throughout the Trump era. There were the border-patrol agents cracking up at the crying immigrant children separated from their families, and the Trump adviser who delighted white supremacists when he mocked a child with Down syndrome who was separated from her mother. There were the police who laughed uproariously when the president encouraged them to abuse suspects, and the Fox News hosts mocking a survivor of the Pulse nightclub massacre (and in the process inundating him with threats), the survivors of sexual assault protesting to Senator Jeff Flake, the women who said the president had sexually assaulted them, and the teen survivors of the Parkland school shooting. There was the president mocking Puerto Rican accents shortly after thousands were killed and tens of thousands displaced by Hurricane Maria, the black athletes protesting unjustified killings by the police, the women of the #MeToo movement who have come forward with stories of sexual abuse, and the disabled reporter whose crime was reporting on Trump truthfully. It is not just that the perpetrators of this cruelty enjoy it; it is that they enjoy it with one another. Their shared laughter at the suffering of others is an adhesive that binds them to one another, and to Trump.

Taking joy in that suffering is more human than most would like to admit. Somewhere on the wide spectrum between adolescent teasing and the smiling white men in the lynching photographs are the Trump supporters whose community is built by rejoicing in the anguish of those they see as unlike them, who have found in their shared cruelty an answer to the loneliness and atomization of modern life.

The laughter undergirds the daily spectacle of insincerity, as the president and his aides pledge fealty to bedrock democratic principles they have no intention of respecting. The president who demanded the execution of five black and Latino teenagers for a crime they didn't commit decries "false accusations" when his Supreme Court nominee stands accused; his supporters who fancy themselves champions of free speech meet references to Hillary Clinton or a woman whose only crime was coming forward to offer her own story of abuse with screams of "Lock her up!" The political movement that elected a president who wanted to ban immigration by adherents of an entire religion, who encourages police to brutalize suspects, and who has destroyed thousands of immigrant families for violations of the law less serious than those of which he and his coterie stand accused now laments the state of due process.

This isn't incoherent. It reflects a clear principle: Only the president and his allies, his supporters, and their anointed are entitled to the rights and protections of the law and, if necessary, immunity from it. The rest of us are entitled only to cruelty, by their whim. This is how the powerful have ever kept the powerless divided and in their place and enriched themselves in the process.

A blockbuster *New York Times* investigation on Tuesday reported that President Trump's wealth was largely inherited through fraudulent schemes, that he became a millionaire while still a child, and that his fortune persists in spite of his fumbling entrepreneurship, not because of it. The stories are not unconnected. The president and his advisers have sought to enrich themselves at taxpayer expense; they have attempted to corrupt federal law-enforcement agencies to protect themselves and their cohorts, and they have exploited the nation's darkest impulses in the pursuit of profit. But their ability to get away with this fraud is tied to cruelty.

Trump's only true skill is the con; his only fundamental belief is that the United States is the birthright of straight, white, Christian men, and his only real, authentic pleasure is in cruelty. It is that cruelty, and the delight it brings them, that binds his most ardent supporters to him, in shared scorn for those they hate and fear: immigrants, black voters, feminists, and treasonous white men who empathize with any of those who would steal their birthright. The president's ability to execute that cruelty through word and deed makes them euphoric. It makes them feel good, it makes them feel proud, it makes them feel happy, it makes them feel united. And as long as he makes them feel that way, they will let him get away with anything, no matter what it costs them.

6

THE CRUELTY OF
THE NATIVISTS

PROVOKING STREET FIGHTS WITH COMMUNISTS WAS A CRUCIAL part of the Nazi strategy in the 1920s and 1930s. The chaos helped stoke fears of a communist takeover and frightened middle-class Germans into accepting the Nazi Party's arguments that it was their only protection against a Bolshevik overthrow.

"Bourgeois Germans across the country had feared the contagion of revolution," the historian Paul Hanebrink wrote in *A Specter Haunting Europe*. "Nazi Party activists preyed on memories of postwar revolutionary upheaval, warning that Germans must defend themselves against a new wave of revolutionary unrest or else become slaves to alien masters."

Combining their propaganda that communism was a Jewish plot with their fomenting of chaos in the streets, "[the] Nazi Party worked tirelessly to present street fights there as a sign that the republic was rotten to the core everywhere," and "presented the Nazi Party's own acts of violence as a justified response to leftist provocations that could redeem Germany from the humiliation of" defeat in World War I. The social and economic instability of the Weimar Republic, fears of the Soviet Union, and a long tradition of anti-Semitism helped the Nazis to win over conservative Germans who might have been skeptical otherwise.

The white nationalists behind the 2017 rally in Charlottesville, Virginia, almost certainly had something similar in mind. The rally, ostensibly to protest the removal of the statue of Confederate General Robert E. Lee, was an attempt by white supremacists to attract violence from Antifa—the loose collective of leftists who have since become an obsession of both the right and the Trump administration—and draw mainstream conservative sympathy as a result. The chaos would work to the advantage of the so-called alt-right, drawing them into an alliance with run-of-the-mill conservatives, uniting them against the scourge of leftism.

"The rally organizers came prepared for violence, and they wanted it. They wanted footage of themselves getting punched and maced so that they could use conservative antipathy to Antifa to erode conservative antipathy to ActualFascists," the conservative writer Michael Brendan Dougherty wrote in *National Review* in 2017. "The organizers don't want heritage, they wanted footage."

Instead, the deadly violence at the rally discredited the white nationalists rather than winning sympathy for them. President Donald Trump's famous equivocation that there were "very fine people on both sides" of the rally wounded his reputation and reportedly inspired his future rival Joe Biden to run for president, and many of the organizers and attendees were either prosecuted for engaging in violence or banned from social-media services. The event was a failure.

In the following years, however, more and more of the ideological arguments behind this rebranded white nationalism made their way into the conservative bloodstream. Fox News hosts spoke loudly and frequently about "demographic replacement," a paraphrase of the white nationalist conspiracy theory of "white genocide." Car ramming would become startlingly common at the Black Lives Matter protests that manifested in response to the killing of George Floyd by police, to the point that Republican elected officials like Florida governor Ron DeSantis would urge the passage of laws that define a tactic popularized by the Islamic State as self-defense. The president and his attorney general, William Barr, would attempt to turn Antifa into a national security threat, even as the Federal Bureau of Investigation warned that white nationalists were far more numerous and deadly.

When I wrote this essay in early 2019, I was trying to trace the intellectual lineage of the Charlottesville rally, a lineage that begins with the anti-immigrant conservationist Madison Grant. Although these ideas were made manifest and executed most infamously and lethally in Nazi Germany, they originated here in the United States as an intellectual justification for nativism and white supremacy. The purpose was to warn that, although a resurrection of the Third Reich was not in the offing, the United States was hardly immune to the contagion of the fraudulent discipline of race science or its implications. Indeed, high-profile members of the Trump administration had already revealed their own affinity for such concepts and were making policy decisions rooted in said calumnies.

The intellectual godfathers of scientific racism in America always recognized that their creed was in tension with American principles of freedom and equality, but saw hope in how insincerely those principles had been historically applied. The solution, for them, was for Americans to stop pretending to believe in them. But hypocrisy can nevertheless be an essential comfort for people who disdain racial equality, because they do not want to think of themselves as people who disdain racial equality. That does not guarantee that the arc of American history will ultimately bend toward justice, but Grantism and its intellectual descendants, including Trumpism, will always find foes even when they appear triumphant.

WHITE NATIONALISM'S DEEP AMERICAN ROOTS

APRIL 2019

ROBERT BOWERS WANTED EVERYONE TO KNOW WHY HE DID IT.

"I can't sit by and watch my people get slaughtered," he posted on the social-media network Gab shortly before allegedly entering the Tree of Life synagogue in Pittsburgh on October 27 and gunning down eleven worshippers. He "wanted all Jews to die," he declared while he was being treated for his wounds. Invoking the specter of white Americans facing "genocide," he singled out HIAS, a Jewish American refugee-support group, and accused it of bringing "invaders in that kill our people." Then–attorney general Jeff Sessions, announcing that Bowers would face federal charges, was unequivocal in his condemnation: "These alleged crimes are incomprehensibly evil and utterly repugnant to the values of this nation."

The pogrom in Pittsburgh, occurring just days before the eightieth anniversary of Kristallnacht, seemed fundamentally un-American to many. Sessions's denunciation spoke to the reality that most Jews have found a welcome home in the United States. His message also echoed what has become an insistent refrain in the Donald Trump era. Americans want to believe that the surge in white-supremacist violence and recruitment—the march in Charlottesville, Virginia, where neo-Nazis chanted "Jews will not replace us"; the hate crimes whose perpetrators invoke the president's name as a battle cry—has no roots in U.S. soil, that it is racist zealotry with a foreign pedigree and marginal allure.

Warnings from conservative pundits on Fox News about the existential threat facing a country overrun by immigrants meet with a similar response. "Massive demographic changes," Laura Ingraham has proclaimed, mean that "the America we know and love doesn't exist anymore" in much of the country: Surely this kind of rhetoric reflects mere ignorance. Or it's just a symptom of partisan anxiety about what those changes may portend for Republicans' electoral prospects. As for the views and utterances of someone like Congressman Steve King ("We can't restore our civilization with somebody else's babies"), such sentiments are treated as outlandish extremism, best ignored as much as possible.

The concept of "white genocide"—extinction under an onslaught of genetically or culturally inferior nonwhite interlopers—may indeed seem like a fringe conspiracy theory with an alien lineage, the province of neo-Nazis and their fellow travelers. In popular memory, it's a vestige of a racist ideology that the Greatest Generation did its best to scour from the earth. History, though, tells a different story. King's recent question, posed in a *New York Times* interview, may be appalling: " 'White nationalist,' 'white supremacist,' 'Western civilization'—how did that language become offensive?" But it is apt. "That language" has an American past in need of excavation. Without such an effort, we may fail to appreciate the tenacity of the dogma it expresses and the difficulty of eradicating it. The president's rhetoric about "shithole countries" and "invasion" by immigrants invites dismissal as crude talk, but behind it lie ideas whose power should not be underestimated.

The seed of Nazism's ultimate objective—the preservation of a pure white race, uncontaminated by foreign blood—was in fact sown with striking success in the United States. What is judged extremist today was once the consensus of a powerful cadre of the American elite, well-connected men who eagerly seized on a false doctrine of "race suicide" during the immigration scare of the early twentieth century. They included wealthy patricians, intellectuals, lawmakers, even several presidents. Perhaps the most important among them was a blue blood with a very impressive mustache, Madison Grant. He was the author of a 1916 book called *The Passing of the Great Race*, which spread the doctrine of race purity all over the globe.

Grant's purportedly scientific argument that the exalted "Nordic" race that had founded America was in peril, and all of modern society's accomplishments along with it, helped catalyze nativist legislators in Congress to pass comprehensive restrictionist immigration policies in the early 1920s. His book went on to become Adolf Hitler's "bible," as the führer wrote to tell him. Grant's doctrine has since been rejuvenated and rebranded by his ideological descendants as "white genocide" (the term "genocide" hadn't yet been coined in Grant's day). In an introduction to the 2013 edition of another of Grant's works, the white nationalist Richard Spencer warns that "one possible outcome of the ongoing demographic transformation is a thoroughly miscegenated, and thus homogeneous and 'assimilated,' nation, which would have little resemblance to the White America that came before it." This language is vintage Grant.

Most Americans, however, quickly forgot who Grant was—but not because the country had grappled with his vision's dangerous appeal and implications. Reflexive recoil was more like it: When Nazism reflected back that vision in grotesque form, wartime denial set in. Jonathan Peter Spiro, a historian and the author of *Defending the Master Race: Conservation, Eugenics, and the Legacy of Madison Grant* (2009), described the backlash to me this way: "Even though the Germans had been directly influenced by Madison Grant and the American eugenics movement, when we fought Germany, because Germany was racist, racism became unacceptable in America. Our enemy was racist; therefore, we adopted anti-racism as our creed." Ever since, a strange kind of historical amnesia has obscured the American lineage of this white-nationalist ideology.

MADISON GRANT CAME FROM OLD money. Born in Manhattan seven months after Robert E. Lee surrendered to Ulysses S. Grant at Appomattox, he attended Yale and then Columbia Law School. He was an outdoorsman and a conservationist, knowledgeable about wildlife and interested in the dangers of extinction, expertise that he soon became intent on applying to humanity. When he opened a law practice on Wall Street in the early 1890s, the wave of immigration from Southern and Eastern Europe was nearing its height. "As he was jostled by Greek ragpickers, Armenian bootblacks, and Jewish carp vendors, it was distressingly obvious to him that the new arrivals did not know this nation's history or understand its republican form of government," Spiro writes in his biography.

Jews troubled Grant the most. "The man of the old stock," he later wrote in *The Passing of the Great Race,* is being "driven off the streets of New York City by the swarms of Polish Jews." But as the title of his 1916 work indicated, Grant's fear of dispossession ran wide and deep:

> These immigrants adopt the language of the native American, they wear his clothes, they steal his name, and they are beginning to take his women, but they seldom adopt his religion or understand his ideals and while he is being elbowed out of his own home the American looks calmly abroad and urges on others the suicidal ethics which are exterminating his own race.

Grant was not the first proponent of "race science." In 1853, across the Atlantic, Joseph Arthur de Gobineau, a French count, first identified the "Aryan" race as "great, noble, and fruitful in the works of man on this earth." Half a century later, as the eugenics movement gathered force in the United States, "experts" began dividing white people into distinct races. In 1899, William Z. Ripley, an economist, concluded that Europeans consisted of "three races": the brave, beautiful, blond "Teutons"; the stocky "Alpines"; and the swarthy "Mediterraneans." Another leading academic contributor to race science in turn-of-the-century America was a statistician named Francis Walker, who argued in *The Atlantic* that the new immigrants lacked the pioneer spirit of their predecessors; they were made up of "beaten men from beaten races," whose offspring were crowding out the fine "native" stock of white people. In 1901 the sociologist Edward A. Ross, who similarly described the new immigrants as "masses of fecund but beaten humanity from the hovels of far Lombardy and Galicia," coined the term "race suicide."

But it was Grant who synthesized these separate strands of thought into one pseudo-scholarly work that changed the course of the nation's history. In a nod to wartime politics, he referred to Ripley's "Teutons" as "Nordics," thereby denying America's hated World War I rivals exclusive claim to descent from the world's master race. He singled out Jews as a source of anxiety disproportionate to their numbers, subscribing to a belief that has proved durable. The historian Nell Irvin Painter sums up the race chauvinists' view in *The History of White People* (2010): "Jews manipulate the ignorant working masses—whether Alpine, Under-Man, or colored." In *The Passing of the Great Race*, the eugenic focus on winnowing out unfit individuals made way for a more sweeping crusade to defend against contagion by inferior races. By Grant's logic, infection meant obliteration:

> The cross between a white man and an Indian is an Indian; the cross between a white man and a Negro is a Negro; the cross between a white man and a Hindu is a Hindu; and the cross between any of the three European races and a Jew is a Jew.

What Grant's work lacked in scientific rigor, it made up for in canny packaging. He blended Nordic boosterism with fearmongering and supplied a scholarly veneer for notions many white citizens already wanted to believe. Americans' gauzy idealism blinded them, he argued, to the reality that newcomers from the Mediterranean and Eastern Europe—to say nothing of anyone from Asia or Africa—could never hope to possess the genetic potential innate in the nation's original Nordic inhabitants, which was the source of the nation's greatness. Grant gleefully challenged foundational ideas:

> Americans must realize that the altruistic ideals which have controlled our social development during the past century and the maudlin sentimentalism that has made America 'an asylum for the oppressed' are sweeping the nation toward a racial abyss. If the Melting Pot is allowed to boil without control and we continue to follow our national motto and deliberately blind ourselves to all 'distinctions of race, creed or color,' the type of native American of Colonial descent will become as extinct as the Athenian of the age of Pericles, and the Viking of the days of Rollo.

His thesis found eager converts among the American elite, thanks in no small part to his extensive social connections. *The New York Times* and *The Nation* were among the many media outlets that echoed Grant's reasoning. Teddy Roosevelt, by then out of office, told Grant in 1916 that his book showed "fine fearlessness in assailing the popular and mischievous sentimentalities and attractive and corroding falsehoods which few men dare assail." In a major speech in Alabama in 1921, President Warren Harding publicly praised one of Grant's disciples, Lothrop Stoddard, whose book *The Rising Tide of Color Against White World-Supremacy* offered similar warnings about the destruction of white society by invading dusky hordes. There is "a fundamental, eternal, inescapable difference" between the races, Harding told his audience. "Racial amalgamation there cannot be."

Harding's vice president and successor, Calvin Coolidge, found Grant's thesis equally compelling. "There are racial considerations too grave to be brushed aside for any sentimental reasons. Biological laws tell us that certain divergent people will not mix or blend," Coolidge wrote in a 1921 article in *Good Housekeeping.*

> The Nordics propagate themselves successfully. With other races, the outcome shows deterioration on both sides. Quality of mind and body suggests that observance of ethnic law is as great a necessity to a nation as immigration law.

Endorsing Grant's idea that true Americans are of Nordic stock, Coolidge also took up his idea that intermarriage between whites of different "races," not just between whites and nonwhites, degraded that stock.

PERHAPS THE MOST IMPORTANT OF Grant's elite admirers were to be found among members of Congress. Reconstruction struggles; U.S. expansion in the Philippines, Puerto Rico, and Hawaii; high levels of immigration—each had raised the specter of white people losing political power and influence to nonwhite people or to the wrong kind of white people. On Capitol Hill, debate raged, yet Republicans and Democrats were converging on the idea that America was a white man's country and must stay that way. The influx of foreigners diluted the nation with inferiors unfit for self-government, many politicians in both parties energetically concurred. The Supreme Court chimed in with decisions in a series of cases, beginning in 1901, that assigned the status of "nationals" rather than "citizens" to colonial newcomers.

A popular myth of American history is that racism is the exclusive province of the South. The truth is that much of the nativist energy in the United States came from old-money elites in the Northeast and was also fueled by labor struggles in the Pacific Northwest, which had stirred a wave of bigotry that led to the Chinese Exclusion Act of 1882. Grant found a congressional ally and champion in Albert Johnson, a Republican representative from Washington. A nativist and union buster, he contacted Grant after reading *The Passing of the Great Race.* The duo embarked on an ambitious restrictionist agenda.

In 1917, overriding President Woodrow Wilson's veto, Congress passed a law that banned immigration not just from Asian but also from Middle Eastern countries and imposed a literacy test on new immigrants. When the Republicans took control of the House in 1919, Johnson became chair of the committee on immigration, "thanks to some shrewd lobbying by the Immigration Restriction League," Spiro writes. Grant introduced him to a preeminent eugenicist named Harry Laughlin, whom Johnson named the committee's "expert eugenics agent." His appointment helped ensure that Grantian concerns about "race suicide" would be a driving force in a quest that culminated, half a decade later, in the Immigration Act of 1924.

Johnson found a patrician ally in Senator David Reed of Pennsylvania, who sponsored the 1924 bill in the Senate. A Princeton-educated lawyer, Reed feared that America was going the way of Rome, where the "inpouring of captives and alien slaves" had caused the empire to sink "into an impotency which made her the prey of every barbarian invader." This was almost verbatim Grant, whose portrait of Rome's fall culminated in the lowly immigrants "gradually occupying the country and literally breeding out their former masters." (His plotline helped him preserve the notion that fair-haired and -skinned people are responsible for all the world's great achievements: Rome's original inhabitants were Nordic, but contemporary Italians were descendants of Roman slave races and therefore inferior.)

Grant's slippery pseudoscience also met with significant resistance. The anthropologist Franz Boas, himself of German Jewish descent, led the way in poking holes in Grantian notions of Nordic superiority, writing in *The New Republic* in 1917 that "the supposed scientific data on which the author's conclusions are based are dogmatic assumptions which cannot endure criticism." Meanwhile, the Supreme Court was struggling mightily to define whiteness in a consistent fashion, an endeavor complicated by the empirical flimsiness of race science. In one case after another, the high court faced the task of essentially tailoring its definition to exclude those whom white elites considered unworthy of full citizenship.

In 1923, when an Indian veteran named Bhagat Singh Thind—who had fought for the United States in World War I—came before the justices with the claim of being Caucasian in the scientific sense of the term and therefore entitled to the privileges of whiteness, they threw up their hands. In a unanimous ruling against Thind (who was ultimately made a citizen in 1936), Justice George Sutherland wrote:

> What we now hold is that the words "free white persons" are words of common speech, to be interpreted

in accordance with the understanding of the common man, synonymous with the word "Caucasian" only as that word is popularly understood.

The justices had unwittingly acknowledged a consistent truth about racism, which is that race is whatever those in power say it is.

As the Immigration Act of 1924 neared passage, some in the restrictionist camp played up Grant's signature Nordic theme more stridently than others. Addison Smith, a Republican congressman from Idaho, proudly invoked the Scandinavian, English, Irish, and other Northern European immigrants of his district, highlighting that among them were no "'slackers' of the type to be found in the cities of the East. We have ample room, but no space for such parasites." Johnson was prepared to be coy in the face of opposition from other legislators—mostly those from districts with large numbers of non–Northern European immigrants—who railed against the Nordic-race doctrine. "The fact that it is camouflaged in a maze of statistics," protested Representative Meyer Jacobstein, a Democrat from New York, "will not protect this Nation from the evil consequences of such an unscientific, un-American, and wicked philosophy."

On the House floor in April 1924, Johnson cagily—but only temporarily—distanced himself from Grant. "As regards the charge . . . that this committee has started out deliberately to establish a blond race . . . let me say that such a charge is all in your eye. Your committee is not the author of any of these books on the so-called Nordic race," he declared. "I insist, my friends, there is neither malice nor hatred in this bill."

Once passage of the act was assured, however, motives no longer needed disguising. Grant felt his life's work had come to fruition and, according to Spiro, he concluded, "We have closed the doors just in time to prevent our Nordic population being overrun by the lower races." Senator Reed announced in a *New York Times* op-ed, "The racial composition of America at the present time thus is made permanent." Three years later, in 1927, Johnson held forth in dire but confident tones in a foreword to a book about immigration restriction. "Our capacity to maintain our cherished institutions stands diluted by a stream of alien blood, with all its inherited misconceptions respecting the relationships of the governing power to the governed," he warned. "The United States is our land. . . . We intend to maintain it so. The day of unalloyed welcome to all peoples, the day of indiscriminate acceptance of all races, has definitely ended."

"IT WAS AMERICA THAT TAUGHT us a nation should not open its doors equally to all nations," Adolf Hitler told *The New York Times* half a decade later, just one year before his elevation to chancellor in January 1933. Elsewhere he admiringly noted that the United States "simply excludes the immigration of certain races. In these respects America already pays obeisance, at least in tentative first steps, to the characteristic *völkisch* conception of the state." Hitler and his followers were eager to claim a foreign—American—lineage for the Nazi mission.

In part, this was spin, an attempt to legitimize fascism. But Grant and his fellow pioneers in racist pseudoscience did help the Nazis justify to their own populations, and to other countries' governments, the mission they were on—as one of Grant's key accomplices was proud to acknowledge.

According to Spiro, Harry Laughlin, the scientific expert on Representative Johnson's committee, told Grant that the Nazis' rhetoric sounded "exactly as though spoken by a perfectly good American eugenist" and wrote that "Hitler should be made honorary member of the Eugenics Research Association."

He wasn't, but some of the American eugenicists whose work helped pave the way for the racist immigration laws of the 1920s received recognition in Germany. The Nazis gave Laughlin an honorary doctorate from Heidelberg University in 1936. Henry Fairfield Osborn, who had written the introduction to *The Passing of the Great Race,* received one from Johann Wolfgang Goethe University in 1934. Leon Whitney, another of Grant's fellow travelers, evidently received a personal thank-you letter from Hitler after sending the führer a copy of his 1934 book, *The Case for Sterilization.* In 1939, even after World War II began, Spiro writes, Lothrop Stoddard, whom President Harding had praised in his 1921 diatribe against race-mixing, visited Nazi Germany and later wrote that the Third Reich was "weeding out the worst strains in the Germanic stock in a scientific and truly humanitarian way."

What the Nazis "found exciting about the American model didn't involve just eugenics," observes James Q. Whitman, a professor at Yale Law School and the author of *Hitler's American Model: The United States and the Making of Nazi Race Law* (2017). "It also involved the systematic degradation of Jim Crow, of American deprivation of basic rights of citizenship like voting." Nazi lawyers carefully studied how the United States, despite its pretense of equal citizenship, had effectively denied that status to those who were not white. They looked at Supreme Court decisions that withheld full citizenship rights from nonwhite subjects in U.S. colonial territories. They examined cases that drew, as Thind's had, arbitrary but hard lines around who could be considered "white."

The Nazis reviewed the infamous "one-drop rule," which defined anyone with any trace of African blood as black, and "found American law on mongrelization too harsh to be embraced by the Third Reich." At the same time, Heinrich Krieger, whom Whitman describes as "the single most important figure in the Nazi assimilation of American race law," considered the Fourteenth Amendment a problem: In his view, it codified an abstract ideal of equality at odds with human experience and with the type of country most Americans wanted to live in.

Grant, emphasizing the American experience in particular, agreed. In *The Passing of the Great Race,* he had argued that "the view that the Negro slave was an unfortunate cousin of the white man, deeply tanned by the tropic sun and denied the blessings of Christianity and civilization, played no small part with the sentimentalists of the Civil War period, and it has taken us fifty years to learn that speaking English, wearing good clothes and going to school and to church do not transform a Negro into a white man."

The authors of the Fourteenth Amendment, he believed, had failed to see a greater truth as they made good on the promise of the Declaration of Independence that all men are created equal: The white man is more equal than the others.

Grant's final project, Spiro writes, was an effort to organize a hunting expedition with Hermann Göring, the commander in chief of the Nazi air force, who went on to become Hitler's chosen successor. Grant died in May 1937, before the outing was to take place. A year and a half later, Kristallnacht signaled the official beginning of the Holocaust.

• • •

AMERICA HAS ALWAYS GRAPPLED WITH, in the words of the immigration historian John Higham, two "rival principles of national unity." According to one, the United States is the champion of the poor and the dispossessed, a nation that draws its strength from its pluralism. According to the other, America's greatness is the result of its white and Christian origins, the erosion of which spells doom for the national experiment.

People of both political persuasions like to tell a too-simple story about the course of this battle: World War II showed Americans the evil of racism, which was vanquished in the 1960s. The Civil Rights Act and the Voting Rights Act brought nonwhites into the American polity for good. The Immigration and Nationality Act of 1965 forever banished the racial definition of American identity embodied in the 1924 immigration bill, forged by Johnson and Reed in their crusade to save Nordic Americans from "race suicide."

The truth is that the rivalry never ended, and Grantism, despite its swift wartime eclipse, did not become extinct. The Nazis, initially puzzled by U.S. hostility, underestimated the American commitment to democracy. As the Columbia historian Ira Katznelson writes in *Fear Itself: The New Deal and the Origins of Our Time* (2013), the South remained hawkish toward Nazi Germany because white supremacists in the United States didn't want to live under a fascist government. What they wanted was a *herrenvolk* democracy, in which white people were free and full citizens but nonwhites were not.

The Nazis failed to appreciate the significance of that ideological tension. They saw allegiance to the American creed as a weakness. But U.S. soldiers of all backgrounds and faiths fought to defend it and demanded that their country live up to it. Their valor helped defeat first the Nazis and then the American laws that the Nazis had so admired. What the Nazis saw as a weakness turned out to be a strength, and it destroyed them.

Yet historical amnesia, the excision of the memory of how the seed of racism in America blossomed into the Third Reich in Europe, has allowed Grantism to be resurrected with a new name. In the conflict between the Trump administration and its opponents, those rival American principles of exclusion and pluralism confront each other more starkly than they have since Grant's own time. And the ideology that has gained ground under Trump may well not disappear when Trump does. Grant's philosophical framework has found new life among extremists at home and abroad, and echoes of his rhetoric can be heard from the Republican base and the conservative media figures the base trusts, as well as—once again—the highest reaches of government.

The resurrection of race suicide as white genocide can be traced to the white supremacist David Lane, who claimed that "the term 'racial integration' is only a euphemism for genocide" and whose infamous "fourteen words" manifesto, published in the 1990s, distills his credo: "We must secure the existence of our people and a future for white children." Far-right intellectuals in Europe speak of "the great replacement" of Europeans by nonwhite immigrants and refugees.

In the corridors of American power, Grant's legacy is evident. Jeff Sessions heartily praised the 1924 immigration law during an interview with Steve Bannon, Trump's former campaign chief. Bannon regularly invokes what has become a cult text among white nationalists, the 1973 dystopian French novel *The Camp of the Saints,* in which the "white world" is annihilated by mass immigration. Stephen Miller, a former Senate aide to Sessions and now among the president's top policy advisers, spent years warning from his perch in Sessions's office that immigration from Muslim countries was a greater threat than immigration from European countries. The president's stated preference for Scandinavian immigrants over those from Latin America or Africa and his expressed disdain for the Fourteenth Amendment's guarantee of birthright citizenship are Grantism paraphrased.

That nations make decisions about appropriate levels of immigration is not inherently evil or fascist. Nor does the return of Grantian ideas to mainstream political discourse signal an inevitable march to Holocaust-level crimes against humanity. But to recognize the homegrown historical antecedents of today's rhetoric is to call attention to certain disturbing assumptions that have come to define the current immigration debate in America—in particular, that intrinsic human worth is rooted in national origin and that a certain ethnic group has a legitimate claim to permanent political hegemony in the United States. The most benignly intentioned mainstream-media coverage of demographic change in the United States has a tendency to portray as justified the fear and anger of white Americans who believe their political power is threatened by immigration—as though the political views of today's newcomers were determined by genetic inheritance rather than persuasion.

The danger of Grantism, and its implications for both America and the world, is very real. External forces have rarely been the gravest threat to the social order and political foundations of the United States. Rather, the source of greatest danger has been those who would choose white purity over a diverse democracy. When Americans abandon their commitment to pluralism, the world notices, and catastrophe follows.

7

THE CRUELTY OF
THE STEPHEN MILLERS

THIS ESSAY HAD BEEN BOUNCING AROUND INSIDE MY HEAD SINCE October 2016. I met more than a few people at Trump rallies who mentioned that their parents or grandparents had come to the United States "the right way" and that undocumented immigrants were unfairly jumping the line by entering the country illegally or by overstaying their visas.

A frequent liberal retort, that the United States has always been a nation of immigrants, was interesting to me, because it also has its flaws. Neither Native Americans nor most black Americans are immigrants: Native Americans were already here when European colonists arrived, and most black Americans' ancestors didn't have a choice about whether to come here. Even the West Indian immigrants who began arriving in large numbers in the 1940s were descendants of enslaved people brought to the West by European powers. Tejanos and others of Mexican descent lived in areas later annexed long before the United States claimed those territories and, with them, the right to treat those populations as they wished.

But, interestingly, both arguments were premised on

a misunderstanding of how massive, byzantine, and, well, *armed* the current U.S. immigration system had become since the heyday of European immigration, and how it got that way. The right-wing narrative assumes that the "line" has remained the same from the late nineteenth century to today, while the left-wing version of the story, while acknowledging that today's immigrants are no less filled with potential than their forebears, often fails to take into account how much lower the barriers were when their own ancestors arrived. The southern border has been militarized for so long that most Americans have forgotten how long it was open.

Over the course of the Trump years I wrote about the horrors of its immigration policy many times. In June 2018, in a piece titled "Family Separation Is the Logic of Trumpism," I wrote about the history of the U.S. government separating families, dating back to slavery, and how deeply it marked even those who spent much of their lives as human chattel. Then as now, these separations follow a logic of dehumanization—of mistreatment based on whom the authorities see as less than a full human being. Such considerations have always shaped American immigration policy, beginning with the 1790 law allowing only free white persons to naturalize, passed two short years after the Constitution was ratified.

For this piece, I wanted to tell another part of that story— why many descendants of European immigrants believe that their ancestors fleeing poverty and injustice were fundamentally different and more deserving than Central American families coming for similar reasons today. Despite the bigoted and anti-Semitic pseudoscience that was the basis of the early-twentieth-century immigration restrictions against Eastern and Southern Europeans, white Americans were still much more forgiving of immigrants who looked like them.

That reality complicates the future of American immigration policy—no matter who ends up in charge.

The Trump administration radicalized many of his opponents into observing how cruel his approach to immigration was, but the history of cruelty in U.S. immigration policy is too complex and bipartisan to be set at the feet of the forty-fifth president alone. Ronald Reagan signed an amnesty legalizing three million undocumented immigrants, and Bill Clinton's 1996 Illegal Immigration Reform and Immigrant Responsibility Act is largely responsible for our contemporary system of immigration detention. Clinton deported more undocumented immigrants than did George W. Bush—and Bush, like Barack Obama, tried and failed to legalize the eleven million undocumented immigrants in the United States. But Obama also deported more immigrants in his first term than Trump did in his, despite Obama's 2012 decision to spare hundreds of thousands of young undocumented immigrants, the "Dreamers," from deportation.

President Joe Biden will be more lenient than the Trump administration, but it would be unusual if Biden represented a radical departure from the bipartisan tradition that existed prior to Trump. The politics and policy of immigration and America have always vacillated between cruel and forgiving, sometimes both at the same time. Who experiences that cruelty, and who is forgiven, has historically fallen along racial lines. The ever-evolving borders of racial identity are an intrinsic part of America's history of immigration policy, and Trump made that history visible again with his expressed preference for white migrants and cruelty toward Muslim and Central American refugees.

What made Trump unusual was his administration's commitment to barbarism as an end rather than a means, with few of the redeeming features that tempered other presidents' approaches to immigration. The story of Trump's top immigration adviser and how his family came to the United States, as poor, rural migrants seeking a better future, seemed like an ideal way to illustrate that.

NOT THE
RIGHT WAY

SPRING 2021

THEY WERE NOT SENDING THEIR BEST. THEY WERE SENDING PEO-
ple with lots of problems, and they were bringing those problems to the United States. They were bringing crime. They
were rapists. Some, you might assume, were good people.

I'm referring, of course, to Great Britain, which historians estimate sent around 50,000 convicts to its American colonies following the 1718 Transportation Act, which allowed
for the purchase of convict labor through indentured servitude. Benjamin Franklin compared the convicts unfavorably
to rattlesnakes, noting that "the Rattle-Snake gives Warning
before he attempts his Mischief; which the Convict does not."
In 1722, both Maryland and Virginia sought to prevent the
importation of convicts from Great Britain, both of which
were overruled by their colonial overseers.

For this reason, the 1931 federal Wickersham Commission report into "crime and the foreign born," found that
"the theory that immigration is responsible for crime, that

the most recent 'wave of immigration,' whatever the nationality, is less desirable than the old ones, that all newcomers should be regarded with an attitude of suspicion, is a theory that is almost as old as the colonies planted by Englishmen on the New England coast." In the colonies, the report notes, there was "new hope for the poor man," and many of these migrants were "able to become useful citizens."

The first immigration scare in America, then, predates the formation of the United States itself. The vocabulary of subsequent immigration scares would change little in the intervening centuries, except that the invention of race would provide new "scientific" justification for arguments that lacked the factual predicate of the first—after all, Britain really was sending convicts to the colonies. But just as the contributions of convicted criminals to the nation's founding population would drift out of public memory, the descendants of those once demonized by nativism would warn that the newcomers would be the end of America, forgetting or rationalizing that the same was once said about their own ancestors.

That historical amnesia helps explain the paradox of American nativism. Immigrants come to America to find work, fleeing religious or ethnic persecution, to go to school, or to escape some other kind of turmoil. Every immigrant's story is fundamentally unique, and yet because the vast majority of Americans come from immigrant stock, the stories of how families from across the globe became American possess unmistakably familiar parallels. But the Trump administration represents the reoccurring backlash to this sentimental story, and the ease with which some immigrants can be portrayed categorically as an invasion to be repelled by force, the familiarity of their stories obscured by the certainty that they must be unlike us.

In 1845, during the height of anti-Irish sentiment, a nativist group warned that "the United States are rapidly becoming the lazar-house and penal colony of Europe," its jails and poorhouses emptied onto American shores "not casually, or to a trivial extent, but systematically."

In 1866, the abolitionist champion Senator Charles Sumner would declare that he had proof from German newspapers that "men convicted of very serious crimes in Germany had been pardoned on condition that they emigrate to this country."

In 1891, a grand jury charged with investigating the mass lynching of eleven Italians and Italian Americans in New Orleans dismissed the allegations and tried and convicted the victims and their country of origin instead. They accused the Italian government of sending its criminals to the United States, surmising that "we doubt not that the Italian government would rather be rid of them than charged with their custody and punishment," but that "the time has passed when this country can be made a dumping ground for the worthless and depraved of every nation."

So when Donald Trump—the descendant of an 1885 German immigrant who came to the United States penniless, illiterate in English, and reportedly fleeing a draft—announced his entry into the 2016 presidential campaign with accusations that Mexico was deliberately sending rapists and drug dealers to the United States, he was engaging in an old American tradition. That tradition is enabled by an equally important one—the collective forgetting that comes with assimilation, the insistence from the descendants of a previous generation of immigrants that their ancestors, unlike these upstart newcomers, were good and virtuous, that they came to America the Right Way.

"The concept of illegal immigration can only exist when there are restrictions on immigration," said Mae Ngai, a professor at Columbia University and the author of *Impossible Subjects: Illegal Aliens and the Making of Modern America.* "So if we have an open system, which we pretty much had for Europeans and for people from the Western Hemisphere into the early twentieth century, [if] there's an open door anybody can more or less anyone go through, then everybody's legal."

The concept of illegal immigration in the United States is a relatively new one, and the massive state apparatus for expelling "illegals" younger still. The ancestors of most of the descendants of European immigrants in the United States simply never had to face it. So for most of the more than 20 million European immigrants who came to the United States between 1880 and 1920, it's true that they immigrated "the right way." But only because for most Europeans who came to the United States around the turn of the twentieth century, there was almost no wrong way to do it.

IN THE FALL OF 1965, in one of the least appreciated accomplishments of the civil-rights era, President Lyndon Johnson signed a bill repealing restrictions adopted at the turn of the century that had curtailed immigration on the basis of race and national identity.

"This system violated the basic principle of American democracy—the principle that values and rewards each man on the basis of his merit as a man," Johnson declared as he signed the bill. "It has been un-American in the highest sense, because it has been untrue to the faith that brought thousands to these shores even before we were a country."

Those restrictions had targeted not only Africans and

Asians but European Jews, Italians, Greeks, and others, considered by nativists to be "inferior" to the "native" white American stock at the time, whom the nativists saw as the mighty Anglo-Saxon descendants of Germanic chieftains. These were people immigration restrictionists believed were prone to criminality and labor radicalism, agents of malign foreign powers hoping to dispose of their miscreants in the United States. For Johnson, and for most of the lawmakers who voted for the bill, the repeal of the eugenics-inspired 1920s-era restrictions—later an inspiration to Nazi Germany—repaired "a very deep and painful flaw in the fabric of American justice," and corrected "a cruel and enduring wrong in the conduct of the American Nation."

But for Stephen Miller, a descendant of Jewish immigrants from Belarus, who would go on to become an architect of the Trump administration's immigration policies, the bill was a tragic mistake. In 2015, as an aide to then-senator Jeff Sessions of Alabama, he urged a young conservative writer named Katie McHugh to write about its "ruinous consequences," then praised her after she published a piece lamenting the growth of the Latino population and the decline of "native born whites." Like his predecessors at the turn of the century, Miller saw national "ruin" in the increased presence of immigrants he considered to be nonwhite.

"This is a person who believes in discredited race science and eugenics in how you craft policy to hurt people, especially people of color, especially Muslims," McHugh told NPR in 2019.

McHugh, who at the time was part of a circle of white nationalists who were seeking to burrow into the federal bureaucracy in order to shape government policy, later recanted and exposed her former friends and associates—including

Miller, whose emails with McHugh were published by the Southern Poverty Law Center. But these revelations did nothing to dislodge Miller from his position of power in the Trump administration, seeking to shape American demography as his ideological heroes like Calvin Coolidge once had. In Trump, who once denigrated immigrants from Latin America, the Caribbean, and Africa as hailing from "shithole countries," Miller found a president who saw the world as he did.

The bitterness of immigration restrictionists over the 1965 law stems in part from their success in shaping it. Democratic senator Ted Kennedy sought to reassure critics at the time that the changes would not "upset the ethnic mix of our society." Although restrictionists now proclaim their affinity for "merit-based" immigration, preference for family members of immigrants—which today's restrictionists derisively refer to as "chain migration"—was crafted by restrictionists as part of the 1965 bill. They believed that it would favor white immigrants and thus undermine the purpose of repealing racist quotas. There is nothing inherently wrong with tailoring immigration policy to job skills or family unification. But American nativists always favor the policy they hope will keep America as white as possible (however they define that), because that is how they conceive of the national interest.

For Miller and the Trump administration, that meant an immigration policy targeting maximum state force at the most vulnerable people seeking residency in the United States. Most infamous was the family separation policy, which was designed to deter illegal immigration by punishing the children of parents seeking a new life in America. The policy left thousands of families shattered, with the government unable to reunite many of them.

Miller also pursued the removal of temporary status for

hundreds of thousands of immigrants from Latin American, Asian, African, and Caribbean nations, a drastic reduction in refugees, and imposed restrictions that effectively "ended asylum at the southern border" and made it easier to deport undocumented immigrants awaiting visas as victims of crimes in the United States.

With the blessing of the Supreme Court, the Trump administration instituted its travel ban, targeting mostly Muslim-majority nations (with Venezuela and North Korea tossed in for superficial deniability), and later expanded it in 2020.

The Trump White House also implemented far-broader criteria for denying green cards or temporary visas on the basis that the applicant was likely to become a "public charge," that is, someone believed likely to "become dependent on the government for subsistence." Although such standards have been part of American immigration policy since 1882, the Trump administration made the benchmarks so broad that, according to the Migration Policy Institute, at least "69 percent of recent green-card recipients had at least one negative factor named in the new rule."

Asked to justify its harsh immigration policies, Trump administration officials would echo the insistence of restrictionists past that the new immigrants were simply inferior to the old ones.

"They don't integrate well, they don't have skills," then–Trump White House chief of staff John Kelly told NPR in 2018. "They're also not people that would easily assimilate into the United States into our modern society. They're overwhelmingly rural people in the countries they come from—fourth-, fifth-, sixth-grade educations are kind of the norm. They don't speak English, obviously that's a big thing."

We've heard it all before. "This was said in the 1890s," David Roediger, the author of *Working Toward Whiteness*, told me. "People predicted that the racial character of the United States was about to change because of immigration. And they meant that, you know, it was changing because Poles were coming in, because Southern Italians were coming in, because Eastern European Jews were arriving, and they were the people who weren't speaking and didn't know how to speak English, weren't assimilating, who were poor prospects."

It would be a mistake to describe it as ironic that Kelly was inadvertently describing the ancestors of the most ardent restrictionists in the Trump White House. After all, the story of immigration in America is that the ramparts of immigration restrictionism are manned by those but a generation or two removed from being described as invaders. The result is a gauntlet of laws, regulations, and militarized enforcement that makes any comparison between the era of open borders for Europeans and the last half century laughable, despite the persistence of the comparison and its role in rationalizing the violence of contemporary American immigration policy.

But the story is nonetheless worth telling. Trump's paternal grandfather came to the United States as a German-speaking teenager from a "small wine village." Kelly's maternal grandfather Giuseppe Pedalino was an Italian American fruit-cart peddler who reportedly "never spoke a word of English." They came, like most European immigrants of the time, fleeing poverty or persecution.

Most dramatically, however, it was Miller's ancestors who came to the United States fleeing religious persecution, ethnic hatred, and extreme poverty, and Miller who devoted all of his efforts to making sure that American immigration policy would punish anyone else who might do the same, echoing the same racist ideology that shut the door on people like his forebears.

WHEN I WAS A CHILD, and I asked my father where our family came from, he told me, "It depends." The answer was confusing but also the closest thing to correct, because our family—like those of millions of Jews in the United States—comes from one of those parts of Eastern Europe that were constantly slipping through the blood-soaked hands of invading armies and ambitious kings, leaving residents with perpetually shifting nationalities. About four hours away from the small lake village in Poland where my father's family is from is Antopol, a small town in the Polesian marshland, with a similar history.

Once Poland, then Russia, now Southern Belarus, this is where Stephen Miller's maternal ancestor, Wolf-Leib Glosser, fled debt and murderous persecution for a new life in the United States. Living in a "thatch-roofed house" with a dirt floor, a chicken coop, and no running water, his family "eked out a living in a small stand in the town square where they sold kerosene, salt, homemade potato bread, dry goods and other small sundry items," according to the Glosser family history, carefully documented by Ruth Glosser, Miller's maternal grandmother.

When Wolf-Leib Glosser was born, sometime in the mid-nineteenth century, the policy of the Russian empire was to force the separation of underage Jewish children from their families and conscript them into the military, where they would be stripped of the knowledge of their own culture and faith but denied the ability to rise in rank, because of their ethnicity. The last decade of the nineteenth century in the Russian empire was part of an era in which Jewish communities lived in constant fear of pogroms, organized campaigns of ethnic cleansing and murder.

Wolf-Leib arrived in the United States in January 1903, with eight dollars to his name and speaking Polish, Russian, Yiddish, and liturgical Hebrew but no English. It was a mere three months before the Kishinev pogrom, in which Russians poured into the streets of that city on Easter weekend, slaughtering Jewish residents and destroying their shops and homes as local police looked on. The incident "sent shockwaves" throughout the United States, where few political leaders who condemned racism and bigotry in Russia publicly recognized the echoes of their nation's own plague of mob violence against minorities.

Wolf-Leib fled in the "dead of night," leaving his wife and children behind to placate his debtors. He spent months peddling a fruit cart in New York City while his brother Nathan worked in a sweatshop, the two of them sending money back home. Seeking more-gainful employment, Nathan went to Johnstown, Pennsylvania, where he worked in a laundry–tailor shop, ultimately securing a loan from a local merchant, which would be the seed money for his own business. Wolf-Leib would join him shortly thereafter.

By 1906, Wolf-Leib and Nathan were able to send for their family in Russia, with the aid of the Hebrew Immigrant Aid Society (now known as HIAS). Founded in 1881, the organization helped hundreds of thousands of Russian Jews flee persecution and immigrate to the United States. The Glosser family, poor, rural, lacking formal educations and the ability to speak English—all of the qualities described by John Kelly as disqualifying current migrants—had begun a thriving business and become valued members of their community. This is a common turn-of-the-century story, but it is also a common story for millions of American immigrants from Vietnam to Guatemala.

Shortly thereafter, nativists fearful of the demographic changes wrought by Jews, Italians, and others successfully choked off immigration from Russia with the restrictions of the 1920s. By 1942, the Glossers' remaining family in Antopol had been wiped out.

"Those of our family who could not make it to the United States, who had not made the decision to leave or had not been able to come before the door was slammed shut, they couldn't get in," David Glosser, who provided me with his mother's account of their family history, told me. "At the start of World War II, they were all murdered by the Nazis."

Glosser was explicit about how the immigration restrictions championed by Wolf-Leib's descendant, Stephen Miller, would have affected his family. "They would have been excluded. They didn't speak English. They had no support. They were impoverished. They would not have been admitted. It's quite clear," Glosser said. "You and I wouldn't be having this chat."

THE STORY OF THE GLOSSERS is one of vicious persecution, crushing poverty, and finally the freedom to live their lives free of the oppression that forced them to flee their ancestral home. But it is also the story of separate standards for the European immigrants of a prior era, one in which both the lack of legal restrictions and the arbitrary lines of racial identity in the United States worked to their advantage.

The public-charge rule, as passed in 1882, was vague and easily met by Wolf-Leib's possession of eight dollars and being able-bodied when he stepped off the boat on Ellis Island in 1903. He was not Chinese and therefore not barred by the Chinese Exclusion Act. By 1917, immigrants were required to be literate—*in their own languages.* There was no large, armed, internal immigration-enforcement apparatus in existence to deport those who did somehow enter the country illegally.

The nation's borders were "soft" and largely "unguarded," Ngai writes. "Inspection at arrival sought to identify excludable persons and to deny them admission, but little could be done if they evaded detection and entered the country." Congress did not appropriate funds for enforcing deportation laws until 1924; today the Department of Homeland Security has a budget of more than fifty billion dollars. All in all, of the more than 20 million European immigrants who arrived between 1890 and the beginning of World War I—those fleeing the Irish potato famine, Italian poverty, or persecution in the Pale of Settlement—only about 2 percent were ultimately barred from entering. The ancestors of most of America's "white ethnics" suffered hardship, oppression, and deprivation—but they never faced the barriers to entry today's huddled masses do.

Being barred from entry and being subject to removal by well-funded government machinery are two distinct things. The massive state bureaucracy to track, detain, and remove undocumented immigrants that exists today under the umbrella of DHS was not present in the era of mass European immigration to the United States at the turn of the century, and to the extent it did exist, its effectiveness against those immigrants was limited by the discretion of its administrators. It is not only that the entry requirements at the height of European immigration were more forgiving; the deportation apparatus was too.

Through the 1920s, the federal government steadily increased its efforts to remove people in the country illegally. But for European immigrants targeted by quotas, there were still options. They could sneak in through the southern border—in the 1920s, "The most heavily traveled route for illegal European immigration was through Mexico," Ngai writes. They could go to Canada, then come to the United States legally after living in Canada for five years. After that, they could send for their relatives, who were not subject to the quotas.

"Even those who sneaked in . . . once people reach their destination—Chicago or Pittsburgh or whatever—the chances of them being apprehended by immigration is practically nil if they're European," Ngai told me.

An irony of American immigration policy is that Western Hemisphere countries were not subject to the entry restrictions—the eugenicists who crafted American immigration policy in the 1920s did see Mexicans as inferior, but they were overruled by diplomatic concerns, including but not limited to retaliation against American business interests across the border. Nevertheless, as Ngai writes, "During the 1920s, immigration policy rearticulated the U.S.-Mexico border as a cultural and racial boundary, as a creator of illegal immigration." For all the hatred historically directed at European immigrants, it was the fear of Latin American immigration that built the American deportation machine we know today.

Backlash from white Americans to zealous border-patrol officers resulted in training that forced them to "act with civility, courtesy, and formality when dealing with Anglo citizens, ranch owners, immigrants arriving from Europe, and 'high class people com[ing] in as tourists' from Canada." Mexican immigrants, on the other hand, were treated with the "quasi- and extra-legal practices associated with rancher vigilantism." Such practices included lynchings, beatings, and "posse shoot- ings," as the historian Kelly Lytle Hernández describes in *Migra! A History of the U.S. Border Patrol.* In one stark example, a future Border Patrol agent named Harlon Carter joined the service after serving a brief prison term—later overturned by a judge—for hunting down and executing a Mexican Ameri- can teenager, Ramón Casiano, with a shotgun. The teenager had "upset" Carter's mother by "loitering" near her home.

Meanwhile, as the Great Depression loomed and "eco- nomic insecurities among Euro-Americans inflamed racial hostility toward Mexicans, efforts to deport and repatriate the latter to Mexico grew," Ngai writes. "The movement did not distinguish between legal immigrants, illegal immigrants, and American citizens." As a result, "nearly 20 percent of the Mexican population in the United States returned to Mexico during the early years of the Depression. The repatriation of Mexicans was a racial expulsion program exceeded in scale only by the Native American Indian removals of the nine- teenth century."

Much of the United States had been ceded from Mexico after its defeat in the Mexican–American War; this meant that some of the up-to-a-million people expelled were removed from land they had lived in for generations, despite the Treaty of Guadalupe Hidalgo's guarantee of full citizenship. Mass deportations of Mexican Americans, from Mexican Repa- triation in the 1920s and 1930s to Operation Wetback in the 1950s, are part of America's long exploitative relationship with Mexican labor. Trump famously praised the latter as a model of "humane deportation."

Attempts to execute the mass deportation of European immigrants, however, met with severe backlash. The Hoover-era Wickersham Commission report on deportation reflected on the expansive powers of immigration enforcement in language that resembles that of today's immigrants' rights activists.

"It is an insufferable reflection upon our humanity that our laws can give such despotic power in deportation and yet provide so little opportunity for even administrative mercy," the report reads. "The absence of discretionary power, both in the deportation of aliens and the readmission of aliens who have been heretofore deported, has had results which should not be tolerated in a civilized country."

The prospect of family separation was at the root of the backlash against deportation—at least as far as European immigrants were concerned. "No matter how long the alien may have resided in this country before his deportation, no matter how technical may have been the nature of the violation of our laws, no matter whether he has an American family in this country whom he can not take with him, his banishment is perpetual."

The report was influential—in the late 1920s, 1930s, and 1940s, government policy was changed to be more merciful toward undocumented immigrants. But those discretionary policies were almost entirely applied to European immigrants, whose humanity and struggles government officials found easier to empathize with. Relief policies were designed to exclude Mexican and Caribbean immigrants, reserving mercy for European immigrants targeted by entry restrictions.

"Thus it became possible to unmake the illegality of

Italian, Polish, and other European illegal immigrants through the power of administrative discretion," Ngai writes. The annihilation of European American families through deportation created the political will for a more forgiving immigration policy—for immigrants considered to be white, or something close to it.

Decades later, under the auspices of Donald Trump and Stephen Miller—both descendants of poor and rural immigrants—the annihilation of Central American families became a policy goal.

JEFF SESSIONS, THEN–ATTORNEY GENERAL OF the United States, told prosecutors in May of 2018 to go after the children.

"We need to take away children," Sessions said, according to notes of a meeting obtained by *The New York Times.* "If [you] care about kids, don't bring them in. Won't give amnesty to people with kids."

The policy provoked a colossal public backlash, doing immense damage to the perception of the federal deportation machine, a bipartisan edifice erected by immigration hawks from both parties. Another irony of American immigration policy is that Barack Obama, a living symbol of American multiculturalism, presided over a much more active removal apparatus than did Donald Trump.

The Obama administration erroneously believed that harsh immigration enforcement would bring Republicans to the table on immigration.

Under continuous pressure from immigrants' rights activists, the administration adopted a more lenient approach toward the conclusion of his first term in 2012. Nevertheless, year by year, Obama deported hundreds of thousands more undocumented immigrants in his first four years as president than Trump did, despite Trump's open contempt for non-white immigrants. It is a reminder that politicians wearing the smiling face of liberalism can provide a more effective façade for cruelty than those who make cruelty their public purpose. Trump did not invent the American deportation machine; he simply took advantage of its powers in ways recent presidents had not contemplated.

Among the results of the backlash against the family-separation policy was the decision by David Glosser to speak out against his nephew Stephen Miller, sharing the history of his family's difficult journey to the United States in order to disprove the premises of the White House's approach to immigration. In 2018, he wrote in *Politico* about having "watched with dismay and increasing horror as my nephew, an educated man who is well aware of his heritage, has become the architect of immigration policies that repudiate the very foundation of our family's life in this country."

"I had a unique platform from which to speak," Glosser told me. "I had no choice other than to reveal the truth to the background of our family and how it relates to the background of the architect of this catastrophe." Miller, for his part, sees his family's ancestral home of Johnstown, Pennsylvania, as having been harmed by "globalists" and the "owners of capital."

Glosser is retired, but his family legacy looms large over his life. He continues to volunteer with HIAS, the organization that helped bring his family to the United States, doing psychological and cognitive evaluations of refugees and those seeking asylum in America, a process Miller has sought to destroy. A few years ago, while going through his grand-father's personal items, Glosser discovered that HIAS was the first beneficiary of his grandfather's will.

Glosser's *Politico* piece detailing his family's immigration history was written in the midst of the 2018 midterms, during which Trump was hoping to preserve his party's control of the House of Representatives by focusing his campaign on a caravan of Central American migrants seeking to enter the United States. Trump called the caravan "an invasion of our country" and warned of "criminals and unknown Middle Easterners" hidden in their midst. The people in the caravan were coming to the United States for the same reasons that Trump's and Miller's ancestors did, with the distinction that, in some cases, migrants from Honduras, El Salvador, and Guatemala were fleeing circumstances partially shaped by American foreign policy.

Just two months after Glosser's piece was published, a gunman angry about the migrant caravan forced his way into the Tree of Life synagogue in Pittsburgh, which Glosser's brother's family attended. The gunman killed eleven worshippers, motivated in part by his hatred for HIAS, which he blamed for bringing in "hostile invaders to dwell among us." It was the kind of violence Wolf-Leib Glosser had fled a century ago.

THE CRUELTY OF CONSPIRACY

THE MACEDONIAN KING LYSIMACHUS SAW THE JEWS AS HAVING "good intentions toward no man." The apostle Paul warned that the Jews were "the enemies of the whole human race." The conservative icon Edmund Burke complained that the French Revolution was unlike others because it had been led by "Jew brokers contending with each other who could best remedy with fraudulent circulation and depreciated paper the wretchedness and ruin brought on their country by their degenerate councils." Karl Marx, in envisioning the emancipation of the working class, determined that "money is the jealous god of Israel, in face of which no other god may exist."

From antiquity to the modern era, Jews have proven tremendously useful as an external enemy, or as a scapegoat for society's ills. In each time period, anti-Jewish thought has been at the service of contemporary politics, from early Christians seeking to discredit their Jewish forebearers, to Protestant Reformers seeking to deny the divinity of the Catholic Church, to Karl Marx attacking capitalism. As the historian David Nirenberg writes, this is something of a historical accident. The centrality of Christianity to the West, and Christians' imperative to defend their faith as a supersession of the Jews' divine covenant, led Western thought to be constructed around reductive binaries that defined Jews as everything Christians were not supposed to be: materialist, divorced from spirituality, severed from the divine due to their own arrogance, and traitors to heaven in their rejection of the true messiah.

Centuries of anti-Jewish thought had conditioned a continent to think of Jewish people not as human beings but as abstract symbols for material greed, spiritual weakness, and moral wickedness. Those beliefs have traveled along with Western thought the same way a plague finds its way around the globe. Long predating the relatively modern political conceptions of liberal and conservative, and even the invention of race, anti-Jewish thought has an ideological flexibility that can find a home anywhere on the political spectrum. In the Trump era, left and right have traded accusations of anti-Semitism. But neither is immune to one of history's oldest and deadliest hatreds, not even those who define themselves by their fight against bigotry and prejudice.

With the rise of communism in the twentieth century, the anti-Jewish philosophical tradition took on a new cast, influenced by *The Protocols of the Elders of Zion*, a czarist hoax presented as a conspiracy "to destroy the white Gentile race, that the Jews may seize the power during the resulting chaos and rule with their claimed superior intelligence over the remaining races of the world, as kings over slaves."

As the historian Paul Hanebrink documents, Winston Churchill saw the Russian Revolution as a Jewish conspiracy that held "the Russian people by the hair of their heads." Polish Catholic leaders warned that "the race that has led

Bolshevism has already made the world subject to gold and banks, and today, driven by the eternal imperialist desire that flows in its veins, turns to the last campaign of conquest." And ultimately Adolf Hitler declared that "if, with the help of his Marxist creed, the Jew is victorious over the other peoples of the world, his crown will be the funeral wreath of humanity and this planet will, as it did thousands of years ago, move through the ether devoid of men."

Presenting Nazi Germany as a bulwark against "Judeo-Bolshevism," Hitler had a tremendous amount of success uniting Europe's nationalist right. Not that Hitler blaming communism on the Jews prevented him from *also* blaming capitalism on the Jews. The führer was just as insistent that "the slave's yoke of international capital" belonged to "its masters, the Jews."

Nazi ideology represented the collision of a long tradition of anti-Jewish thought with the invention of race and racism. Whereas in prior eras Jews might have escaped persecution and destruction through conversion, when Jews became a "race" in the minds of Europe's intellectuals, their religious traits became ingrained biological ones.

Perhaps you're wondering what this has to do with Louis Farrakhan, the leader of the Nation of Islam and the subject of the following essay. The answer is that, although it may seem peculiar, Farrakhan's anti-Semitism is more or less the same old anti-Jewish arguments and conspiracies, repurposed as a way to blame Jews as the architects of white supremacy. This may seem like a remarkable feat of rhetorical alchemy, but it isn't: It is mostly ideological plagiarism, repackaged for an audience that happens not to be European. The politics of Farrakhanism are really no different than they were in early, mid-, or late twentieth-century Europe: They are a way for a nationalist demagogue to rally a community against a foreign threat. Even today, Jews remain an easy target for amoral opportunists.

Echoing the Nazis' concern that "cultural Bolshevism" was degrading authentic German culture, Farrakhan has said, "Jews were responsible for all of this filth and degenerate behavior that Hollywood is putting out: turning men into women, and women into men." Farrakhan believes that "Jews control the media. They said it themselves! Jews and some gentiles control the banking industry, international banks. They do!" Farrakhan even draws on themes from antiquity, quoting the apostle Paul in Romans that "the Jew is not the Jew outwardly by the circumcision of the flesh. The Jew is the Jew inwardly by the circumcision of the heart," and condemning Jews as "the synagogue of Satan." Louis plays all the hits.

There are anti-Jewish tropes in Islam—Muslim extremists frequently invoke the Battle of Khaybar, which led to the expulsion of Jews from the Arabian Peninsula—but Farrakhan rarely if ever makes use of them. Instead, his arguments are borrowed from the long and well-documented history of Western anti-Semitism: The Jews have all the financial power, the Jews are degrading our glorious traditional culture, the Jews control the government, the Jews have been forsaken by the divine for their rejection of Jesus, a great spiritual and political renewal awaits when the Jews are defeated. Ideologically, Farrakhan talks like a far-right European nationalist. He is just also black.

There is a certain irony in the leader of the Nation of Islam drawing on a millennium of white, Christian, anti-Jewish themes to make his argument—but black Americans are part of the West, and, regrettably, such themes are part of the West's intellectual inheritance. Farrakhan's main innovation is that he has baselessly deployed such themes to explain white supremacy as a Jewish invention, arguing that Jews are "the master of segregation . . . You brought that to South Africa, you brought it to America." Similarly, Farrakhan's Nation of Islam has published literature accusing Jews of controlling the international slave trade.

Here again, there is a consonance with the old anti-Semitism of Europe. As the historian David Brion Davis has written, "Jews had no important role in the British Royal African Company or in the British slave trade of the eighteenth century, which transported by far the largest share of Africans to the New World." Similarly, the historian Seymour Drescher calculates that "it is unlikely that more than a fraction of 1 percent of the twelve million enslaved and relayed Africans were purchased or sold by Jewish merchants. . . . At no point along the continuum of the slave trade were Jews numerous enough, rich enough, and powerful enough to affect significantly the structure and flow of the slave trade."

The notion that Jews invented white supremacy is also risible, an inversion of the actual history. Modern race science was largely constructed around the idea that the Jews were not white but rather a "race" of "Asiatic" origin whose physical features and mental qualities separated them from true "whites." Farrakhan's insistence that Jews control black Americans is a nationalist transposition of long-standing white supremacist mythology. As Nell Irvin Painter writes in *The History of White People*, "Among white race chauvinists, the belief that Jews manipulate the ignorant working masses—whether Alpine, Under-Man, or colored—has proved extremely durable." Delve into the online cesspools of the far right and you can find an endless series of images implying that black-rights movements, from Martin Luther King Jr. to Black Lives Matter, are covert Jewish plots.

When Burke determined the French Revolution was led by Jews, there were "at most forty thousand Jews" in the entire country. Farrakhan identifies Jews as the Southern planter elite, but according to Davis, "in the American South, in 1830, there were only 120 Jews among the 45,000 slaveholders owning twenty or more slaves and only twenty Jews among the 12,000 slaveholders owning fifty or more slaves." Anti-communist propaganda all over Eastern Europe identified Jews as the masters of communism, even though, as Hanebrink writes, "The Communist Party would have flourished throughout the region without any Jews at all."

Farrakhan's case, like those of all anti-Semitic demagogues before him, relies on a kind of one-drop theory, where the involvement of any Jews at all signifies Jewish control. A kernel of truth—the existence of Jewish racists, Jewish movie producers, Jewish bankers, Jewish communists, or Jewish slaveowners—makes the entire system "Jewish," much as one drop of "black" blood makes the lightest-skinned person black.

In asking why Farrakhanism retains some support within the black community, one might ask why similar ideas have held sway in the West for centuries and still do in Europe, where nationalist strongmen continue to use thinly veiled code words to attack "globalism" and "cosmopolitanism," finding convenient bogeymen in targets like liberal financier George Soros. Or in the United States, where conspiratorial fantasies about men like Soros or theories like QAnon draw on implicit and explicit anti-Semitic themes. For centuries, anti-Jewish rhetoric has provided Western communities across the political spectrum with the comfort of believing external enemies hold the door to paradise closed, enemies whose destruction will allow those doors to swing open.

A key distinction, of course, is that white supremacy in America is a history of conspiracies. The Middle Passage was a conspiracy to use black people as forced labor; the Confederacy was a conspiracy to keep black people as chattel; the end of Reconstruction was a conspiracy to overturn black citizenship; Jim Crow was a conspiracy to maintain black people as a subservient labor caste; the Tuskegee medical experiment on black men was a conspiracy; redlining was a conspiracy; the exclusion of most black people from many of the benefits of the New Deal was the result of a conspiracy; the theft of Henrietta Lacks's cells was a conspiracy; lending discrimination is a conspiracy; and so on and so forth. And for the most part, black Americans must go about their lives every day with knowledge of such conspiracies as most white Americans deny they exist, or that they have been of any significance in shaping modern life whatsoever. The remarkable thing is that Farrakhanism, for all its harms, remains as unpopular as it does.

That is not to say there is no danger in it. These beliefs have been used to justify hatred against Jews and in some cases outright violence and murder. They act as a solvent upon the natural bonds between religious and ethnic minorities with shared political interests. And they help keep alive the flame of one of history's oldest and most destructive prejudices. In the Trump era, it has proven a useful bludgeon for attempting to break apart the coalition between black Americans and Jews, one of the most fruitful progressive alliances in American history, at a perilous moment for both communities.

It also significantly shaped my childhood. I can remember sitting alone in my D.C. homeroom the day of the Million

Man March and wondering if my classmates hated me. I can remember asking friends in the Nation if they could hear what Farrakhan said about Jews and reconcile it with what they knew of me. I remember feeling a tremendous loneliness in this separation from people I cared about and who I thought cared about me. I wanted to understand why.

I still regard Farrakhanism as noxious, but its resilience is no longer a mystery. I wrote this essay in early 2018 to explain to others why it persists, as someone who has been personally wounded by it. I hope it helps you understand and empathize with those who have found some comfort in the Nation of Islam, without excusing the anti-Semitism that remains central to its religious doctrine.

WHY TAMIKA MALLORY WON'T CONDEMN FARRAKHAN

MARCH 11, 2018

WHEN I WAS SEVENTEEN, I WAS A SCRUFFY-HEADED BIRACIAL black and Jewish teenager, and a furious Louis Farrakhan hater. In the mid-1990s, Farrakhan's fame and influence was at its height; I had once been thrown out of a middle-school gym class for calling the Nation of Islam leader a racist. His Million Man March, a massive collective act of solidarity and perhaps the most important black event of the decade, had been one of the loneliest days of my young life. I sat in home-room, one of just a few dozen kids in school, wondering why so many people hated people like me.

It was a story my high school English teacher Cullen Swinson told me, years later, that helped me understand why people might associate with the Nation. Scott Montgomery Elementary School was located in what *The Washington Post* called "the Wicked District" in a grim series on black youth in D.C. in the 1950s. Things were still bleak in the late '60s when

Swinson began attending Scott—one year, there was a crime scare that enveloped the whole neighborhood.

"Fear would soon become a daily companion in the short walk to and from school every day," Swinson told me, until "a host of clean-cut, friendly, polite, and ramrod-straight, bow-tied young men from the Masjid took up daily residence on every street corner from 7th Street to 1st Street." They were from the Fruit of Islam, the Nation's paramilitary wing. "I will never forget how they calmed the fears of so many mothers and children, just by their mere presence," Swinson said.

From the outside, seeing a liberal activist associating with an organization like the Nation of Islam can seem incomprehensible—particularly if you're Jewish and you hear in Farrakhan's speeches the venom that poisoned Europe for millennia and led to the annihilation of a third of the world's Jews in the twentieth century. But I thought back to the story Swinson told me after Farrakhan made national news again in recent weeks in connection with the Women's March, the organization that led a massive protest the day after Donald Trump's inauguration. It's a reminder that the sources of the Nation of Islam's ongoing appeal, and the reasons prominent black leaders often decline to condemn Farrakhan, may have little to do with the Nation's prejudiced beliefs.

The national co-chair of the Women's March, Tamika Mallory, was present at the Nation of Islam's annual Saviours' Day event in late February, where Farrakhan railed against Jews for being "the mother and father of apartheid," declared that "the Jews have control over those agencies of govern-ment," and surmised that Jews have chemically induced homosexuality in black men through marijuana. The Nation continues to produce volumes of propaganda blaming Jews for the world's ills. After the Anti-Defamation League posted a write-up of the event, noting Mallory's presence, Mallory and her colleagues were accused of dismissing the concerns of critics on social media who felt they were, if not endorsing anti-Semitism, homophobia, and sexism, failing to publicly rebuke it.

"There were people speaking to me as if I was anything other than my mother's child—it was very vile, the language that was being used, the way I was called an anti-Semite," Mallory told me. "I think that my value to the work I do is that I can go into many spaces as it relates to dealing with the complexity of the black experience in America. It takes a lot of different types of people to help us with our struggle."

Then there's the timing—at a moment of rising anti-Semitism in the United States and abroad, resurgent white nationalism, and anxiety among many liberal Jews about their place in the progressive movement, Mallory's presence at the NOI event shocked many who identified with the Women's March.

The incident is the latest episode in a pattern that has repeated itself ever since Farrakhan's entry onto the national stage. The Nation of Islam leader first rose to national prominence defending Jesse Jackson from accusations of anti-Semitism, after Jackson referred to New York as "Hymietown" during the 1984 Democratic presidential primary. Farrakhan called Judaism a "dirty religion" and warned Jews against attacking Jackson: "If you harm this brother, it will be the last one you harm." Farrakhan's defense of Jackson, which many black voters felt was unfairly maligned and taken out of context, helped establish his reputation as someone who, right or wrong, would not cave to the white establishment.

Since then, the cycle has repeated for one black leader after another. Farrakhan says something anti-Semitic, which draws press attention; he is roundly condemned, which draws more press attention but also causes some black people to feel he is being disproportionately attacked; and the controversy further burnishes his credibility within the black community as someone who is unacceptable to the white establishment and is therefore uncompromised. It is a cycle he has fueled, and benefited from, for decades. After the Saviours' Day story blew up on social media, Farrakhan and the Nation of Islam began promoting clips of the most inflammatory sections of the speech on Twitter, including a clip in which he says that Jews control the FBI. Currently, his pinned tweet asks, "What have I done to make Jewish people hate me?"

Yet because of the NOI's ongoing presence in many poor and working-class black communities, time and again Farrakhan is able to threaten the mainstream political ambitions of black public figures who, for good reasons and bad, choose to deal with him. There was Jackson, who ultimately condemned Farrakhan's anti-Semitism as "reprehensible." The Democratic National Committee's deputy chair, Representative Keith Ellison, disavowed his earlier membership in the Nation of Islam, saying that they "organize by sowing hatred and division, including anti-Semitism, homophobia, and a chauvinistic model of manhood." According to *The Washington Post*, Ellison also met privately with Farrakhan in 2016 (Ellison put out a statement on March 13 denying he has met with Farrakhan since a chance meeting in 2013). There's even Barack Obama, whose presidential ambitions might have been curtailed had a black photographer not buried a photo of the Illinois senator meeting Farrakhan in 2005, conscious of how the image might be exploited. Obama formally "rejected and denounced" Farrakhan during the 2008 campaign.

"Farrakhan knows who his constituents are. If he can cause some controversy and grab some headlines, he's gonna do it. I think it's kind of a hustle. He's been doing it for years, it's not going to change," said Amy Alexander, a journalist who edited an anthology of black writers on Farrakhan called *The Farrakhan Factor.* "It's almost like he's that kid on the schoolyard who in front of the teacher will drop the f-word just to get the teacher riled up. And if the teacher falls for it every time, what's that kid's incentive to stop doing it?"

Most people outside the black community come into contact with the Nation of Islam this way—Farrakhan makes anti-Semitic remarks, which generate press coverage and then demands for condemnation. But many black people come into contact with the Nation of Islam as a force in impoverished black communities—not simply as a champion of the black poor or working class but of the black underclass: black people, especially men, who have been written off or abandoned by white society. They've seen the Fruit of Islam patrol rough neighborhoods and run off drug dealers, or they have a family member who went to prison and came out reformed, preaching a kind of pride, self-sufficiency, and entrepreneurship that, with a few adjustments, wouldn't sound out of place coming from a conservative Republican. The self-respect, inner strength, and self-reliance reflected in the polished image of the men in suits and bow ties can be a powerful sight.

"Even before Farrakhan, the Nation was the first group to really go into the prisons to rehabilitate, or to call incarcerated men and women towards a kind of rehabilitative lifestyle," said Zain Abdullah, a professor at Temple University who used to teach Islam to people in prison. "They command some respect because of their visibility and presence in lower-class communities. People don't see them selling out to corporate America, selling out to government. I think people see them as a grassroots organization. They still speak to the poor, to racial injustices, and that's where their power lies."

The Nation of Islam had an estimated fifty thousand members as of 2007, far from its heyday in the 1960s. Farrakhan's inability to grow the Nation's ranks indicates that sympathy with his critiques of white racism does not necessarily translate into broad affection for the man himself.

"What's interesting is, why is Farrakhan still relevant to these communities, and why is he still as visible as he is? He still commands twenty, thirty thousand people," Abdullah said. "I think people see the Nation as a voice of dissent. A viable voice of dissent. Leadership in these communities— few are as visible as Farrakhan."

I spoke with several civil-rights leaders who reject Farrakhan's views but didn't want to go on record criticizing Farrakhan—in part out of respect for the constituency he represents, but also because they are aware of precisely how he exploits such condemnations to strengthen his own credibility. One prominent civil-rights activist cautioned against reading some black Americans' sympathy with Farrakhan's critique of white racism as a wholesale embrace of his message. "The message and appeal of Barack Obama is the polar opposite of Louis Farrakhan. That is more emblematic of the black community's sentiments than Louis Farrakhan," said the activist. "In this era of mass incarceration, the Nation still maintains a presence in the prisons, where we have too many people of color locked up, too many men, they are in many of our communities. So the unsparing critique of racism that he provides has a certain appeal."

For all its attempts at curbing urban violence, the Nation itself has a bloody history. Malcolm X was assassinated by members of the Nation in 1965 after his break with Elijah Muhammad and turn toward orthodox Sunni Islam; in 1973, former members of the Nation were convicted of murdering seven members of the Hanafi Muslim sect in Washington, D.C., five of them children. In 2000, Farrakhan apologized to Malcolm's surviving family, saying that he felt "regret that any word that I have said caused the loss of life of a human being." While Malcolm was still alive, Farrakhan said he was "worthy of death."

Nevertheless, the Nation retains credibility in many black communities as a force for reducing street violence.

It was in that context that Mallory came into contact with the Nation of Islam. Mallory turned to anti-violence activism after her son's father was murdered, eventually becoming the national director of Al Sharpton's National Action Network. "In that most difficult period of my life, it was the women of the Nation of Islam who supported me, and I have always held them close to my heart for that reason," Mallory wrote in a statement published in *NewsOne* on Wednesday.

She soon realized that all the women she knew who had lost loved ones to gun violence had also lived in poor, segregated neighborhoods, and she concluded that the circumstances that led to these deaths were systemic and not just individual. And in those neighborhoods, the Nation was present when others were not.

"The Nation of Islam was the place where most of the black men and women that I knew had been there and really had been reformed. Men particularly in my family, people who had been arrested, and people who had been through really troubled situations, I saw them cleaning themselves up and were successful," Mallory told me. "I found that the Nation had been influential in helping them to turn their lives around."

Mallory was surprised by the backlash to her presence at the Saviours' Day event, in part because she's been going to the annual Nation of Islam function since she was a child—her parents were activists. Although she is a Christian, she says it was common for her to work with the Nation of Islam on anti-violence initiatives, such as the NOI's "Occupy the Corner" program, which involves members of the Fruit of Islam patrolling dangerous areas to prevent violence. In 1989, after the Fruit of Islam's "Dopebuster" patrols proved successful in the Mayfair housing projects, *The Washington Post* reported that other neighborhoods were clamoring for their help.

That reputation has endured; in 2012, Chicago's first Jewish mayor, Rahm Emanuel, said that the Nation of Islam had a role to play in reducing violence in the city. "They have decided, the Nation of Islam, to help protect the community. And that's an important ingredient, like all the other aspects of protecting a neighborhood." Emanuel echoed what many black communities had long since concluded—the Nation can be the least bad of the available options, especially in a city like Chicago, where the police retain a reputation for lawlessness and brutality in minority neighborhoods.

This is also where the resistance to condemning Farrakhan or the Nation can come from: a sense that despite the Nation's many flaws, it is present for black people in America's most deprived and segregated enclaves when the state itself is not present, to say nothing of those who demand the Nation be condemned. Then there is the sense that while Farrakhan's views are vile, he lacks the power or authority to enforce them. Denouncing the marginalized Farrakhan can seem ridiculous to those who feel like white people put their own Farrakhan in the White House.

"The NOI has kind of faded, because of Farrakhan's virulent racism and sexism and bizarre crap; I don't think he's a leader anyone can follow," said Alexander. "Some of these hardcore anti-Farrakhan people always want black people to denounce Farrakhan and the Nation of Islam, which I reject. Their footprint has shrunk, but in a lot of communities, for a long time, they were helping people and families when nobody else would."

But with the Women's March, Mallory is no longer just doing anti-violence work. She's become a leader of a diverse, national political movement, of which Farrakhan's most frequent targets—Jews, women, LGBT people—are irreplaceable members.

"We would hope that public figures that aspire to be the leaders of social movements are truly equitable in the way that they tackle intolerance," said Jonathan Greenblatt, the national director of the Anti-Defamation League. "We don't think it should take very much to call out when somebody makes claims like, 'The Jews control the government. The satanic Jews are behind all the world's ills.' I think the response for this is a layup."

The more politically expedient path indeed seems obvious—but the stakes here for Mallory are personal and not simply political. I asked Mallory if she thought Farrakhan was anti-Semitic, or sexist, or homophobic. "I don't agree with everything that Minister Farrakhan said about Jews or women or gay people," said Mallory. "I study in a tradition, the Kingian nonviolent tradition. I go into prisons and group homes and I don't come out saying, 'I just left the criminals or the killers.' That's not my language. That's not something I do. I don't speak in that way. In the tradition that I come out of, we attack the forces of evil but not people."

Trying to understand anti-Semitism has required something of a cultural adjustment for Mallory, who grew up in Harlem and didn't know many Jewish people. She told me that once, in a conversation with colleagues, she remarked that Jewish people were good with money. "I've personally been checked on things like saying, 'Well, you help us with the money, because I know that you guys know how to handle money,' and one activist, she immediately followed up with me offline and said, 'Listen, that's anti-Semitic.'

"I asked her, 'Could it possibly be ignorant language? . . . I know that it's ignorant to say that, because it's a negative stereotype and you reinforce that, but again when you say anti-Semitic it's very dangerous for a person like me. It sounds really bad,'" Mallory said. "So she and I had a conversation. The two things that happened in that moment were one—she basically arrested my language and explained to me why that language was not good for the Jewish community, and at the same time I explained to her why using the terminology that she used was cause for me to feel attacked. And she understood that."

Mallory said that she now understands why her original remarks were hurtful to her colleague. "Now when I have conversations with other people and they say those things to me, I explain to them, 'Hey, this is what I've learned recently about this language,'" Mallory said. "It's very similar to any person outside of the black community looking at us saying, 'Get you some watermelon and fried chicken.' It's a negative stereotype that's being reinforced, so this is the kind of unpacking we need to be doing."

That fear of being labeled anti-Semitic, and the consequences of being a black leader associated with that term, was part of why she reacted so defensively on social media when CNN's Jake Tapper began a tweetstorm on February 28, highlighting the anti-Semitic statements in Farrakhan's speech and Mallory's attendance at the event. One tweet, in which Mallory wrote, "If your leader does not have the same enemies as Jesus, they may not be THE leader! Study the Bible and u will find the similarities. Ostracizing, ridicule and rejection is a painful part of the process . . . but faith is the substance of things!," was interpreted by some of her critics as Mallory invoking the anti-Semitic canard that the Jews killed Jesus, a meaning Mallory said she did not intend.

"When you are labeled an anti-Semite, what follows can be very, very devastating for black leaders. To have someone say that about you, it almost immediately creates a feeling of defensiveness, because you know the outcome," Mallory said. "The same photos that people have pulled up on the Internet that showed my relationship with the Nation of Islam have been there for years. And yet I was still able to build an intersectional movement that brought five million people together, and the work that I have done for over twenty years, and it's very clear that I have worked across the lines with very different people."

I asked Mallory what she would tell a Jewish activist who was disturbed by her associating with the Nation. "I would say that I hear and understand that, and I hope that as I'm able to understand how they feel, I hope that they will also take the time to understand why I have partnered with the Nation of Islam and been in that space for almost thirty years," Mallory responded.

On Tuesday, the Women's March released a statement saying, in part, "Minister Farrakhan's statements about Jewish, queer, and trans people are not aligned with the Women's March Unity Principles." In her essay for *NewsOne,* Mallory wrote that "as historically oppressed people, Blacks, Jews, Muslims and all people must stand together to fight racism, anti-Semitism and Islamophobia."

Neither statement explicitly condemned Farrakhan, and Greenblatt said he was unsatisfied with the responses of both the Women's March and Mallory. "Even if they respect certain programs his organization runs, that in no way mitigates the malicious things he's saying about Jews and the responsibility for people in leadership positions to recognize it for what it is and reject it in a clear and unambiguous manner," Greenblatt said.

Therein lies the key conflict for Mallory, and her colleagues at the Women's March, going forward. The Nation of Islam may be essential to anti-violence work in poor black neighborhoods. The Nation may be an invaluable source of help for formerly incarcerated black people whose country has written them off as irredeemable. The Nation may offer a path to vent anger at a system that continues to brutalize, plunder, and incarcerate human beings because they are black. And it may also be impossible to continue working with the Nation and at the same time lead a diverse, national, progressive coalition that includes many of the people Farrakhan and the Nation point to as the source of all evil in the world.

I asked Mallory if she intended to keep working with the Nation. "The brothers and sisters that I work with in the Nation of Islam are people too," she said. "They are a part of the work that I've been doing for a long time, and they are very much so ingrained in my anti-violent work of saving the lives of young black men and women.

"So that's the answer to that."

From the perspective of her critics, Mallory's refusal to denounce Farrakhan or the Nation appears as a condemnable silence in the face of bigotry. For her supporters, Mallory's refusal to condemn the Nation shows an admirable loyalty toward people who guided her through an unfathomable loss.

But watching Farrakhan bask in the media attention, as yet another generation of black leadership faces public immolation on his behalf, it is impossible to see him as worthy of her loyalty.

THE CRUELTY OF
EXCLUSION

THE CONSERVATIVE INTELLIGENTSIA WERE HELPLESS TO STOP DONald Trump in the 2016 Republican primary. They launched a half-hearted effort—most famously, *National Review* launched its "Against Trump" issue, featuring many writers who have since settled comfortably into roles offering intellectualized after-the-fact justifications of whatever Trump does.

Why did Trump understand the Republican base better than the intellectuals who purport to define "conservatism" did? Partly it's a consequence of Trump's constant imbibing of Fox News, which is so influential in shaping the perceptions of the conservative rank and file. But the other part is that conservative writers misled themselves about what motivated the Republican base, what divergences they would consider heresies, and what they truly wanted. That self-deception arguably begins with the Tea Party, the anti-Obama movement that swept the GOP and the midterm elections in 2010.

After Barack Obama's resounding victory over the late Arizona senator John McCain in 2008, the press was inundated with postmortems about the death of the Republican

Party, which was becoming a "regional" institution. Those who assumed the imminent death of the GOP had no idea of the backlash to come or how broad it would be. Obama took office in what was at the time the worst recession since the Great Depression, and Republican intransigence and Democratic timidity foiled an adequate policy response. Democrats lost big in the 2010 midterms, and conservatives credited the rise of the Tea Party movement with helping secure the Republican victory. Obama's personal popularity helped him overcome Mitt Romney to win a second term in 2012, but midterm losses for Democrats in both 2010 and 2014 were devastating.

But what was the Tea Party movement? To most conservative writers, it was the revival of small-government constitutionalism. Others discerned something more complex. In *The Weekly Standard,* a conservative outlet whose demise was a direct consequence of its criticism of Trump, Matthew Continetti wrote that the Tea Party had two faces. "One looks to the future. The other looks to the past. One wants to repair deformities in the American political structure and move on. The other is ready to scrap the whole thing and restore a lost Eden."

Conservative intellectuals misunderstood that Eden and what it looked like. They projected their low-tax, federalist, small-government beliefs onto a Republican rank and file whose views were far more complex and far more motivated by identity than conservative commentators wanted to admit. So when an authoritarian reality-show star who insincerely vowed not to touch Medicare or Medicaid and to raise his own taxes appeared, promising to "Make America Great Again," they believed the conservative base would reject him. But Republican voters embraced him, because the version of the electorate that conservative intellectuals imagined was a fantasy.

"Not a single grassroots Tea Party supporter we encountered argued for privatization of Social Security or Medicare along the lines being pushed by ultra-free-market politicians like Representative Paul Ryan (R-WI) and advocacy groups like FreedomWorks and Americans for Prosperity," wrote the political scientists Theda Skocpol and Vanessa Williamson in their comprehensive 2013 study of the Tea Party, *The Tea Party and the Remaking of Republican Conservatism.* The Tea Party "worries about racial and ethnic minorities and overly entitled young people signal a larger fear about generational social change in America. . . . When Tea Partiers talk about 'their rights,' they are asserting a desire to live again in the country they think they recall from childhood or young adulthood." A country that never would have elected someone like Obama.

Trump's victory in the 2016 primary came from understanding that motivation better than the people paid to be professional conservatives. The "Against Trump" case was largely built around the idea that Trump's heresies meant he wouldn't be a "true" conservative, in the sense of being anti-abortion, protax cuts for the wealthy, and in favor of privatizing as much of the welfare state as possible. Most Republican voters, though, don't actually care about "big government" in the sense that pious disciples of William F. Buckley do. Trump's divergences from conservative orthodoxy—his overt prejudice against immigrants, his rhetorical support for popular programs like Medicare and Medicaid, his opposition to free trade—didn't bother Republican voters, because they already agreed with Trump on those issues long before he showed up.

Just as conservative intellectuals were in denial about the

motives of the Republican base, they were in denial about their own. After all, Trump's attacks on multiracial democracy were no more of a deal breaker for many of them than his insincerely held positions on Medicare or Medicaid were to GOP primary voters. There are a handful of conservative intellectuals who resisted the social and economic pressure to turn MAGA—and I think liberals sometimes fail to appreciate the courage necessary to adhere to your principles despite the enmity of former friends and colleagues—but most ultimately accepted Trump's hegemony over the Republican Party and the conservative movement. Trump is a tremendously dishonest person, but he's forced an exceptional number of people to reveal their true selves.

This essay is about a key moment of conservative denial about the significance of Trumpism, and how Trump himself raised the stakes of his own defeat. I wrote this prior to Trump's first impeachment, and in hindsight, the Democrats became much more aggressive once it was clear to them that Trump's lawlessness was a threat to their party and not just to their constituents. I also believe the closing line was too strident. At the time, I was considering the international significance of a nation of America's power and influence falling to authoritarian nationalism, and I overstated the possibility that other nations would be unable to resist that tide. Despite Trump's loss, the resurgence of right-wing nationalism around the globe is hardly over. It would be a mistake to assume that its appeal in America has fully dissipated.

WHAT WE DO NOW
WILL DEFINE US FOREVER

JULY 18, 2019

THE CONSERVATIVE INTELLIGENTSIA FLOCKED TO THE RITZ-Carlton in Washington, D.C., this week for the National Conservatism Conference, an opportunity for people who may never have punched a time clock to declare their eternal enmity toward elites and to attempt to offer contemporary conservative nationalism the intellectual framework that has so far proved elusive.

Yoram Hazony, the Israeli scholar who organized the conference, explicitly rejected white nationalism, barring several well-known adherents from attending, my colleague Emma Green reported. But despite Hazony's efforts, the insistence that "nationalism" is, at its core, about defending borders, eschewing military interventions, and promoting a shared American identity did not prevent attendees from explicitly declaring that American laws should favor white immigrants.

Some other attendees, such as *National Review*'s Rich Lowry, took pains to distance themselves from the president's brand of nationalism. "We have to push back against Donald Trump when he does things to increase that breach between the right and African Americans," Lowry said. But in the fall of 2017, when Trump attempted to silence black athletes protesting police brutality, Lowry praised his "gut-level political savvy," writing, "This kind of thing is why he's president."

The conference stood solidly within the conservative intellectual tradition, as a retroactive attempt by the right-wing intelligentsia to provide cover for what the great mass of Republican voters actually want. Barry Goldwater did not break the solid South in 1964 because the once-Democratic voters of the Jim Crow states had suddenly become principled small-government libertarians; voters who backed Donald Trump in 2016 did not do so because they believed a nonracial civic nationalism had been eroded by liberal cosmopolitanism.

The consensus that American civic nationalism recognizes all citizens regardless of race, creed, color, or religion was already fragile before Trump took office. That principle has been lauded, with varying degrees of sincerity, by presidents from both parties, and in particular by the first black president, who reveled in reminding audiences that "in no other country in the world is my story even possible." The nationalism that conservatives say they wish to build in fact already existed, but it was championed by a president whose persona was so deformed by right-wing caricature that they could not perceive it. Instead, they embraced the nationalism that emerged as a backlash to his very existence and all it represented.

Trump's nationalist innovation is not taking pride in his country, supporting a principled noninterventionism, or even advocating strict enforcement of immigration laws. The only new thing Trump brings to the American nationalism of recent decades is a restoration of its old ethnic-chauvinist tradition. Conservative intellectuals cannot rescue national-ism from Trump, any more than they could rescue Goldwa-ter from Jim Crow, because Trump's explicit appeals to racial and religious traditionalism, and his authoritarian approach to enforcing those hierarchies, are the things that have bound conservative voters so closely to him. The failure of the con-servative intelligentsia to recognize this is why it was caught so off-guard by Trump's rise to begin with.

At a rally last night in North Carolina, Trump was reminding the country of this truth. Last week, the president told four Democratic congresswomen—Alexandria Ocasio-Cortez, Ayanna Pressley, Rashida Tlaib, and Ilhan Omar—to "go back" to their countries, even though all of them are American citizens. This is literally textbook racism. The Equal Employment Opportunity Commission offers "Go back to where you came from" as its example of potentially unlawful harassment on the basis of national origin.

Trump's demand is less a factual assertion than a moral one, an affirmation of the president's belief that American citizenship is conditional for people of color, who should be grateful we are even allowed to be here. Some elected Repub-licans offered gentle rebukes; others defended the president's remarks. But at his rally in North Carolina, Trump showed them all that the base is with him. The crowd erupted into chants of "Send her back" when the president mentioned Omar, the Minnesota representative who came to the United States as a refugee from Somalia.

Republicans, in the week since Trump's initial tweet attacking the four representatives, have tried to argue that the president was criticizing their left-wing views and "hatred for

America" or that the attacks on Omar were justified because of her past remarks about Israel. This is belied by the nature of the attack itself—not only did Trump say "countries" in his tweet telling the representatives to "go back," but much of the bill of particulars against Omar that his supporters use to justify calling for her banishment also applies to the president, long a hyperbolic critic of the American political establishment.

Some of Omar's remarks in the past (for which she has apologized) have echoed anti-Semitic language about Jewish conspiracies and dual loyalty, but the president has described Israeli prime minister Benjamin Netanyahu as "your prime minister" to American Jewish audiences and is a proponent of the anti-Semitic conspiracy theories around immigration that terrorists have used to justify killing American Jews. No apology from the president on these matters is forthcoming, and the right will not demand one. The ancient anti-Semitic charge of dual loyalty does not somehow become more justifiable when applied to Muslims. As James Kirchick wrote for *The Atlantic*, "Trump's invocation of Israel to attack four ethnic-minority women is breathtakingly cynical, effectively working to pit Jews and people of color against each other."

Trump has falsely accused Omar of supporting al-Qaeda, of betraying her country. But when a foreign power attacked American elections, it was the president who first sought to profit from that attack, and then to obstruct the investigation into it, and finally to offer a vocal defense of the perpetrators.

The argument that Omar's criticisms of her adopted country for failing to live up to its stated ideals justify revoking her citizenship substantiates the very criticism she lodged. Trump has said, "If you hate our country, or if you are not happy here, you can leave!" but his entire 2016 campaign was premised on the idea that many Americans not only are deeply unhappy but also have every right to demand that things be better. That Trump's supporters believe Omar's sins justify her banishment and Trump's similar transgressions justify his presence in the White House helps illustrate exactly what is going on here. Under Trumpism, no defense of the *volk* is a betrayal, even if it undermines the republic, and no attack on the *volk*'s hegemony can be legitimate, even if it is a defense of democracy.

Faced with the president's baldly expressed bigotry toward four women of color in Congress, Republicans turned to reporters to argue that his attacks are part of a clever political strategy, elevating four left-wing women of color into the faces of his opposition. I suspect these Republicans, and some political reporters, believe that this somehow exonerates Trump from the charge of bigotry, as though prejudice ceases to be prejudice if it becomes instrumental. In fact, the admission that fomenting racism and division is central to Trump's strategy is a stunning rebuke to those political reporters and pundits who, for four years, have insisted that the rise of Trump is about anything else. Trump and his most ardent liberal critics are in full agreement about the nature of his appeal, even as they differ on its morality. Only the Trumpists, and those who wish to earn their respect, fail to see it.

It also speaks to the futility of trying to somehow rescue a Trumpian nationalism from Trump. Racism is at the core of Trumpism. The movement cannot be rescued from its bigotry, and those at the National Conservatism Conference who believe it can are in denial. Conservatives can make their case for limited government, or for religious traditionalism, but as long as it is tied to Trump or Trumpism, it will be tainted. Trump is not a champion of the civic nationalism Hazony and others claim they want to see. He is a mortal threat to it.

I often open my articles on Trumpism with explorations of American history. I've spent much of the past four years trying to illuminate the historical and ideological antecedents to Donald Trump, to show how America got to this point.

So I want to be very clear about what the country saw last night, as an American president incited a chant of "Send her back!" aimed at a Somali-born member of Congress: America has not been here before.

White nationalism was a formal or informal governing doctrine of the United States until 1965, or for most of its existence as a country. Racist demagogues, from Andrew Johnson to Woodrow Wilson, have occupied the White House. Trump has predecessors, such as Calvin Coolidge, who imposed racist immigration restrictions designed to preserve a white demographic majority. Prior presidents, such as Richard Nixon, have exploited racial division for political gain. But we have never seen an American president make a U.S. representative, a refugee, an American citizen, a woman of color, and a religious minority an object of hate for the political masses, in a deliberate attempt to turn the country against his fellow Americans who share any of those traits. Trump is assailing the moral foundations of the multiracial democracy Americans have struggled to bring into existence since 1965, and unless Trumpism is defeated, that fragile project will fail.

Nevertheless, most of Trump's predecessors had something he does not yet have: the support of a majority of the electorate. Ilhan Omar's prominence as a Republican target comes not, as conservatives might argue, simply because her policy views are left-wing. Neither is it because, as some liberals have supposed, she is an unmatched political talent. She has emerged as an Emmanuel Goldstein for the Trumpist right because, as a black woman, a Muslim, an immigrant, and a progressive member of Congress, she represents in vivid terms a threat to the nation Trumpists fear they are losing.

To attack Omar is to attack a symbol of the demographic change that is eroding white cultural and political hegemony, the defense of which is Trumpism's only sincere political purpose. Many of the president's most outrageous comments have been delivered extemporaneously, when he departs from his prepared remarks. Last night, though, his attacks on Omar were carefully scripted, written out by his staff and then read off a teleprompter. To defend the remarks as politically shrewd is to confess that the president is deliberately campaigning on the claim that only white people can truly, irrevocably be American.

Still, a plurality of Americans in 2016 and 2018 voted against defining American citizenship in racial terms, something that has perhaps never happened before in the history of the United States. There was no anti-racist majority at the dawn of Reconstruction, during the heyday of immigration restriction, or in the twilight of the civil-rights movement. The voters of this coalition may yet defeat Trumpism, if they can find leaders who are willing and able to confront it.

That is not a given. In the face of a corrupt authoritarian president who believes that he and his allies are above the law, the American people are represented by two parties equally incapable of discharging their constitutional responsibilities. The Republican Party is incapable of discharging its constitutional responsibilities because it has become a cult of personality whose members cannot deviate from their sycophantic devotion to the president, lest they be ejected from office by Trump's fanatically loyal base. The Democratic Party is incapable of discharging its constitutional responsibilities because its leadership lives in abject terror of being ejected from office by alienating the voters to whom Trump's nationalism appeals. In effect, the majority of the American electorate, which voted against Trump in 2016 and then gave the Democrats a House majority in 2018, has no representation.

The electoral coalition that gave Democrats the House represents perhaps the strongest resistance to the rising tide of right-wing ethno-nationalism in the West, yet observe what the party has done with that mandate. The great victory of the House Democrats has been to halt the Republican legislative effort to deprive millions of health-care coverage, a feat they accomplished simply by being elected. But over the past seven months, Democrats have proved unable to complete a single significant investigation, hold many memorable hearings, or pass a single piece of meaningful legislation that curtails Trump's abuses of authority. Instead, they held their breath waiting for Robert Mueller to save them, and when he did not, they, like their Republican predecessors, took to issuing sternly worded statements, tepid pleas for civility, and concerned tweets as their primary methods of imposing accountability.

As the president's declarations of immunity from oversight have grown more broad and lawless, the Democrats have slow-walked investigations, retreated from court battles, and unilaterally surrendered the sword of impeachment. They have only just begun to call witnesses from the Mueller inquiry; they have only just begun to challenge the president's lawlessness in court; they have only just begun to hold Trump officials in contempt for their defiance of Congress's constitutional prerogatives. This foot-dragging will leave them with little time to actually look into presidential abuses before campaign season begins, effectively forfeiting a massive political advantage, to say nothing of abdicating their constitutional duties. The leadership of the Democratic Party has shown more appetite for confronting and rebuking legislators representing the vulnerable communities Trump has targeted most often than it has for making the president mildly uncomfortable.

Although two prior presidents, Bill Clinton and Richard Nixon, faced articles of impeachment over obstruction of justice, Speaker Nancy Pelosi offered the gibberish analysis that the president was "self-impeaching," so no actual impeachment was necessary. When confronted with yet another woman accusing the president of sexual assault, Pelosi said, "I haven't paid much attention to it." When the politically connected financier Jeffrey Epstein was indicted again on charges of sex-trafficking minors, and Pelosi was asked what she would do about now-ousted labor secretary Alex Acosta, who negotiated a previous sweetheart deal with Epstein, she said, "It's up to the president. It's his Cabinet," a position indistinguishable from that of Senate majority leader Mitch McConnell, who is a member of the president's party.

"If you start endangering children, I become a lioness," Pelosi declared, before caving on a funding bill for border security that will do nothing to relieve the systematic abuse of migrants at the border and whose restrictions the Department of Homeland Security is already ignoring. Chuck Schumer, the Democratic minority leader in the Senate, took the occasion of federal prosecutors in New York mysteriously closing their investigation into the president's hush-money payments to former girlfriends to ask the FBI to look into a popular app that ages pictures of people's faces. The president's racist attacks on Omar and her colleagues were precipitated by Democrats leaking a poll of "white, non-college voters," supposedly showing that they might cost the party the House and the presidency. Having publicly told the school bully where and how to take their lunch money, the Democrats were surprised when he showed up.

One could protest that the Democrats' timidity is a cold, calculated strategy. Republicans hold the Senate, the argument goes, so an impeachment inquiry would only lead to the president's acquittal. The whiter, more conservative voters who form much of Trump's base are geographically distributed in a way that maximizes their political power. Democrats may need to win over some of these voters, who would be alienated by impeachment, to take the White House. If the Democrats cannot hold the House, they cannot hold back Trump.

But Democrats now hold the House, and they are not holding Trump back. The president has abetted a foreign attack on American democracy, he has obstructed justice, he has vowed to turn federal law enforcement on his political enemies. There are squalid camps at the border where families are being separated and children are being sexually assaulted, their existence justified as a necessary response to a foreign "invasion." Trump has sought to rig American democracy in favor of white voters and refused to recognize the oversight authority of Congress and now assails the cornerstone principle of multiracial democracy that none of us is more American than any other. What, exactly, would be enough to rouse Democrats to action?

In the face of such a challenge to the American idea, tactics become intertwined with morality. If the Democrats convince themselves that anything they do to attack the president risks alienating white voters who believe the country belongs only to them, then they will be partially responsible for the path the country is taking and the standard it is upholding. The Democrats' weakness has not appeased the president. Instead, it has only invited bolder challenges to democracy and the rule of law. This will not change. If congressional Democrats cannot or will not defend the principle that America belongs to all of its citizens, regardless of race, creed, color, or religion, their oaths to defend the Constitution are meaningless.

Ilhan Omar must be defended, but not because of her views on Israel, gay rights, or progressive taxation. You needn't agree with her on any of those things; in fact, you needn't like her at all. But she must be defended because the nature of the president's attack on her is a threat to all Americans—black or white, Jew or gentile—whose citizenship, whose belonging, might similarly be questioned. This is not about Omar anymore or the other women of color who have been told by this president to "go back" to their supposed countries of origin. It is about defending the idea that America should be a country for all its people. If multiracial democracy cannot be defended in America, it will not be defended elsewhere. What Americans do now, in the face of this, will define us forever.

10

THE CRUELTY OF
PHILO-SEMITISM

AMERICAN JEWS WERE NOT ONE OF THE RELIGIOUS OR ETHNIC minorities that Donald Trump explicitly demonized on his path to victory in 2016. At least on the surface, Trump seemed favorably disposed. His son-in-law and a trusted adviser were Jewish, and his daughter Ivanka had converted.

Yet most American Jews were wary of Trump, and in neither 2016 nor 2020 did the perennial speculation about the Jewish vote going Republican because of left-wing anti-Semitism pan out. That's because most American Jews are liberal, sure, but it's also because Trump's style of demagoguery, despite not being directed at American Jews, was nevertheless resonant of the Jewish experience in the Diaspora with leaders who don't like Jews very much. And Trump's frequent invocation of anti-Semitic stereotypes, even as bizarre compliments, confirmed that instinct.

"A lot of you are in the real estate business, because I know you very well. You're brutal killers, not nice people at all," Trump told the Israeli-American Council in Florida in 2019. "But you have to vote for me—you have no choice.

You're not gonna vote for Pocahontas, I can tell you that. You're not gonna vote for the wealth tax. Yeah, let's take 100 percent of your wealth away!" The assumption that Jews are both rich and greedy is classic anti-Semitism—even as Trump apparently finds such traits admirable.

What Trump did have was a coterie of right-wing pro-Israel Jewish advisers, whose contempt for liberal American Jews mirrored the stereotypes Trump was familiar with. Setting aside for a moment the fact that Trump was an inspiration to Jew-haters globally, he was also being advised by the kind of extremists who believe liberal Jewish nationalists are worse than people who aided the Nazis in wiping out a third of global Jewry. When Trump intervened in the internal Jewish American debate over Israel by accusing American Jews of "disloyalty," he was echoing the rhetoric of Jews he is friendly with.

I wrote this piece because I felt that part largely got lost in the ensuing uproar over Trump's remarks—in keeping with the tendency of minority communities to keep their internal disputes, well, internal. But the ongoing confusion over both Trump's motivations and the reasons for uncritical Republican support of Israel—as well as their increasingly strident deployment of Jewish stereotypes against their liberal and left-wing opposition—were worth exploration. Jewish American liberalism is often characterized as hopeless naïveté, and I also wanted to show that it represents a mixture of idealism, pragmatism, and faith that long predates contemporary arguments over Israeli policy.

If you're rolling your eyes at yet another angsty piece on internal Jewish politics over Israel, I don't blame you at all. A great deal of American coverage of the conflict is seen through that prism, and the Palestinian view is rarely received with as much charity or understanding. There are other writers who are more qualified to explore that perspective.

What I can do is offer a historical argument for why pluralism became so central to the political identities of American Jews and why it remains so resistant to pressure from the conservative movement and from their Israeli cousins abroad. Seeing that commitment as a kind of weakness and failing to appreciate how well it has served American Jews is one reason why its opponents have not succeeded in undermining it.

THE JEWISH DIVIDE

SPRING 2021

THE PRESIDENT OF THE UNITED STATES DID NOT UNDERSTAND why the Jews were being so ungrateful. After nearly two years in office, Trump moved the U.S. Embassy to Jerusalem, recognized Israeli sovereignty over the Golan Heights, and rescinded the Iran nuclear agreement that Israeli prime minister Benjamin Netanyahu opposed.

And what did these faithless Jews do? In 2018, they went to the polls and pulled the lever for Democrats in overwhelming numbers, with 79 percent of Jews voting Democratic. Concerned about reelection, Trump lashed out, calling Jewish support for the Democratic Party the result of "total lack of knowledge or great disloyalty." After all, as Trump put it to a group of American Jews at a Rosh Hashana celebration in 2020, Israel is "your country."

Accusing Jews of "disloyalty" is a classic anti-Semitic canard, a justification for repression and violence. But the president turned the canard on its head when he explained that what he meant was that American Jews were insufficiently *loyal to Israel,* affirming not only that he believes American Jews are fundamentally citizens of a foreign country and guests in the United States but that Jewish "dual loyalty" is both expected and admirable.

Only publicly, however. Privately, the president's staffers have overheard him angrily complaining that Jews "are only in it for themselves." Trump spent much of his administration attacking two Muslim congresswomen, Democratic representatives Ilhan Omar and Rashida Tlaib, for holding anti-Semitic beliefs, even though Trump fundamentally agrees with the sentiments Omar and Tlaib were accused of expressing—that American Jews are loyal to Israel rather than the United States.

Attacks on religious and ethnic minorities are a predominant theme in Trump's speeches and policies. But his relationship to Jews is unique, in that, as the writer Yair Rosenberg puts it, Trump believes anti-Semitic stereotypes—like the idea that Jews are clannish and miserly—to be positive traits. He has courted the American Jewish community by pursuing a close alliance with the Israeli government and received scorn from most Jewish voters in return. Trump's enthusiastic reception from the Israeli right misled him into believing that American Jews would be a natural addition to his nationalist coalition. But the majority of American Jews, despite their support for Israel, identify with the cultural and political pluralism that has allowed them to live relatively safe and prosperous lives in the United States.

All Trump's crude entreaties have done is highlight the contradictions between the experiences of American Jews and their Israeli cousins, baffling a president who thinks in broad ethnic stereotypes, despite the fact that his daughter

and son-in-law are both Jews. The reason for Trump's erup-
tion is that, having given Jews what he thought they wanted,
he finds it baffling that they do not literally worship him; in
2019, Trump quoted a right-wing conspiracy theorist dub-
bing him the "King of Israel," a title similar to the one the
Gospels applied to Jesus. Trump only understands certain
kinds of loyalty: fealty to him, which is paramount, and ethno-
nationalism, which he understands as a kind of self-interest.
Left-leaning American Jews, in the eyes of the president, fail
both tests, for reasons he finds incomprehensible. Even so,
Trump is still looking out for number one: In Trump's reasoning, by being "disloyal" to Israel, American Jews are being
ungrateful to Trump for all he's done for them.

The disconnect, however, is easy to explain: The geostra-
tegic interests of the right-wing party governing the state of
Israel are not the same as the political interests of American
Jews—in fact, they are increasingly divergent. Netanyahu,
Israel's longest-serving prime minister, has made a tacti-
cal decision to ally with illiberal, even anti-Semitic parties
and governments in Europe, betting that right-wing ethno-
nationalist governments will be less likely to object to Israel's
decades-long occupation of Palestinian territory. That has
extended to the United States, where much to the horror of
liberal Zionists—those who have an ideological commitment
to a Jewish state but also want an end to the occupation—
Netanyahu has made a strategic bet that the Republican Party's Evangelical base will be a stronger source of uncritical
support for Israel than American Jews are. This has led to,
among other bizarre Trump-era spectacles, the now-common
absurdity of right-wing gentiles attacking their left-wing Jewish critics as anti-Semites for being insufficiently supportive
of Israel.

The moral implications of such a strategy aside, Netanyahu's basic calculus appears to be correct. There is a wider range of opinions about Israel at the average American or Israeli seder table than there is in the U.S. Congress. The bipartisan American consensus on Israel is less a product of Jewish influence than of Israel's popularity among American gentiles, including the Evangelical Christians who are a crucial Republican constituency. Most American Jews support Israel but disapprove both of the current Israeli government and of Trump's policies on Israel; a foreign policy toward Israel that catered to the preferences of the majority of American Jews would be significantly to the left of the one that exists today. As Trump later acknowledged ruefully, "Christians are more excited by [the embassy move] than Jewish people."

But Netanyahu's strategy means that the Israeli prime minister is willing to enable the erosion of the American pluralist tradition that has made the United States a safe haven for religious and ethnic minorities of all kinds, but particularly for Jewish people, if that advances his own international strategy. That strategy runs parallel to that of the Republican Party, which hopes to split the Democratic coalition over support for Israel, even if that means scuttling bipartisan support for the Jewish state. That strategy has yet to succeed, and Israel may rue pursuing it if it does. At the center of both strategies stands Donald Trump, whose uncritical support for Israel and belief that America is fundamentally a nation for white Christians exacerbates a divide between the two largest Jewish populations in the world.

The president's frame, then, has it exactly backward. It is not American Jews who have betrayed their Israeli cousins. It is the Netanyahu-led Israeli government that has betrayed Jews outside Israel, by aligning itself with nationalist parties in countries like Poland and Hungary, who are hostile to the ideals that make it possible for Jews in the Diaspora to live free of persecution. Chief among those betrayals is Netanyahu's role in helping Trump erode the religious and ethnic pluralism to which most American Jews have devoted themselves for decades, seeking to preserve the United States not just as a haven for Jewish people but for persecuted minorities of all backgrounds.

That ideal was born, much as the idea of multiracial American democracy was, in the conflict over slavery and abolition. Contrary to the assumptions of the Israeli right and their American allies, for American Jews this is not a question of blind faith but a strategy for survival that has helped move the United States closer to its founding principles. Jewish Americans have maintained a commitment to pluralism that has helped make the United States among the safest places in the world to be a Jew.

AS THE CIVIL WAR LOOMED, American Jews had many reasons to distrust the abolitionists and their crusade for social justice. Fervently Christian, some of the most ardent abolitionists were given to age-old expressions of anti-Jewish rhetoric. The abolitionist William Lloyd Garrison referred to the proslavery Mordecai Noah as a "Shylock" and a "miscreant Jew," describing him as a "lineal descendant of the monsters who nailed Jesus to the cross between two thieves." Garrison's colleague Edmund Quincy, the sometime editor of his newspaper, *The Liberator*, commented that if Noah was "a fair specimen of the race, it is no wonder they have been an insulted and despised people."

Long before the large-scale immigration of Jews to the

United States, in antebellum America the center of Jewish life was arguably in Charleston, South Carolina, the first state to secede. Two Southern senators, Judah Benjamin of Louisiana—later the treasury secretary of the Confederacy—and David Levy Yulee of Florida, were Jews. Senator Benjamin Wade of Ohio once described Judah Benjamin as an "Israelite with Egyptian principles," while the anti-slavery newspaper tycoon Horace Greeley described him as an "oily Jew."

As the nation teetered on the brink of war, the Jewish community in America was also divided. Jews in the South, having fled persecution in Europe, were largely accepting of the nation's racial hierarchy—the American color line was more welcoming to Jews than the sectarianism of the old world. And in the North, past persecution encouraged Jews to avoid political conflicts, lest the oppression they fled follow them to their new home. The last thing America's small community of Jews must have wanted was to insert themselves into a bitter political conflict over slavery—the kind of national upheaval that frequently led to Jews being slaughtered in their former homelands. But much like the rest of the country, the American Jewish community could not avoid becoming divided over the question of slavery—and it is arguably here, in the tumult of the Civil War, where the modern American Jewish community and its commitment to social justice was born.

That divide split open when a New York rabbi named Morris Raphall gave a widely publicized sermon that was both pro-Union and pro-slavery, offering a theological justification of slavery while mildly chastising Southern slaveowners for not adhering to the standards for human bondage set by the Bible.

"Slaveholding is no sin, and that slave property is expressly placed under the protection of the Ten Commandments," Raphall declared, adding that "the unfortunate negro is indeed the meanest of slaves. Much has been said respecting the inferiority of his intellectual powers, and that no man of his race has ever inscribed his name on the Pantheon of human excellence, either mental or moral."

As a path forward, Raphall offered a sensible centrism—Southern slaveholders should moderate the cruelty of the institution, and abolitionists should stop advocating for the end of human bondage.

Two hundred miles away in Baltimore, the abolitionist Rabbi David Einhorn was disgusted. Calling Raphall's sermon a "deplorable farce," he offered a detailed and witheringly sarcastic rebuke to the argument that slavery was divinely sanctioned. "The Jew, a descendant of the race that offers daily praises to God for deliverance out of the house of bondage in Egypt, and even today suffers under the yoke of slavery in most places of the old world, crying out to God," Einhorn wrote in a tone of disbelief, "undertook to designate slavery as a perfectly sinless institution, sanctioned by God. And the impudent persons who will not believe this are met with fanatical zeal, with a sort of moral indignation." Responding to Raphall's assertion that the curse of Ham justified slavery, a favorite argument of Southern theologians, Einhorn wrote, "God created man in His image. This blessing of God ranks higher than the curse of Noah."

Einhorn believed Jews, in fact, had an obligation, despite their fear of drawing attention to themselves, to fight on behalf of other oppressed people. "Israel, the people of peoples, is called upon to fight against the whole world for the whole world," he wrote in 1861. This was both a religious moral obligation and a matter of political self-interest. "Once we start to evaluate people by the country of birth, next will come an evaluation by religion and in this case surely, the Jews, the so-called crucifiers of the crucified, will be in great danger."

Einhorn's sermon, delivered in the slave state of Maryland, was not well received. After the buildings housing two abolitionist publications were destroyed, his congregation asked him to leave town, fearing that he would be the target of mob violence. Einhorn left Baltimore and never returned.

Einhorn's beliefs were not "assimilationist" in the sense of abandoning Jewish religious practice, despite the fact that they were infused by the spirit of the abolitionist strain of American liberalism. Rather, they were rooted in what he saw as the religious obligation of Jews to fight for justice on behalf of others—even if some of those others were not exactly friendly to Jews. For the majority of American Jews, that commitment persists to this day.

Einhorn "challenged the long-held concern among Jewish leaders that their Judaism was their business and that they had better not speak out collectively as Jews and jeopardize their sense of belonging in the United States," the historian Steven Weisman wrote in *The Chosen Wars: How Judaism Became an American Religion*. "His beliefs were a foreshadowing of the emerging doctrine that Jews were exponents of universal ethical precepts, and that it was their 'mission,' their duty, to disseminate them to the world." These beliefs were no doubt influenced by the fact that Jewish immigrants were among the "forty-eighters," German immigrants who were expelled following the liberal revolutions of 1848, and saw an opportunity to realize those ideals in their new homeland.

Although in the argument between Raphall and Einhorn, the former is the traditionalist, it would be a mistake to therefore see Einhorn as assimilationist. On the contrary, the religious obligations of Jews as imagined by Einhorn restricted Jewish Americans from accepting one of the most important elements of American assimilation—its traditional racial hierarchy. Einhorn's beliefs are now the prevailing interpretation of Jewish values in America, one whose tenets continue to confound nationalists of all stripes who believe that loyalty to blood and soil are paramount commitments. Not only nationalists like Donald Trump, but their Israeli cousins who built a garrison state on the banks of the Jordan River after millennia of exile.

SINCE THE CIVIL WAR, AMERICAN Jews have built a place for themselves here much the way other minorities have—by holding the United States accountable to its own principles. The survival of American Jews in the West was secured through pluralism and civil rights for all. American Jews opposed the racist immigration restrictions of the 1920s and led the fight for their repeal in 1965, they helped battle Jim Crow in the 1950s and '60s, and they remain a crucial part of the liberal coalition today. This is as much the idealism of American Judaism's liberal ethos as it is a matter of self-interest—only in a truly pluralistic nation could American Jews be secure as less than 5 percent of the population.

The lesson of the Jewish experience in the United States is, as Einhorn wrote, that when the rights of other minorities are threatened, American Jews are threatened. The rise of a nativist demagogue at the head of one of the two major parties, a man whose rhetoric resonates with the kind of men who walk into synagogues and gun down Jews at worship, has only solidified that conviction among the majority of American Jews.

Israelis have learned, if anything, the opposite lesson. The terrorist attacks during the Second Intifada, the escalation of Israel's regional rivalry with Iran, and the failure of negotiations between then–prime minister Ehud Barak and Palestinian leader Yasser Arafat scarred the Israeli electorate. Just as the ideological perspective of Jewish American immigrants in the nineteenth and early twentieth centuries was shaped by the nature of the illiberal right-wing governments they fled, Israel's politics are informed by the experiences of Jewish immigrants who left other nations in the Middle East and parts of the old Soviet Union.

"Israel feels under siege and sees its very survival as at risk. In this situation, questions of identity become crucial," wrote the Johns Hopkins professor Raffaella Del Sarto in *Israel Under Siege,* her exploration of the political dominance of the Israeli right. That sense of siege produced a domestic political consensus that "combines the perception of an inherently hostile environment—hence the need for forceful policies and deterrence—with ethnoreligious conceptions of politics and the principle of territorial maximalism." Nevertheless, she writes, "Israel's prevailing sense of besiegement remains remarkably at odds with the country's military superiority and regional power status." That its standard military might is less effective against asymmetric tactics may further contribute to that sense of "besiegement." But it is also the case that any society that spends decades denying people their fundamental political rights will talk itself into previously unfathomable cruelties in order to perpetuate that injustice.

Where in the United States the younger generation of

Jews has proven resistant to a nationalist right inclined to define American identity in racial and religious terms, a great deal of Israeli youth have grown more nationalist and more intolerant. Where most American Jews have found safety in a multiracial, multireligious coalition, many Israeli Jews have found theirs in defeating or destroying their enemies. Most American Jews have found refuge in pluralism, many Israeli Jews in nationalism.

Perhaps nowhere is this divide clearer than on the issue of West Bank settlements: Only 28 percent of American Jews believe Israel should dismantle none of the settlements, compared to fully 50 percent of Jewish Israelis. Netanyahu himself has proclaimed his intention to annex large portions of the West Bank, dooming the possibility of a Palestinian state, but without committing to equal rights for all people between the river and the sea.

American Jews have typically resolved the tension between their universalist values and Zionism by seeing Israel as a necessary exception, due to thousands of years of anti-Semitism, the post-1948 expulsion of Jews from Arab countries, sectarian violence endemic to the region, and the Holocaust. The United States was also born in blood and fire, and at incalculable cost to North America's indigenous population. Sure, there's bigotry against Palestinian citizens of Israel, the thinking goes, but like the United States, that country deserves the chance to evolve into a more perfect union.

But this vision of a more accepting Zionism is increasingly in tension with Israel's political trajectory: not just the occupation but Israel's treatment of African refugees, its subsidizing and construction of settlements on Palestinian territory, its adoption of a "nation-state" law implicitly downgrading the status of non-Jewish citizens, and the explicitly racist politics of its longest-serving prime minister. Trump and Netanyahu's relationship forced American Jews to confront the contradiction between the pluralism they support at home and the Jewish nationalism they have made peace with abroad. This does not mean that the long-predicted erosion of American Jewish support for Israel is imminent—but it made those tensions harder to dismiss or ignore than they once were.

If you're an American Jew from my generation, you remember a time before Netanyahu's ironclad grip on Israeli politics. In the mid- to late nineties, it looked like peace between Israelis and Palestinians might be possible. I remember Yitzhak Rabin and Yasser Arafat shaking hands in front of Bill Clinton, and the sneering face of Rabin's assassin, Yigal Amir. I remember Netanyahu's disgrace and defeat at Barak's hands and the feeling that, despite the Israeli left's history of violent land grabs, peace might actually be within reach.

But Palestinians in the West Bank and Gaza have been living in what has been for them an ongoing catastrophe since the founding of Israel in 1948, hemmed in by an Israeli government ideologically committed to depriving Palestinians of national self-determination, or political rights within the state of Israel, and their own ineffectual or corrupt leadership. That crisis has only worsened in the past two decades. While many left-leaning American Jews, including me, remembered the peace process as a tragic near-miss, to many Palestinians it was an insincere ruse designed to obscure an Israeli land grab.

"As seemingly fruitless negotiations dragged on for a decade, many Palestinians came to perceive that vital segments of the 22 percent of historic mandatory Palestine composed of the West Bank, Gaza Strip, and East Jerusalem on which they had hoped to establish a sovereign state were being inexorably absorbed into Israel by this creeping process of settlement and de facto annexation," the historian Rashid Khalidi wrote in *The Iron Cage*. "Equally seriously in terms of Palestinian perceptions, over this decade of negotiations (and later during the four-plus years of the intifada that followed), Israel came to exercise a far greater measure of control than ever before over the Palestinian population and over the 83 percent of the territory of the West Bank wherein, by the Oslo and subsequent accords, it had full or partial jurisdiction."

The bloody scenes of the Second Intifada are also a formative trauma for the Israelis who remember them. But during and after that conflict, Israeli casualties were dwarfed by Palestinian ones. Israelis deserve to live unafraid that a suicide bomber will turn the bus they ride or the restaurant they dine at into an abattoir. So, too, do Palestinians deserve a right to political representation and due process, to move through their own land without being subjected to a spider-web of military checkpoints, and to live without the fear that regular military incursions will incinerate their loved ones and destroy their homes.

While most American Jews maintain hope of a two-state solution, the Israeli government has created a one-state real-ity in which Palestinians in the West Bank and Gaza have few real political rights, an arrangement the Israeli human rights group B'Tselem has joined generations of Palestinians in describing as a form of apartheid. Nevertheless, American Jews might have been able to continue to ignore the realities of that conflict indefinitely, hoping that peace might someday manifest—if Netanyahu and his Republican allies had not made that impossible with their shortsighted interference in American politics.

• • •

WHEN NETANYAHU, AT TRUMP'S REQUEST, barred Rashida Tlaib and Ilhan Omar from visiting Israel in August 2018, it was a logical extension of the approach he had pursued since the Obama administration. In 2015, Republicans held a special session of Congress in which they invited Netanyahu to attack Obama's pursuit of a deal to prevent Iran from developing nuclear weapons. Opposing Obama's policy was one thing. Inviting a foreign leader to use Congress to humiliate a sitting president was another. Accepting that invitation showed that Netanyahu was perfectly willing to use his power and prestige to aid his Republican allies, and they would happily reciprocate.

Trump supporters have argued that Netanyahu was correct to bar Omar and Tlaib because of their support for the Boycott, Divestment, and Sanctions—or BDS—movement against Israel. But Obama was a liberal Zionist who publicly reiterated his commitment to Israeli security and statehood on many an occasion, and still, Netanyahu accepted a Republican invitation to debase him before Congress.

Netanyahu's strategy has paid dividends for him and for the Republican Party, but it has also made it clear to Democrats that as long as Netanyahu is in charge, the Israeli government is willing to interfere in American domestic politics on the GOP's behalf. The Republican Party that Netanyahu has allied himself with—one that is increasingly nativist, whose leader views American citizenship in racial terms and sees American Jews as temporarily displaced Israelis, whose intellectuals treat the presence of nonwhites as a danger to the republic—is anathema to the universalist values that have allowed American Jews to make a home here.

American Jews owe no allegiance to the Israeli state, just as Israeli Jews owe no allegiance to the United States. But they do owe something to each other, as individual members of a historically persecuted people: They owe each other solidarity against those who would oppress, marginalize, or otherwise harm them because they are Jews.

The divide between liberal American Jews and their right-wing counterparts at home and abroad is ultimately an argument over who is shirking their obligations. The Jewish American right sees its lefty co-religionists as kowtowing to Israel-haters whose anti-Zionism is a thin cloak for anti-Semitism. The Jewish left sees the right as bolstering a right-wing nationalism that inspires the fanatics who gun down Jews at prayer in American synagogues and who are willing to ally themselves with anti-Semites all over the world as long as they support Israeli territorial maximalism.

Trump has walked into the middle of this dispute with his characteristic sensitivity. Among the president's genuine political skills is rubbing open wounds with salt. As with so many other things, Trump's accusation of disloyalty toward American Jews follows the logic of Republican rhetoric across the line of plausible deniability. And as with the president's attacks on "the Squad," calling American Jews disloyal assumes that they are not truly American.

Many left-leaning American Jews saw this coming. When they heard Trump tell representatives like Ayanna Pressley, Alexandria Ocasio-Cortez, Omar, and Tlaib to go back where they came from, they heard the echoes of powerful anti-Semites throughout history. The current Israeli government apparently heard such remarks as the endorsement of the ethno-nationalism that it also embraces.

Prominent Republicans from the president on down have previously offered remarks that echoed the subtext of Omar's comments, which they attacked. Trump famously told a group of Jewish Republicans in 2015, "You're not gonna support me because I don't want your money. You want to control your politicians, that's fine," and late last year told a group of American Jews that Israel was "your country." These remarks are almost identical in substance to the most damning interpretations of Omar's comments; they drew little complaint from the right.

Similarly, House Republican leader Kevin McCarthy sent a tweet in late October 2018 blaming Jewish Democratic donors Tom Steyer, George Soros, and Michael Bloomberg for trying to "buy the election." Soros has figured heavily in conservative conspiracy theories for years, with Republican pundits morphing the Hungarian American Holocaust survivor into a Nazi, a classic anti-Semitic inversion of history used to justify the invocation of Soros as a shadowy puppet master.

McCarthy deleted the tweet only after a white supremacist committed the biggest anti-Semitic massacre in American history at the Tree of Life synagogue in Pittsburgh, inflamed by the conspiracy theory that formed the core of Republican messaging during the 2018 midterms: that some sinister force—likely Soros—was responsible for a Central American migrant caravan headed for the southern border. The worst single instance of anti-Semitic violence in American history did not occur during the Civil War, or at the height of nativism in the 1920s, or even during the heyday of the second or third iterations of the Ku Klux Klan. It happened in 2018, as part of a racist backlash fomented by a sitting American president who prided himself on his close ties to Israel.

Right-wing Jews may wonder how their liberal counterparts can countenance what they see as the unapologetic anti-Semitism of Omar and Tlaib and of a left that is increasingly suspicious of symbols of Jewish pride but comfortable with icons of Palestinian nationalism. Omar has apologized in the past for using anti-Semitic language, and in 2019 both Omar and Tlaib planned to visit Israel on the invitation of a Palestinian-rights group, Miftah, which has published articles accusing Jews of using gentile blood in matzoh, an ancient anti-Semitic myth. (Not that it matters to anti-Semites, but Jewish dietary laws bar the consumption of blood of any kind.) Miftah later apologized. The two congresswomen also support the BDS movement against Israel that the Israeli government and its supporters in both parties consider anti-Semitic. Although there are anti-Semites who support BDS, to characterize even nonviolent protest methods as inherently anti-Semitic because they target Israel is to say that no legitimate protest of the Israeli government's actions is possible—and for some people that is the point.

Liberal American Jews who are uncomfortable with Omar and Tlaib's remarks and associations still regard Trumpism's rejection of multiracial citizenship as a far more immediate threat, because it undermines what they see as the cornerstone of their acceptance in the United States. Just as Einhorn saw the principle of anti-slavery as more important than the anti-Semitism of some abolitionists, most American Jews are unwilling to sacrifice their commitment to pluralism over the anti-Semitism of some in their coalition. Tlaib and Omar make some liberal American Jews feel uncomfortable; Trump makes them feel unsafe.

Many American Jews also regard one-sided Republican concern for anti-Semitism as a cynical attempt to pit vulnerable groups against each other, in order to exploit rifts in the Democratic coalition, and understandably refuse to participate in what they see as a disproportionately vicious response that has nothing to do with defending Jews and everything to do with demonizing Omar and Tlaib and the vulnerable minority groups they represent.

This is not to say that nothing Omar and Tlaib have said or done is deserving of criticism, even though some of the reactions have been disproportionate to the offenses. When Republicans say "law and order," most people on the left understand that they mean impunity for police who abuse their power, particularly against people of color. When conservatives denigrate undocumented immigrants as "illegals" and their children as "anchor babies," liberals recognize this as an effort to dehumanize the undocumented, particularly those of Latin American origin. When Trump inveighs against "terrorism" as a justification for discriminatory policies against Muslims, Democrats recognize it as a pretext. When it comes to the insistence that American support for Israel is about money, Jewish allegiance to foreign powers, or the result of supernatural hypnosis, the implications should be similarly obvious. A left that treats anti-Semitism the way the American right treats racism, as a largely imaginary phenomenon exaggerated by bad-faith actors, is a left that has failed to oppose bigotry in all its forms.

Both criticism of Israel in anti-Semitic terms, and attempts to conflate justifiable criticism of Israel with anti-Semitism are common, and many people on both sides of the argument are uninterested in distinguishing them unless forced to do so. Yet the longer that Israel insists on maintaining its dominance over millions of Palestinians while denying them political rights, the more urgent it becomes for uncritical supporters of Israel to characterize any condemnation of that dominance as anti-Semitic—whether it is or not.

Right-wing Jews baffled by the calculus that Trump is a

greater danger to Jews than Tlaib and Omar should consider that they have adopted the mirror image of that logic: While Trump's decades-long adherence to anti-Semitic stereotypes makes them uncomfortable, Omar and Tlaib's harsh criticism of Israel makes them feel unsafe. America's embrace of Jews is, after all, an anomaly in Jewish history. Assimilated Jews have found themselves ambushed by murderous anti-Semitism in the past—Jews were among the educated and commercial elite of Germany, until they weren't. Trump's anti-Semitism, if nothing else, speaks to the urgency of defending Israel—anti-Semitism is permanent, they argue, and American pluralism may not be.

Yet this uncritical embrace of nationalism has also led some Jews to describe their liberal co-religionists in terms that validate anti-Semitic perceptions of Jews more broadly; the conservative pundit Ben Shapiro has referred to liberal Jews as "JINOs" and "bad Jews" who "vote Democrat" and therefore "undermine [the Jewish people] from within." Shapiro and his comrades seem unaware that by validating anti-Semitic stereotypes about liberal American Jews, who comprise the majority of American Jewry, they are affirming the ideological beliefs of anti-Semites while presenting themselves as worthy exceptions.

If the vast majority of American Jews are "bad Jews," as Shapiro maintains, then hating them is rational. This is why Shapiro, himself a frequent target of anti-Semites, has drawn the interest of white-nationalist terrorists, including Alexandre Bissonnette and Anders Breivik, and is praised on white-nationalist forums. They may not like Shapiro personally, but he is saying what they want to hear. When the president said that liberal Jews are dumb or disloyal, he was echoing a prevailing theme of right-wing Jewish discourse in the Trump era.

Those themes are echoed by the American Jews in Trump's inner circle. Trump's ambassador to Israel, David Friedman, compared the liberal Zionists of J Street to Nazi collaborators before excommunicating them from the faith entirely. This kind of rhetoric offers a threefold blessing to Jew haters: It tells anti-Semites they are free to hate liberal Jews; it tells them that doing so does not even count as anti-Semitism, because their targets are not truly Jews to begin with; it redefines anti-Semitism exclusively as criticism of Israel or her right-wing defenders. Zionist gentiles, from this perspective, can have their anti-Semitism excused, while left-wing Jews who advocate for Palestinian rights or who simply oppose the occupation can be smeared as anti-Semites.

Yet amid the mutual recriminations and accusations of bigotry that characterize the discourse over the conflict, there remain only two choices: two states where both peoples realize their nationalist aspirations, or one democratic state based on one person one vote. Anything else—further occupation, displacement, genocide, apartheid, war—is a moral catastrophe. As the more powerful actor in the conflict, Israel has the most influence over whether this story ends in further tragedy.

Nor is it reasonable to expect Muslim or Palestinian Americans—or anyone else really, but particularly them—to be Zionists or to be uncritical supporters of policies that deny basic rights to people who share their ethnic background or religion. Netanyahu has explicitly said that Israel is "the national state, not of all its citizens, but only of the Jewish people." Are the Israeli citizens who are not Jewish, non-Jews who live under Israeli control in the territories—or their loved ones who live elsewhere—supposed to simply accept that without protest or objection? Do American Jews—or anyone else—owe their silence to a country that has decided to maintain control over millions of people without granting them basic political rights or representation? Defending Israeli and American Jews alike from anti-Semitism is not the same thing as protecting Israeli territorial ambitions, no matter how much the Israeli and American right wish it to be so.

Israel is a fact; it exists. The Israeli insistence on denying Palestinians the right of national self-determination they expect for themselves is, as the Israeli historian Gershom Gorenberg writes, a direct path to undoing that existence. Anti-Semites cannot be talked out of their beliefs, but the easiest and quickest way for Israel to limit the impact of anti-Israel protest movements, and neutralize the ability of anti-Semites to disguise their motives as human rights advocacy, would be to end its decades-long hegemony over the Palestinian people.

The path that Israel's current political leadership has chosen instead is empowering right-wing ethno-nationalists all over the world, supporting the kind of governments that make life for Jews in the Diaspora difficult. Yet believing that right-wing ethno-nationalist governments are incapable of turning on Israel is no less naïve than believing that American pluralism will last forever. It is arguably more naïve. American religious pluralism, however imperfectly practiced, is centuries older than the European commitment to purging anti-Semitism, which is younger than Israel itself.

This is why the vast majority of American Jews have refused Republican entreaties, a dynamic unlikely to change in the near future. American Jews will not give up the pluralism of their home in America simply to defend their Israeli co-religionists from the consequences of their illiberalism. It is an unreasonable demand, and denying it is no act of disloyalty.

The October before the 2020 election, Trump held a public phone call with Netanyahu in which he invited the Israeli prime minister to mock his Democratic opponent, Joe Biden, as "Sleepy Joe." Trump's smile "visibly faded" as Netanyahu dodged the offer, instead thanking the president for his support.

A few weeks later, about eight out of ten American Jewish voters contributed to Biden's victory in the 2020 election. The next day, as Trump was still falsely claiming victory, Netanyahu publicly congratulated Biden, referencing their "long and warm personal relationship." It was, you might say, a lesson in loyalty.

11

THE CRUELTY OF
THE COVID CONTRACT

THIS PIECE WAS WRITTEN JUST A COUPLE OF WEEKS BEFORE THE nation watched George Floyd die on video, a police officer's knee on his neck. When I look back at this, it reads to me like a description of the factors that would lead to the largest civil-rights protest movement in American history.

The federal government had failed to contain the pandemic or protect the essential workers it depended on. People were stuck at home, unable to work, go out, or spend time with friends and family. Armed Trump supporters were gathering at state capitols to protest the restrictions as tyranny; they would soon be cheering police crackdowns on Americans protesting murder by armed agents of the state. Governors were essentially left to figure out on their own how to contain the pandemic in the absence of leadership from the federal government, which was too preoccupied with placating the president's ego for public-health officials to do their jobs as effectively as they should have or wanted to. By the spring, tens of thousands of Americans had died, and many more had lost their livelihoods.

When I first posited that the Trump administration and conservative media had reacted to the emerging data on racial disparities by concluding that containing the pandemic was not worth the harm to the economy, there were critics who said that I was foolish—the Trump administration didn't know or care, and Trump himself was too stupid or oblivious to be aware of such details. The idea that the Trump administration would condition its response to the pandemic based on its perception of who was bearing the brunt of it was a fevered symptom of a different affliction, Trump Derangement Syndrome.

Subsequent reports vindicated my conclusions. In July, *The Washington Post* reported that desperate White House advisers had begun presenting Trump with maps and data showing spikes in coronavirus cases "among 'our people' in Republican states," as a way to convince the president to take the pandemic more seriously. That same month, *Vanity Fair* reported that advisers close to Trump's son-in-law, Jared Kushner, believed that "because the virus had hit blue states hardest, a national plan was unnecessary and would not make sense politically." Nonpolitical concerns, such as keeping people alive, were of negligible importance by comparison.

Then, in September, the president himself simply blurted out that "if you take the blue states out, we're at a level that I don't think anybody in the world would be at. We're really at a very low level, but some of the states—they were blue states, and blue-state managed." The sentiment was grotesque but illuminating. Trump did not imagine himself as much more than, as my *Atlantic* colleague Ron Brownstein put it, "a wartime president, with blue states, rather than any foreign nation, as the enemy." For Trump, holding him responsible for protecting lives of Americans who did not vote for him—or who merely lived in states where a majority of voters preferred the other candidate—was nonsensical.

What I did not anticipate was that the White House itself would become the center of a coronavirus outbreak and that Trump would contract the disease. Conservative propaganda lulled White House officials into believing that the coronavirus could not reach them. But once it did, they could not change course, because defiance of public-health measures—even the simplest ones, like wearing a mask—had become a gesture of loyalty to the president, while adherence to them was an expression of disloyalty. A constant of the Trump years was that counting on Trump supporters to reach the limit of their commitment to him was a losing bet.

These factors all converged into a bizarre spectacle, in which Trump sycophants in the administration and right-wing media not only returned to downplaying the virus but insisted that Trump overcame it through sheer force of will, as if the more than 400,000 Americans who perished were simply weak, and as if they had access to the same level of care that the president did. Trump initially dismissed the pandemic as a "blue state" problem, and that meant that even when it became both a "red state" problem and a problem for him personally, his supporters were primed to accept his dismissals, at great cost to themselves. Trump spent the last few months of his campaign holding rallies that were functionally superspreader events, as if to advertise his disdain for the safety of his most loyal supporters, a disdain they misinterpreted as reciprocating their devotion.

I do not think Americans, including myself, have wrapped our minds around the catastrophe of the pandemic, and how much of the suffering it caused was simply unnecessary. I'm not sure that recognition will fully come to bear until it ends, and the firm embraces of our friends and loved ones remind us of the time that was stolen from all of us. Even then, it will take years to fully assess the costs, which were borne disproportionately by working-class communities whose labor was deemed essential but whose bodies were not. The only certainty is that in the final accounting, the president's depraved indifference to the loss of life will be remembered as decisive.

THE CORONAVIRUS WAS AN EMERGENCY UNTIL TRUMP FOUND OUT WHO WAS DYING

MAY 8, 2020

SIX WEEKS AGO, AHMAUD ARBERY WENT OUT AND NEVER CAME home. Gregory and Travis McMichael, who saw Arbery running through their neighborhood just outside Brunswick, Georgia, and who told authorities they thought he was a burglary suspect, armed themselves, pursued Arbery, and then shot him dead.

The local prosecutor, George E. Barnhill, concluded that no crime had been committed. Arbery had tried to wrest a shotgun from Travis McMichael before being shot, Barnhill wrote in a letter to the police chief. The two men, who had seen a stranger running and decided to pick up their firearms and chase him, had therefore acted in self-defense when they confronted and shot him, Barnhill concluded. On Tuesday, as video of the shooting emerged on social media, a different Georgia prosecutor announced that the case would be put to a grand jury; the two men were arrested and charged with murder yesterday evening after video of the incident sparked national outrage across the political spectrum.

To see the sequence of events that led to Arbery's death as benign requires a cascade of assumptions. One must assume that two men arming themselves and chasing down a stranger running through their neighborhood is a normal occurrence. One must assume that the two armed white men had a right to self-defense and that the black man suddenly confronted by armed strangers did not. One must assume that state laws are meant to justify an encounter in which two people can decide of their own volition to chase, confront, and kill a person they've never met.

But Barnhill's leniency is selective—as *The Appeal*'s Josie Duffy Rice notes, Barnhill attempted to prosecute Olivia Pearson, a black woman, for helping another black voter use an electronic voting machine. A crime does not occur when white men stalk and kill a black stranger. A crime does occur when black people vote.

The underlying assumptions of white innocence and black guilt are all part of what the philosopher Charles Mills calls the "racial contract." If the social contract is the implicit agreement among members of a society to follow the rules— for example, acting lawfully, adhering to the results of elections, and contesting the agreed-upon rules by nonviolent means—then the racial contract is a codicil rendered in invisible ink, one stating that the rules as written do not apply to nonwhite people in the same way. The Declaration of Independence states that all men are created equal; the racial contract limits this to white men with property. The law says murder is illegal; the racial contract says it's fine for white people to chase and murder black people if they have decided that those black people scare them. "The terms of the Racial

Contract," Mills wrote, "mean that nonwhite subpersonhood is enshrined simultaneously with white personhood."

The racial contract is not partisan—it guides staunch conservatives and sensitive liberals alike—but it works most effectively when it remains imperceptible to its beneficiaries. As long as it is invisible, members of society can proceed as though the provisions of the social contract apply equally to everyone. But when an injustice pushes the racial contract into the open, it forces people to choose whether to embrace, contest, or deny its existence. Video evidence of unjustified shootings of black people is so jarring in part because it exposes the terms of the racial contract so vividly. But as the process in the Arbery case shows, the racial contract most often operates unnoticed, relying on Americans to have an implicit understanding of who is bound by the rules and who is exempt from them.

The implied terms of the racial contract are visible everywhere for those willing to see them. A twelve-year-old with a toy gun is a dangerous threat who must be met with lethal force; armed militias drawing beads on federal agents are heroes of liberty. Struggling white farmers in Iowa taking billions in federal assistance are hardworking Americans down on their luck; struggling single parents in cities using food stamps are welfare queens. Black Americans struggling in the cocaine epidemic are a "bio-underclass" created by a pathological culture; white Americans struggling with opioid addiction are a national tragedy. Poor European immigrants who flocked to an America with virtually no immigration restrictions came "the right way"; poor Central American immigrants evading a baroque and unforgiving system are gang members and terrorists.

The coronavirus pandemic has rendered the racial

contract visible in multiple ways. Once the disproportionate impact of the pandemic was revealed to the American political and financial elite, many began to regard the rising death toll less as a national emergency than as an inconvenience. Temporary measures meant to prevent the spread of the disease by restricting movement, mandating the wearing of masks, or barring large social gatherings have become the foulest tyranny. The lives of workers at the front lines of the pandemic—such as meatpackers, transportation workers, and grocery clerks—have been deemed so worthless that legislators want to immunize their employers from liability even as they force them to work under unsafe conditions. In East New York, police assault black residents for violating social-distancing rules; in Lower Manhattan, they dole out masks and smiles to white pedestrians.

Donald Trump's 2016 election campaign, with its vows to enforce state violence against Mexican immigrants, Muslims, and black Americans, was built on a promise to enforce terms of the racial contract that Barack Obama had ostensibly neglected or violated by his presence. Trump's administration, in carrying out an explicitly discriminatory agenda that valorizes cruelty, war crimes, and the entrenchment of white political power, represents a revitalized commitment to the racial contract.

But the pandemic has introduced a new clause to the racial contract. The lives of disproportionately black and brown workers are being sacrificed to fuel the engine of a faltering economy, by a president who disdains them. This is the COVID contract.

As the first cases of the coronavirus were diagnosed in the United States, in late January and early February, the

Trump administration and Fox News were eager to play down the risk it posed. But those early cases, tied to international travel, ensnared many members of the global elite: American celebrities, world leaders, and those with close ties to Trump himself. By March 16, the president had reversed course, declaring a national emergency and asking Americans to avoid social gatherings.

The purpose of the restrictions was to flatten the curve of infections, to keep the spread of the virus from overwhelming the nation's medical infrastructure, and to allow the federal government time to build a system of testing and tracing that could contain the outbreak. Although testing capacity is improving, the president has very publicly resisted investing the necessary resources, because testing would reveal more infections; in his words, "By doing all of this testing, we make ourselves look bad."

Over the weeks that followed the declaration of an emergency, the pandemic worsened and the death toll mounted. Yet by mid-April, conservative broadcasters were decrying the restrictions, small bands of armed protesters were descending on state capitols, and the president was pressing to lift the constraints.

In the interim, data about the demographics of COVID-19 victims began to trickle out. On April 7, major outlets began reporting that preliminary data showed that black and Latino Americans were being disproportionately felled by the coronavirus. That afternoon, Rush Limbaugh complained, "If you dare criticize the mobilization to deal with this, you're going to be immediately tagged as a racist." That night, the Fox News host Tucker Carlson announced, "It hasn't been the disaster that we feared." His colleague Brit Hume mused that "the disease turned out not to be quite as dangerous as we thought." The nationwide death toll that day was just 13,000 people; it now stands above 70,000, a mere month later.

As the commentator Matt Gertz writes, some of these premature celebrations may have been an overreaction to the changes in the prominent coronavirus model designed by the Institute for Health Metrics and Evaluation at the University of Washington, which had recently revised its estimates down to about 60,000 deaths by August. But even as the mounting death toll proved that estimate wildly optimistic, the chorus of right-wing elites demanding that the economy reopen grew louder. By April 16, the day the first anti-lockdown protests began, deaths had more than doubled, to more than 30,000.

That more and more Americans were dying was less important than who was dying.

The disease was now "infecting people who cannot afford to miss work or telecommute—grocery store employees, delivery drivers and construction workers," *The Washington Post* reported. Air travel had largely shut down, and many of the new clusters were in nursing homes, jails and prisons, and factories tied to essential industries. Containing the outbreak was no longer a question of social responsibility but of personal responsibility. From the White House podium, Surgeon General Jerome Adams told "communities of color" that "we need you to step up and help stop the spread."

Public-health restrictions designed to contain the outbreak were deemed absurd. They seemed, in Carlson's words, "mindless and authoritarian," a "weird kind of arbitrary fascism." To restrict the freedom of white Americans, just because nonwhite Americans are dying, is an egregious violation of the racial contract. The wealthy luminaries of conservative media have sought to couch their opposition to restrictions as advocacy on behalf of workers, but polling shows that those most vulnerable to both the disease and economic catastrophe want the outbreak contained before they return to work.

Although the full picture remains unclear, researchers have found that disproportionately black counties "account for more than half of coronavirus cases and nearly 60 percent of deaths." The disproportionate burden that black and Latino Americans are bearing is in part a direct result of their overrepresentation in professions where they risk exposure and of a racial gap in wealth and income that has left them more vulnerable to being laid off. Black and Latino workers are overrepresented among the essential, the unemployed, and the dead.

This is a very old and recognizable story—political and financial elites displaying a callous disregard for the workers of any race who make their lives of comfort possible. But in America, where labor and race are so often intertwined, the racial contract has enabled the wealthy to dismiss workers as both undeserving and expendable. White Americans are also suffering, but the perception that the coronavirus is largely a black and brown problem licenses elites to dismiss its impact. In America, the racial contract has shaped the terms of class war for centuries; the COVID contract shapes it now.

This tangled dynamic played out on Tuesday, during oral arguments over Wisconsin governor Tony Evers's statewide stay-at-home order before the state Supreme Court, held remotely. Chief Justice Patience Roggensack was listening to Wisconsin assistant attorney general Colin Roth defend the order.

"When you see a virus like this one that does not respect county boundaries, this started out predominantly in Madison and Milwaukee; then we just had this outbreak in Brown County very recently in the meatpacking plants," Roth explained. "The cases in Brown County in a span of two weeks surged over tenfold, from sixty to almost eight hundred—"

"Due to the meatpacking, though, that's where Brown County got the flare," Roggensack interrupted to clarify. "It wasn't just the regular folks in Brown County."

Perhaps Roggensack did not mean that the largely Latino workers in Brown County's meatpacking plants—who have told reporters that they have been forced to work in proximity with one another, often without masks or hand sanitizer, and without being notified that their colleagues are infected—are not "regular folks" like the other residents of the state. Perhaps she merely meant that their line of work puts them at greater risk, and so the outbreaks in the meatpacking plants, seen as essential to the nation's food supply, are not rationally related to the governor's stay-at-home order, from which they would be exempt.

Yet either way, Roggensack was drawing a line between "regular folks" and the workers who keep them fed, mobile, safe, and connected. And America's leaders have treated those workers as largely expendable, praising their valor while disregarding their safety.

"There were no masks. There was no distancing inside the plant, only [in the] break room. We worked really close to each other," Raquel Sanchez Alvarado, a worker with American Foods, a Wisconsin meatpacking company, told local reporters in mid-April. "People are scared that they will be fired and that they will not find a job at another company if they express their concerns."

In Colorado, hundreds of workers in meatpacking plants

have contracted the coronavirus. In South Dakota, where a Smithfield plant became the site of an outbreak infecting more than seven hundred workers, a spokesperson told BuzzFeed News that the issue was their "large immigrant population." On Tuesday, when Iowa reported that thousands of workers at meat-processing plants had become infected, Governor Kim Reynolds was bragging in *The Washington Post* about how well her approach to the coronavirus had worked.

Although, by the official tally, more than 70,000 Americans have died from the coronavirus, many governors are rushing to reopen their states without sufficient testing to contain their outbreaks. (Statistical analyses of excess deaths in comparison with years past suggest that COVID-19 casualties are approaching and may soon exceed 100,000.) Yet the Trump administration is poised to declare "mission accomplished," engaging in the doublespeak of treating the pandemic as though the major risks have passed, while rhetorically preparing the country for thousands more deaths. The worst-case scenarios may not come to pass. But federal policy reflects the president's belief that he has little to lose by gambling with the lives of those Americans most likely to be affected.

"We can't keep our country closed down for years," Trump said on Wednesday. But that was no one's plan. The plan was to buy time to take the necessary steps to open the country safely. But the Trump administration did not do that, because it did not consider the lives of the people dying worth the effort or money required to save them.

The economic devastation wrought by the pandemic, and the Trump administration's failure to prepare for it even as it crippled the world's richest nations, cannot be overstated. Tens of millions of Americans are unemployed. Tens of thousands line up outside food banks and food pantries each week to obtain sustenance they cannot pay for. Businesses across the country are struggling and failing. The economy cannot be held in stasis indefinitely—the longer it is, the more people will suffer.

Yet the only tension between stopping the virus and reviving the economy is one the Trump administration and its propaganda apparatus have invented. Economists are in near-unanimous agreement that the safest path requires building the capacity to contain the virus before reopening the economy—precisely because new waves of deaths will drive Americans back into self-imposed isolation, destroying the consumer spending that powers economic growth. The federal government can afford the necessary health infrastructure and financial aid; it already shelled out hundreds of billions of dollars in tax cuts to wealthy Americans. But the people in charge do not consider doing so to be worthwhile—Republicans have already dismissed aid to struggling state governments that laid off a million workers this month alone as a "blue-state bailout," while pushing for more tax cuts for the rich.

"The people of our country are warriors," Trump told reporters on Tuesday. "I'm not saying anything is perfect, and will some people be affected? Yes. Will some people be affected badly? Yes. But we have to get our country open and we have to get it open soon."

The frame of war allows the president to call for the collective sacrifice of laborers without taking the measures necessary to ensure their safety, while the upper classes remain secure at home. But the workers who signed up to harvest food, deliver packages, stack groceries, drive trains and buses, and care for the sick did not sign up for war, and the unwillingness of America's political leadership to protect them is a policy decision, not an inevitability. Trump is acting in accordance with the terms of the racial contract, which values the lives of those most likely to be affected less than the inconveniences necessary to preserve them. The president's language of wartime unity is a veil draped over a federal response that offers little more than contempt for those whose lives are at risk. To this administration, they are simply fuel to keep the glorious Trump economy burning.

Collective solidarity in response to the coronavirus remains largely intact—most Americans support the restrictions and are not eager to sacrifice their lives or those of their loved ones for a few points of gross domestic product. The consistency across incomes and backgrounds is striking in an era of severe partisan polarization. But solidarity with the rest of the nation among elite Republicans—those whose lives and self-conceptions are intertwined with the success of the Trump presidency—began eroding as soon as the disproportionate impact of the outbreak started to emerge.

The president's cavalier attitude is at least in part a reflection of his fear that the economic downturn caused by the coronavirus will doom his political fortunes in November. But what connects the rise of the anti-lockdown protests, the president's dismissal of the carnage predicted by his own administration, and the eagerness of governors all over the country to reopen the economy before developing the capacity to do so safely is the sense that those they consider "regular folks" will be fine.

Many of them will be. People like Ahmaud Arbery, whose lives are depreciated by the terms of the racial contract, will not.

12

THE CRUELTY OF
THE CODE OF SILENCE

THE YEAR THAT PRESIDENT DWIGHT D. EISENHOWER APPOINTED Earl Warren as chief justice of the Supreme Court, he wrote in his diary that civil-rights activists were pushing too far too fast.

"The improvement of race relations," Eisenhower wrote in 1953, "is one of those things that will be healthy and sound only if it starts locally. I do not believe that prejudices, even palpably unjustified prejudices will succumb to compulsion. Consequently, I believe that Federal law imposed upon our States . . . would set back the cause of race relations for a long, long time." At a dinner with Warren in 1954, while the court was deliberating over *Brown v. Board of Education*, the case that would outlaw school segregation, he told the chief justice that white segregationists were "not bad people. All they are concerned about is to see that their sweet little girls are not required to sit in school alongside some big overgrown Negro."

Warren would later write the majority opinion in *Brown*, being less sympathetic than the president to that sort of reasoning. Eisenhower's logic was not fully correct, but it was also not exactly wrong. The backlash to the *Brown* decision was vast, and schools today remain largely segregated by social custom and business practice rather than state or federal law. Yet the shift in the culture caused by the decision is real, in that both those who advocate for policies that maintain school segregation and those who advocate for policies that would ameliorate it try to claim the mantle of *Brown*. Chief Justice John Roberts memorably quipped, in the *Parents Involved* decision that gutted *Brown*, "The way to stop discrimination on the basis of race is to stop discriminating on the basis of race," which actually meant, ignore the effects of discrimination by pretending to be color-blind.

Nevertheless, one of the lessons of *Brown*'s aftermath is that it is not enough to change minds as long as the underlying imbalance of power remains unaddressed. Although systemic discrimination is hardly a thing of the past, both sides generally see themselves as opposed to racism. There is a similar feedback loop happening with law enforcement, where a superficial commitment to anti-discrimination is at odds with the plain results of public policy. The lesson of *Brown* is that it is not enough to change minds as long as the underlying imbalance of power remains unaddressed.

Nor is it simply a phenomenon of the right. It is somewhat surreal to look back on all the grand gestures and rhetoric in the summer of 2020, when organizations of all kinds embraced Black Lives Matter slogans, gave employees time off for Juneteenth, capitalized the *b* in *black*, and in most cases changed very little about how they do business. Similarly, while activists were pursuing substantive changes to public policy, other people embraced Black Lives Matter as a means of consumerist self-expression and individual virtue rather than a movement against systemic injustice. It is easier to embrace abstract ideals and slogans than to consider how the world might change if we were truly committed to them. The Black Lives Matter movement is arguably a product of this discontinuity between what Americans say we believe and what we actually do.

Back in 2015, when I was covering the unrest in Ferguson, Missouri, over the death of Michael Brown, one of the big questions was whether Darren Wilson, the officer who shot him, would be indicted by a grand jury. Although the documents from the grand jury suggested that there wasn't enough evidence to indict Wilson for killing Brown, a federal civil-rights investigation revealed the Ferguson police department was rife with discrimination and abuse, and that the local government was funding itself by using the police to squeeze its black population with fines and fees. Death is what draws national headlines, but millions of Americans' lives are shaped by more prosaic forms of dispossession by law enforcement. That is not an inevitability but a policy choice.

The protest movement in Ferguson drew attention to an issue many Americans had previously ignored: that police officers are very rarely indicted for misconduct in the line of duty, even if that misconduct is lethal. In the ensuing five years, this same issue of police impunity would emerge again and again. One side of it was simply cultural and ideological: Many white Americans on grand juries were predisposed to believing that officers were acting in fear of their lives when confronted with black men allegedly threatening them. The dead were often described by the officers who killed them in near supernatural terms—Wilson described Brown as "bulking up" to "run through" a hail of bullets. Grand juries composed of people who are inclined to share racialized fears of black men endowed with super strength are not going to indict an officer who acts on them. What is a "reasonable" use of force is inherently subjective and shaped by history.

So the impunity of police who abuse their powers is defined by a legal regime that turns almost anything—gunning down a child playing with a toy gun in a public park, choking a man to death for selling loose cigarettes, severing a man's spine with a rough ride in a police van—into a justifiable act.

That legal regime is substantially shaped by police unions, which have spent decades attempting to insulate their members from accountability for misusing their authority. This regime has shaped the culture of policing itself, exacerbating a callousness toward the public that is one of the oldest and most pernicious aspects of the job. Getting rid of police unions would not solve all of the problems with policing, any more than *Brown* or the Civil Rights Act fixed racism, but it would solve some important ones, and alter the culture of impunity in law enforcement to which Americans have become accustomed. As *Brown* shows, you can't stop discrimination on the basis of race if all you do is say you're no longer discriminating on the basis of race.

With this piece, I was trying to explain the origins of police impunity as an outgrowth of the backlash to the civil-rights movement as well as a structural problem exacerbated by the role that police unions play in our political system. But I also wanted to show how Trump himself was shaped by the politics of police unions, which have long taken center stage in New York City. As the writer Ezekiel Kweku noted several years ago, Trump's "vision of the city is not drawn from the lived experience or statistical reality of life in the average

American city in 2017. For him, the city is a nightmare vision of the New York of the '70s, '80s, and early '90s—Old Future New York."

This is the politics of dystopian John Carpenter movies. But it is also the politics of police unions.

ABOLISH
POLICE UNIONS

THE WAY MAYOR DAVID DINKINS SAW IT, HE DID ALL HE COULD. He hired six thousand new police officers. He avoided pay cuts for cops while New York City was in the midst of a fiscal crisis. The city's first black mayor had, *The New York Times* reported in 1992, "largely sacrificed his ambitious social agenda to expand the police force to record levels."

But he hadn't done everything the police unions wanted. He opposed a measure to upgrade officers' sidearms. In the midst of riots sparked by the shooting of Jose Garcia, a Dominican immigrant whom police suspected of selling drugs, Dinkins had visited the family in an attempt to cool things down. The Patrolmen's Benevolent Association—the largest of New York's five police unions—took out a full-page ad in the *New York Post* attacking Dinkins, saying the mayor had "callously ignored the traumatic plight of the police officer involved and managed to transform a drug villain into a martyr," and blaming him for exacerbating "the rioting, looting and burning, as misguided individuals and street punks rallied around a convoluted cause." And perhaps worst of all, Dinkins supported an effort to establish a civilian review board. In response the head of the PBA warned, "The forces of evil are all around. . . . They are trying to surround us. They are trying to defeat us."

But the unions didn't stop at public relations.

On September 16, 1992, police rioted.

"Thousands of off-duty police officers thronged around City Hall," *The New York Times* reported, "swarming through police barricades to rally on the steps of the hall and blocking traffic on the Brooklyn Bridge for nearly an hour in the most unruly and angry police demonstration in recent memory." Dinkins's Republican rival, future mayor and Trump counsel Rudy Giuliani, was there "leading the crowd in chants," a role he would reprise three decades later on January 6, 2021, helping incite the mob that assaulted the Capitol. The rally, which had been organized by the PBA, "degenerated into a beer-swilling, traffic-snarling, epithet-hurling melee that stretched from the Brooklyn Bridge to Murray Street." Giuliani paid no price for his role in the riot, defeating Dinkins in the mayoral election months later. The union had successfully helped depose a mayor who had failed to submit to its authority.

"It was a white racist rally. I will never forget it. I had two or three years on the job," said Corey Pegues, a black former NYPD officer who wrote a memoir, *Once a Cop*, about his time on the force. One of the uniformed officers assigned to monitor the protest, Pegues was expected to maintain order at a rally where off-duty police were hurling racist epithets at the mayor and cheering his prospective replacement. "I'm a lowly cop and I got drunk lieutenants and captains coming out and I was supposed to stop them. How was I supposed to police them?"

THE NEW YORK CITY POLICE unions are not outliers—police unions have been the most aggressive defenders of cops accused of misconduct for decades—but in recent years Black Lives Matter has brought national scrutiny to the unions' success in protecting officers who abuse their powers. As president, Trump embraced them not only as political allies, but as a voice of the unions' particular vision of "law and order," one that elevates some groups of people above the law and leaves others with no choice but to submit to it. In Trump's apocalyptic warnings of the consequences of liberal political ascendancy, one can hear the echoes of New York City police-union officials arguing that the police are the thin blue barrier between civilization and collapse. "Americans know the truth," Trump said during the 2020 campaign, falsely accusing his Democratic rival of wanting to abolish the police. "Without police, there is chaos. Without law, there is anarchy. And without safety, there is catastrophe."

Police unions have used this kind of apocalyptic rhetoric to cement their power in cities and states across the country. If the police are the sole force that staves off anarchy, then every elected official's power is dependent on an alliance with that force, in accordance with a deeper law only the police get to define. Following this logic, every target of police misconduct is a criminal who had it coming, and anyone who objects to such conduct is probably a criminal too and, by implication, a legitimate target of state violence. Due process is a privilege reserved for the righteous—that is, police who might lose their jobs, not the citizens who lose their lives in a chance encounter with law enforcement. The most modest attempts at reform—from banning choke holds to gathering data on police misconduct—are typically met with fierce resistance. If the police are the force that transcends law to protect society, unions are the force that protects the police, by whatever means they deem necessary.

"The problem with unions is that they begin to protect everybody for everything. No matter how grievous a crime or the misconduct, they just automatically defend them. And when that happens, you lose all accountability," said Michael Quinn, a white retired Minneapolis police officer and author of *Walking with the Devil*, a detailed account of what he calls "the police code of silence," the informal pact between officers to turn a blind eye to abuse and corruption.

This resistance to oversight of their powers has been part of police culture for decades; the unions have exacerbated that culture's most imperious tendencies. When individual officers behave badly, unions ensure they get away with it, alternately intimidating or ingratiating themselves to elected officials until review boards are dismantled and disciplinary records scrubbed. But both the integrity of the law and effective police work require public servants who are conscious of the limits of their authority, and who can maintain a commitment to political neutrality on the job. There is a direct connection between authoritarianism on the street and authoritarianism in government, in that both contemplate no distinction between the use and misuse of the gravest of powers. This logic of impunity cannot be contained to those on society's margins. Eventually anyone who supports democratic accountability for those who wield such power must become an enemy.

When Trump pardoned servicemembers who committed

war crimes or police officers in prison for abusing their authority, he was reiterating the message that certain people are exempt from the protection of the law, while others are immune to its restrictions. Trump was also rewarding a constituency he expected to reward him in return. From his rhetoric, it was clear that in exchange for his unwavering support, Trump expected the police and military to aid him in punishing his political foes.

The question of police unions is fraught. Republicans have supported them because they are politically conservative and a useful wedge against the rest of organized labor. Liberals may be ambivalent, but support their existence on the grounds that all workers have the right to organize, and that the arguments against police unions can be deployed against other public-sector employees with unions, such as teachers. Police abolitionists either disregard the idea that police count as workers at all, or see eliminating police unions as a worthy goal only as a step on the path to abolishing policing as a whole.

There is a simpler argument. Police should not have unions because armed agents of the state empowered with the authority to use lethal force should not have the capacity to use that authority to advance their own political purposes. It is a fundamental principle of democracy that those who wield state force be accountable to the people, lest that force be turned against the public. That principle applies to the military. It should also apply to the police.

THE INVENTION OF THE POLICE is like the invention of race; memory and history have conspired to make the recent seem eternal. And yet both are recent innovations.

For much of the history of the United States, there were no professional police departments. In the rural South, whites organized slave patrols in fear of rebellion from the enslaved, while in the more urban North, men were expected to take turns serving in the local watch. "With few watchmen on duty, there was little they could do in response to crime or disorder. Cities were in fact very disorderly in those years, with much public drunkenness, clashes between different ethnic groups, and periodic riots," Samuel Walker, a historian of American policing and a professor at the University of Nebraska Omaha, writes in *The Police in America.*

Modern police departments didn't emerge in the United States until the 1830s and 1840s, in part as a reaction to riots in the urban North. Walker writes that the newly established police departments were ineffective and politically corrupt, and the officers themselves were often unpopular. With no two-way radios or squad cars, they were inefficient at responding to complaints and bad at solving crime. The departments were often partially financed by the black-market businesses they were supposed to be policing, with saloons, gambling halls, and brothels paying officers to leave them alone, effectively becoming managers of cities' vice industries. As the labor movement gained steam in the early twentieth century, police were used to break strikes and halt organizing campaigns.

"There was never a 'golden age' of policing in which the police were friendly, knowledgeable about their neighborhoods, and enjoyed good relations with the public," Walker writes. "The idea of the friendly neighborhood cop is pure myth." To this day, that myth remains a cherished one—a cornerstone of both political rhetoric and popular entertainment.

This widespread ineffectiveness and corruption sparked the police-professionalization movement of the early twentieth century, which sought to turn the police into upright civil servants who answered to the public rather than the local political machine. Across the country, police reformers set recruitment standards, instituted specialized training, and dedicated units to handling specific crimes. Reformers re-organized police departments along military-style structures and tried to reduce the use of the police as an element of political patronage. They also tried to rein in the physical abuse that had flourished unchecked.

The 1930s Wickersham Commission report on "Lawlessness in Law Enforcement" documented the extensive use of torture in criminal investigations, known colloquially as "the third degree."

"Physical brutality, illegal detention, and refusal to allow access of counsel to the prisoner is common. Even where the law requires prompt production of a prisoner before a magistrate, the police not infrequently delay doing so and employ the time in efforts to compel confession," the report reads. "While third-degree methods are most frequently practiced by policemen and detectives, there are cases in which prosecuting officers and their assistants participate in them." Torture methods, which "were particularly harsh in the case of Negroes," were simply a regular part of the criminal-justice system.

"There were no controls over routine police-officer activity, on use of force, on just simple standards of work," Walker told me. "In terms of current problems, all of the concern about police reform today, we are still trying to dig ourselves out of the hole that we dug ourselves into in the late nineteenth century and most of the twentieth century." Old habits are hard to break, and most of the problems with American policing are older than many appreciate.

Police responded to the era of reform and the commission with language that is familiar from our own time. The Wickersham Commission report quotes "the police and their advocates" dismissing the objections of defense attorneys and civil libertarians as the whining of "sob sisters of both sexes," who were "more interested in the criminals than in the protection of law abiding citizens." The rhetoric used by police union leaders is so old that it predates the unions themselves.

Police first tried to unionize around World War I, but their efforts faded after then–Massachusetts governor and future Republican president Calvin Coolidge crushed the 1919 Boston police strike for higher wages. After Boston, the police-unionization movement didn't resurrect itself until the 1960s and 1970s. In the meantime, scholars like William Westley published the first serious academic studies of policing. Their assessments of police work are blunt; in our time their descriptions, like those of the Wickersham Commission, would be considered anti-police. The police officer, Westley wrote in 1952, "regards the public as his enemy, feels his occupation to be in conflict with the community, and regards himself as a pariah." That "experience and the feeling give rise to a collective emphasis on secrecy, an attempt to coerce respect from the public, and a belief that almost any means are legitimate in completing an important arrest." In a small survey of officers published in Westley's study, they were most likely to say that the use of force was justified not by resisting arrest, certain guilt, or even interrogation, but by "disrespect for police."

Some scholars believed these sentiments were cultivated by the job, with cops expected to prevent the inequalities of modern society from harming the wealthy and privileged, while being looked down upon for their methods in doing so. Egon Bittner wrote in 1970 that "policemen are required to deal with matters involving subtle human conflicts and profound legal and moral questions, without being allowed to give the subtleties and profundities anywhere near the consideration they deserve," and were expected to be "wise, considerate, and just, without providing them with opportunities to exercise these virtues."

These contradictory expectations, Bittner concluded, bred a kind of contempt for the public they were meant to serve. All of these factors contribute to the sense cops have that they are constantly under siege, even as they wield tremendous power.

In short, all of the contemporary conflicts over American policing—due process, brutality, internal police culture, discrimination—have been present since the invention of the police. But attempts to ameliorate those flaws were hobbled when police unions emerged again in the 1960s and 1970s alongside a larger public sector unionization push, at the crucial moment when the most heavily policed communities in the country sought to turn America into a true multiracial democracy.

THE CIVIL-RIGHTS MOVEMENT WAS A rebellion against the law. It had to be. And the police were called upon to crush it.

From marches to sit-ins to protests, many of the most iconic images of the era were representations of police brutality: the Birmingham police siccing dogs on protesters, Alabama state troopers beating marchers on the Edmund Pettus Bridge, Atlanta cops manhandling Martin Luther King Jr. after an arrest at a sit-in. These images showed white Americans who had averted their eyes from the realities of segregation—from their restaurants to their schools to their neighborhoods— that it was enforced at the point of a gun in their name.

"The civil-rights movement contributed to greater attention to police misconduct, police violence, police harassment, and it did so in part because the police reacted so badly and in such a heavy-handed way and racist way to a lot of what the civil-rights movement was trying to accomplish," said David Sklansky, a professor at Stanford Law and the author of *Democracy and the Police.*

A crucial series of Supreme Court decisions sought to curtail police abuses, compelling cops to inform suspects of their rights, barring the use of evidence obtained through illegal search and seizure, and giving poor defendants a right to counsel. These decisions reined in—even if they did not eliminate—many of the lawless practices described in the Wickersham Commission report.

For many police officers and their political allies, civil-rights protest was anarchy and lawlessness, and the Supreme Court's decisions were pro-criminal. "The police unionism movement, which emerged in the late 1960s and early 1970s, was a reaction to new efforts to bring the police under democratic control," Sklansky said. And the police were not alone in their reaction and backlash. As the civil-rights movement sought further progress on questions of economic justice as well as civic equality, many white Americans recoiled.

For most white voters, the unrest simply confirmed that liberal efforts to alleviate inequality had failed, and that overwhelming force was the answer. Riots and clashes with police in 1967 and 1968 bolstered the conservative movement, which increasingly couched its criticisms of American liberalism in the language of "law and order." White voters gravitated toward politicians like Richard Nixon, who argued that the riots were caused by "permissiveness toward violation of the law and public order by those who agree with the cause in question" and that "the first responsibility of government and a primary responsibility of the judicial system is to guarantee to each citizen his *primary* civil right—the right to be protected from domestic violence."

Nixon famously carried the 1968 presidential election with his message of law and order. But that message, which characterized even the nonviolent civil-rights protests of the 1950s and early 1960s as an invitation to "anarchy," was too moderate for some of the newly ascendant police unions. They were far more enthusiastic about the segregationist Democrat George Wallace of Alabama, who, in a speech to the Fraternal Order of Police convention at Miami Beach in 1967, called for a literal police state.

"If the police of this country could run it for about two years, then it would be safe to walk in the streets," Wallace said, blaming "bearded beatnik bureaucrats" and a collective of "world guerrilla-warfare chieftains in Havana" for the riots, foreshadowing themes Trump would embrace with complaints about "George Soros" and "the deep state." According to the *Miami Herald*, Wallace got a "roaring response" from the cops, "lifting the cheering policemen to their feet" when he called for them to run the country.

Employing a staple of police-union rhetoric, Wallace implicitly compared the suffering of police under new legal restraints on the use of force to that of Black Americans fighting segregation. "The police are a beleaguered group," Wallace told *The Birmingham News* in 1967, saying police deserved "praise" for beating civil-rights marchers on the Edmund Pettus Bridge—or, as he put it, shutting down the "unlawful assembly" in Selma. He won the FOP's endorsement that year.

Wallace lost, but his racist populism provided the Republican Party with a path to victory they didn't have four years earlier. Nixon "prevailed by adopting much of Wallace's rhetoric and pulling together a broad electoral alignment that drew various ethnicities into a white political identity that opposed racial liberalism," the historian Joseph Lowndes writes in *From the New Deal to the New Right*. Adjusting Wallace's approach, Nixon could more subtly link rising crime with demands for black equality without incurring the same level of backlash, cracking the New Deal coalition as Barry Goldwater never could.

Nixon's appeal was also effective because fears surrounding crime and riots were hardly just white concerns. As the historian Michael Flamm writes in *Law and Order*, as many as 65 percent of black Americans told pollsters they were afraid for their personal safety in 1967. "Americans of all races agreed that the riots had hurt the civil rights cause, harmed blacks the most, and attracted only limited support," Flamm wrote. But where most black Americans "blamed the unrest on discrimination, poor housing, and unemployment," as well as pointing to "police brutality as a major factor," white Americans "overwhelmingly (by an 8–1 margin) rejected it." As the Yale law professor James Forman Jr. writes in *Locking Up Our Own*, black political leaders in the 1970s and 1980s pushed for strict punitary measures like mandatory minimum sentencing with the strong support of their constituents.

Unlike more government aid to fight poverty and discrimination, which those leaders also sought, harsher criminal punishments were something their political allies were willing to countenance. In a recurring pattern, black communities across the country would suffer both from high crime and the government's efforts to suppress it.

Popular demand for a heavy-handed response to crime strengthened the hands of the emergent police-unionism movement. Americans who would never have personally identified with Wallace nevertheless tacitly took a version of the trade that he offered: Give the police impunity, and they will give you order.

"It was the sixties that really galvanized a lot of public support for the police," Walker told me. "'The police are gonna protect us from these rioters. They're the ones who are gonna put down riots.' And the police very skillfully exploited that.

"Unions discovered that they had a lot of power, that in union contract negotiations, they could play the crime card," Walker told me. "The other side of the crime card, of course, is the race card. Unspoken but clearly understood everywhere is that people are gonna be victimized by black criminals."

THE NEWLY ORGANIZED POLICE SKILLFULLY marshaled fears of rising crime to foil efforts at accountability. In New York City in 1966, supporters of the Patrolmen's Benevolent Association ran an ad campaign showing an anxious white woman exiting the subway, with the text reading: "The Civilian Review Board must be stopped! . . . Her life . . . your life . . . may depend on it." The PBA president at the time warned that "you won't satisfy these people until you get all Negroes and Puerto Ricans on the board and every policeman who goes in front of it is found guilty." The police and their allies won a landslide victory against adding citizens to the board.

In Philadelphia in 1967, the Fraternal Order of Police successfully sued to shut down a civilian advisory board, its national organization having warned that such boards were "spearheads for the Communists." Similar stories played out across other big cities; police unions and their conservative allies successfully persuaded voters that any oversight of the police would put them in danger.

Despite its depiction on television, in film, and in the heated rhetoric of conservative politicians and police-union representatives, very little of policing involves physical peril, or even solving crimes. "The vast majority of police work involves order maintenance and peacekeeping," Walker writes. "Reporting data from a major study of police services shows that crime-related calls represent only 19 percent of all 911 calls for service." The behavior and reputation of the police in communities suffering from violent crime in fact cripples their ability to solve crimes—a 2019 *Washington Post* investigation of America's largest cities found that half of homicides failed to even result in an arrest. The bargain of safety in exchange for impunity is never actually fulfilled. But both police unions and their allies understand that the most effective political rhetoric presents the police as the lone barrier between civilization and barbarism, even when advocating their own right to barbarism.

Where Coolidge's conservatism had led him to oppose police unions, the new right saw them as comrades. In New York City in 1965, in the midst of a quixotic run for mayor, famed *National Review* editor William F. Buckley Jr. praised the "restraint" of state troopers beating civil-rights marchers in Selma, to a crowd of 5,600 cheering and clapping policemen, who gave the conservative intellectual a "standing ovation." In Buckley's view, the troopers in Selma were standing for a world of "order and values," which in a certain sense was true. It was an explicitly racist order built on explicitly racist values, and the politics of policing allowed Buckley, and by extension the conservative movement, to defend that order and those values in the name of public safety rather than white supremacy.

The Supreme Court's extension of due-process rights, the backlash to the civil-rights movement, and the alliance with the new conservative movement created an environment in which police unionism could thrive. The unions' alliance with the conservative movement would pay off decades later when, in states like Wisconsin, police were exempted from Republican attacks on public-sector unions.

Until the late 1970s, however, their contracts, according to Walker, lacked the "really offensive provisions that we know today." They were largely about wages and benefits. But the success of "law and order" politics drew in both parties, creating a bipartisan consensus that amounted to, as the historian Elizabeth Hinton has written, "disinvesting from social welfare measures while escalating crime control and penal programs."

A key part of that consensus was embracing the idea that criticism of abuses by law enforcement was advocacy for criminality. This was the same argument police and their advocates had been making going all the way back to early-twentieth-century reform efforts—but now it had been adopted by politicians across the political spectrum, whether they truly believed it or simply believed that opposing tough on crime politics was unwise. It was in this political context that police unions began using their power to create a system in which holding officers accountable for misconduct in the line of duty is nearly impossible.

Looking at eighty-two active police-union contracts in major American cities, a 2017 Reuters investigation found that a majority "call for departments to erase disciplinary records, some after just six months." Many contracts allow officers to access investigative information about complaints or charges against them, so they can get their own stories straight without risking legal trouble. Some require the officer's approval before making public information regarding misconduct; others set time limits on when citizens can file complaints. When city officials attempt to make changes to foster greater accountability, they are buried in a mountain of cash accumulated by police unions through dues and donations. Like Dinkins, elected officials who support the mildest reforms are inundated with ads warning that any restraints on the ability of the police to use force will result in the collapse of civilization. Impunity for misconduct can supersede concerns about compensation. In San Antonio, the local police union accepted caps to pay and benefits as the then–city manager abandoned her efforts to, among other reforms, prevent police from erasing past misconduct records.

"Officers who are fired for egregious conduct or who are recommended for termination and then quit, there's no record of them anywhere. So the protection they get for capricious termination, the collateral cost of that, turns into protection of serial abusers," Dr. Phillip Atiba Goff, the founder of the Center for Policing Equity, told me. "That's a way in which unions end up perpetuating the worst within law enforcement, even if we don't assign them malicious intent."

On the rare occasions officers are fired for misconduct, they are often reinstated by sympathetic arbitrators. The most common explanation for overturning a disciplinary procedure, according to a 2020 study by Stephen Rushin of the Loyola University School of Law, was that the punishments were "disproportionate" to the offense, a conclusion that replaces the "judgment of police chiefs, sheriffs and city leaders with [that of the arbitrator]." A 2017 *Washington Post* investigation found that, since 2006, of the 1,881 officers fired for misconduct, 451 were reinstated through requirements in union contracts. In one recent survey, the economist Rob Gillezeau of the University of Victoria found that after departments unionize, there is a "substantial increase" in police killings of civilians. Neither crime rates nor the safety of the officers themselves is affected.

"You get into a shooting, the first thing they tell you, 'Call your union delegate. And don't say anything. Don't talk to nobody 'til you speak to the union delegate.' That's even before calling a lawyer," Pegues told me. "They know they're going to be protected. So it's almost like open season on the community."

These bureaucratic barriers to accountability established by police unions do more than simply protect bad actors. They cultivate an authoritarian culture within police departments by exacerbating a phenomenon often described as the police code of silence.

Beneath the strident rhetoric of police union officials, rank-and-file officers are well aware of how impunity corrupts the profession. The National Institute of Justice published a survey in 2000 showing that 67 percent of police officers believe that "an officer who reports another officer's misconduct is likely to be given the cold shoulder by his or her fellow officers." Fifty-two percent affirmed that "it is not unusual for a police officer to turn a blind eye to improper conduct by other officers." Only 39 percent agreed with the statement that "police officers always report serious criminal violations involving abuse of authority by fellow officers."

"The whole problem with the code of silence is not so much that cops don't want to report misconduct, but that there's no accountability for the officers that are involved in misconduct. And if a department's not gonna hold them accountable, why should they step up, make their life miserable on the job, to do something that the department's not gonna follow through with them or even have an impact on them?" Quinn told me. "They're labeled as snitches or rats, or you don't get people responding [to calls] to back them up. They get ostracized on the job, so that life just becomes really hard for them to go to work."

Officers themselves might not believe in the code, despite adhering to it. According to the survey conducted by the National Institute of Justice, more than eight out of ten "reported that they do not accept the 'code of silence'" as an "essential part of the mutual trust necessary to good policing." Despite the fact that officers say they "do not believe in protecting wrongdoers, they often do not turn them in." From the officers' perspective, there's little reason to speak up, and plenty of incentive to ignore their consciences while on the job.

The code of silence, the rationalization of brutality, and the culture of contempt for outsiders—particularly for groups of people law enforcement has traditionally been charged with repressing—all predate police unions. But police unions not only thrive on these dysfunctions and rely on them for their own existence; they have successfully helped embed them in the bureaucracy of policing by establishing rules that make it extremely difficult to permanently fire bad cops, or to prevent bad cops who have been fired from being rehired in a different jurisdiction, and that also ensure police who engage in misconduct can count on the silence of their colleagues. Then they use their financial resources and political influence to prevent these rules from being changed, and they intimidate politicians who might consider changing them.

This is not a system ruined by a few bad apples. This is a system that creates and protects bad apples by design. Most people who become police officers enter the profession because it is held in high esteem and because they wish to provide a public service. But individual good intentions cannot overcome a system carefully designed to render them meaningless. Trying to be a good cop can actually get you in trouble with your superiors, your fellow officers, and the union that represents you.

"I came in and I really thought that I was going to change the world, you know, because everybody traditionally looks up to police," Pegues told me. "And then when you get into the culture, it leaves a bad taste in your mouth."

Technology has diminished the ability of police unions to frame the narrative. In the mid-twentieth century, both de facto and de jure segregation made it difficult for white Americans to observe for themselves the disparate treatment black people received at the hands of the police, which is one reason why the photographs of police abusing civil-rights protesters in the South awakened the conscience of a nation. Those protests, however, were organized public events.

The inventions of the cellphone camera and social media made it possible for millions of Americans to witness for the first time not only capricious use of lethal force by police, but the sort of daily humiliations by abusive officers that are never reported by their colleagues or by the people who experience them: the shopper who is profiled and arrested without cause, the student who is needlessly brutalized for youthful defiance, the motorist who is detained and harassed for an officer's amusement. In 2020, Darnella Frazier, a seventeen-year-old with a cellphone camera, documented the killing of George Floyd by a Minneapolis police officer for the world to witness. That eight-and-a-half-minute video became the spark for what were reportedly the largest civil-rights protests in the history of the United States.

Most Americans who watched the video of Floyd begging for his life for eight and a half minutes, as a Minneapolis police officer kneeled on his neck, saw a human being. Robert Kroll did not. The head of the Police Officers Federation of Minneapolis saw a "violent criminal" and viewed the protests that followed as a "terrorist movement." The "liberal media" was to blame, he wrote in a letter to union members, complaining that the officers involved in Floyd's death had been "terminated without due process," suggesting the officers had a right to keep their jobs but the man who died in their custody had no right to be alive. The effectiveness of this rhetoric, so powerful in years past, was blunted by what Americans could see with their own eyes.

The dark underside of the national awakening regarding police abuse that took place in the summer of 2020 is, for all the millions of Americans whose consciences were shocked, millions of others saw these same images and came away even more convinced of the virtue of the brutality they depicted. Even as cellphone cameras provided a means to expose conduct protected by the police code of silence, that national awakening also produced a counterrevolution in Blue Lives Matter, a popular movement devoted to valorizing those very abuses the code was meant to hide. Blue Lives Matter was founded in 2014, following the murders of NYPD officers Rafael Ramos and Wenjian Liu. Mustered as a retort to Black Lives Matter, one linking criticism of police misconduct intrinsically to murder, the slogan became popular as an ideological statement of support for the notion that impunity for police is an integral part of civilized society. The designer of the "blue lives matter flag," a black and white American flag with a blue line in the middle, explained to *Harper's* in 2018 that "the black above represents citizens . . . and the black below represents criminals." This is consonant with the ideological worldview of police unions: "Citizens" have rights, "criminals" do not, and police unilaterally get to decide who is who.

The heavy-handed police response to the 2020 Black Lives Matter protests, then, was a form of political violence, in the eyes not just of the protesters but of those who justified abusive behavior by law enforcement. For the latter, cops who beat and injured protesters were manning the ramparts of civilization against a movement that was threatening not mere disorder or civil unrest, but war on their way of life. For some people, the sight of officers brutalizing protesters was a moral abomination, a perversion of the law. For others, it was the world as it should be.

Conservatives who recognize such abuses as a serious dilemma often argue that the dysfunctional culture of police unions is one that all unions cultivate—particularly public-sector unions. That is, it is a union's job to advocate for its workers no matter the circumstances, and with public-sector unions, that means prioritizing the needs and priorities of their members over those of the public.

Even if one accepted these premises, however, there is one big difference between police unions and every other type of union, public or private: The police can kill you.

IN 2014, IN THE MIDST of protests over the shooting of Michael Brown in Ferguson, Missouri, *The Washington Post* ignited a small social-media firestorm when it published an op-ed by a former police officer in which the headline stated plainly, "I'm a cop. If you don't want to get hurt, don't challenge me." He elaborated, "Don't argue with me, don't call me names, don't tell me that I can't stop you, don't say I'm a racist pig, don't threaten that you'll sue me and take away my badge." Not a single one of those behaviors is a crime, yet each of them is punishable by injury or death.

That headline was an assertion that was both literally true and that inadvertently acknowledged the challenge that police pose to democratic societies: Empowered by the state with the use of violence, police might exercise that power in contempt of the rights of the citizens who have conferred it to them—not to enforce laws, but to enforce their own authority and political prerogatives.

In democratic societies, the use of state-sanctioned violence is meant to be constrained by the rule of law. Instead, led by their unions, the police in America have developed into a constituency with a strong interest in the ability to dispense violence with impunity against the very population it is charged with protecting. It is only this impunity, cultivated by police unions and their political allies, that allows a former officer to state, with complete unfettered confidence, that those who disrespect him are potentially subject to summary execution.

There is no other public profession of which this can be said. A teacher who pulls out a gun and shoots a student cannot avoid prosecution if the school fails to investigate the incident within five days. A librarian with a tendency to beat visitors who refuse to heed demands for silence unconscious with large books will not be reinstated because an arbitrator determined management failed to properly follow procedure in firing them. And while these professions provide essential services, withholding their labor cannot constitute a threat of violence.

But in the Blue Lives Matter ideology of police unions and the Trumpist right, failing to adhere to the correct politics constitutes a forfeiture of police protection; as Trump attorney general William Barr told an audience of police officers and prosecutors in 2019, communities that protest maltreatment by police "might find themselves without the police protection they need." This amounts to armed agents of the state, whose authority to use force is theoretically granted to them by the people to enforce the law, using that authority to determine the acceptable parameters of political expression. That is both a perversion of democracy and a mockery of free speech.

It's also the kind of fear, prolonged by memories of British occupation, that delayed the creation of police departments until the middle of the nineteenth century. As James Madison wrote in 1795, "The separation of the power of declaring war, from that of conducting it, is wisely contrived, to exclude the danger of its being declared for the sake of its being conducted. The separation of the power of raising armies from the power of commanding them is intended to prevent the raising of armies for the sake of commanding them. . . . No nation could preserve its freedom in the midst of continual warfare."

Madison's argument is commonly cited in favor of civilian control of the military. But it applies as much to the police and their "war on crime," in which the "enemy" is not some foreign power but the public, or some portion of the public. "There's now a dominant military culture within modern police agencies," writes Radley Balko in *Rise of the Warrior Cop.* "Cops are told all the time that the public presents a threat to them, and that the threat grows more dire by the day."

In Trump, the unions found a politician whose worldview matched their own. The Fraternal Order of Police mobilized heavily for Trump in 2016, which "contributed to a significant swing in vote share from Romney to Trump," according to the political scientist Michael Zoorob. In 2020, Michael McHale, the head of the National Association of Police Organizations, a lobby group for police unions, called Joe Biden, the author of the pro-police 1994 crime bill, and Kamala Harris, a former prosecutor, the "most radical anti-police ticket in history."

Police unions' endorsement of Trump did not go unnoticed among black officers—who are often underrepresented among union officials. In 2016 and in 2020, black police organizations attempted to counter the FOP's enthusiastic backing for Trump.

"Police unions are involved in activities that are to the detriment of officers of color. And an example of that is the National FOP endorsing President Trump recently before the election," said Sonia Pruitt, a retired Montgomery County Police captain and a former chair of the National Black Police Association. "And there was an outcry from black officers because they were like, 'Well, nobody asked us,' you know, 'We don't support him.'"

The political dilemma would not be solved if police unions' allegiance were to the Democratic Party—in either case, their overt partisanship would risk the possibility that officers would see themselves as members of a political faction to whom they owe their ultimate loyalty, instead of the public. More bipartisan support would simply insulate them further from democratic control.

The question is why there should be police unions at all. Because the defining labor of police is violence, any police union is bound to eventually want to negotiate leniency for the misuse of violence by its members and to advocate not only for policies that guarantee that leniency but for politicians who will secure it. That guarantee is rooted in part in the racial disparities of police misconduct, which also insulate police from political backlash. That makes the preservation of such disparities a political interest for police unions, which can easily override the preferences of black officers, who tend to have more sympathy for the targets of police misconduct.

Some liberals acknowledge that police unions are an obstacle to reform but argue that workers—even police—have a fundamental right to organize for better wages and benefits. Indeed, the former officers I spoke to argued that unions helped secure financial stability or protected them from capricious decisions by management. "Police unions are valuable in that they were created to ensure due process for police officers and great working conditions. My retirement benefits are outstanding because of the union's negotiation with the county that I worked in," Pruitt told me.

Similarly, Quinn pointed out that there are instances where "departments do go after cops that they don't like for one reason or another," recalling an instance where management tried to get one of his colleagues fired for reporting misconduct by a supervisor.

The military is hardly exempt from questions of fair pay, or capricious or ineffective leadership, or even politics. But civilian control of the armed services is nevertheless considered sacrosanct, because a democracy where government officials with guns and uniforms make the decisions has ceased to be one. Because it lacks an organized political entity like police unions that can place it beyond democratic accountability, the military relies instead on public support, which means maintaining an outward stance of political neutrality—it is no coincidence that high-ranking former members of the otherwise deeply conservative military establishment spoke out following rumors that Trump might invoke the Insurrection Act to interrupt the transition of power between the Trump and Biden administrations.

Plenty of veterans can and do participate in politics, and so do some veteran-run organizations. But they cannot be said to speak for the military as a whole the way police unions do. If police unions were abolished, officers and former officers could still, as individual citizens and as part of police organizations, speak out in favor of their politics. But they would lack the power to negotiate getting away with murder as a condition of employment, or to collectively withdraw the state's cloak of protection from citizens who protest their conduct. The existence of powerful organizations that advocate for armed agents of the state at the expense of the public they serve is not simply an obstacle to reform. It is dangerous.

IN EARLY JANUARY 2021, HOPING to reverse his loss to Joe Biden in the 2020 election, Trump incited an armed mob to storm the Capitol Building as legislators were preparing for the ceremonial accounting of electoral votes. The rioters sought out Vice President Mike Pence—Trump had misled the crowd into believing Pence could overturn the election—and Democratic House Speaker Nancy Pelosi, chanting "Hang Mike Pence" and "Where's Nancy?"

Lawmakers and their staff evacuated before the mob forced their way into the building, but there were at least five deaths connected to the riot. One rioter was shot when she tried to breach a hallway "just yards" away from federal lawmakers. Several dozen Capitol Police officers were injured by the mob, which reportedly included a number of off-duty police and former military. Six Capitol Police officers were suspended for their actions during the riot—at least twenty-nine others were under investigation by late February. One officer, a black Iraq War veteran named Eugene Goodman, led a crowd away from an unprotected wing of the Senate and in doing so may have prevented lawmakers from being lynched.

The badly outnumbered Capitol Police were eventually reinforced by riot cops from the local metropolitan police, after political appointees at the Pentagon denied requests for assistance from the D.C. National Guard. As police tried to disperse the rioters, a reporter from *The Nation* heard a woman cry out, "They're shooting at us. They're supposed to shoot BLM, but they're shooting the patriots." It took three days for Trump to lower the White House flag in honor of Brian Sicknick, an officer who suffered multiple strokes hours after confronting rioters at the Capitol.

Trump's reluctance to honor a police officer who fell in the line of duty—one who was also an outspoken supporter of his—may seem strange. But in repelling the rioters' assault on democracy, the Capitol Police who resisted the mob had breached their contract with the Trump supporters drawn to Blue Lives Matter. That slogan was never an assertion of the value of police officers' individual lives. It was an affirmation of the role of police in maintaining the racial order Trump had promised to restore. The Capitol riot was their last opportunity to make America great again, by overturning the election. The Capitol Police officers who did their duty became traitors, because they placed the oaths they swore to the Constitution over the corrupt bargain that Trump had offered them, and over their responsibility to maintain America's traditional racial hegemony. Those officers' "blue lives" thus ceased to matter to the mob. This was, in a way, the logic of police unions turned upon individual officers: They had broken the code, and forfeited their elevated status in doing so.

"I got called [the n-word] a couple of dozen times today" while protecting the Capitol, Harry Dunn, a black Capitol Police officer, told ABC News. "Is this America? They beat officers with Blue Lives Matter flags. They fought us. They had Confederate flags in the U.S. Capitol."

The Capitol riot also strained the brotherly bond of police unions. The National Fraternal Order of Police quietly released a letter condemning the mob and expressing sympathy with the dead and injured officers. But there was no parade of police-union officials on cable television condemning the MAGA mob as "terrorists" or "animals." There were no announcements that off-duty cops would refuse to work security at political events supportive of the mob or the lie that motivated them. That kind of heat is reserved for those who protest on behalf of black people killed by the police, not those willing to kill cops in the name of white rule. Given a choice between defending democracy or maintaining the political alliances that protect their impunity, the unions made the obvious choice.

Some police-union leaders refused even a perfunctory condemnation of the attempted coup. The day after the rioters ransacked the Capitol, the head of the Chicago Fraternal Order of Police, John Catanzara, told a local news station how much he sympathized with an armed mob that attempted to overturn the results of a presidential election.

"It was a bunch of pissed-off people that feel an election was stolen, somehow, some way," Catanzara said. "You're not going to convince me that that many people voted for Joe Biden. Never for the rest of my life will you ever convince me of that." Compared to the Black Lives Matter protests that followed Floyd's death, the insurrection at the Capitol was "very different than what happened all across this country all summer long in Democratic-ran cities and nobody had a problem with that."

This is an argument that must be savored. It is fundamentally true that protesting against unjust murder by armed agents of the state is different from violently attempting to reverse the outcome of an election, even if one is outraged by the riots that occurred in some cities. One is a right explicitly protected by the Constitution; the other threatens the inalienable right of the people to choose their leaders. Yet for Catanzara, a Trump supporter who leads a union that represents some twelve thousand sworn officers, the BLM protests were a form of anti-police oppression, while a deadly insurrection in the name of forcibly installing Donald Trump as president is the language of the unheard.

The mob failed to overturn the results of the election. But the willingness of police-union leaders to defend the insurrection after the fact, and the presence of off-duty police officers in the mob, illustrate the dangers of organizations that condition sworn officers to think of themselves as soldiers at war with the public they are meant to serve.

13

THE CRUELTY OF
THE PRESIDENT

THE BIG QUESTION FOR ME WHILE I WAS WRITING AND REPORT-
ing this essay in the summer of 2020 was, did the moment
already pass?

Most of this book has been about the historical and ideological forces behind the rise of Donald Trump. This story
is about the backlash to his rise and how it led to a moment
of possibility we haven't seen since the 1960s, when America
became, at least on paper, a nation for all its people, with the
passage of the Voting Rights Act. These moments of enlightenment don't last, however, and they don't operate on legislative
schedules. By fall, it was clear that views of Black Lives Matter
had trended downward from their peak during the summer,
in part because Trump himself was campaigning against the
protesters, hoping to capitalize on fears of crime and disorder.

Trump lost, but the rebuke was much less total than the
polls had suggested. Republicans made substantial gains in
the House and initially looked to have kept control of the Senate. With Republican control, the ambitious agenda that liberals were imagining when the polling averages showed Joe

Biden ahead of Trump by seven or eight points seemed dead. There was no Biden landslide, only a stalemate—one that would ensure that Trumpism would continue to dominate the Republican Party for years to come. But unseating an incumbent president is no small feat, and Trump's loss owes a debt to the work Black Lives Matter activists and other organizers did in the intervening years, not simply in traditional political work like voter registration but in connecting the nation's ongoing problems to the historical scourge of white supremacy. Just as the white North in the late 1860s turned against Andrew Johnson because his commitment to white supremacy threatened to render the bloody sacrifices of the Civil War meaningless, millions of Americans were able to connect Trump's callousness and bigotry to his inability to govern.

The political outlook shifted when Raphael Warnock and Jon Ossoff won the Senate runoffs in Georgia. The Senate was still on a razor's edge, but the Democrats now had majority control. The Democrats' fragile trifecta would enable them to govern, but a Reconstruction-size regeneration of American democracy—the admission of new states, the revitalization of the Voting Rights Act, a large federal effort to remedy economic inequality—nevertheless seemed out of reach. That became clearer in early January, when moderate Democratic senators Joe Manchin of West Virginia and Kyrsten Sinema of Arizona reaffirmed their opposition to repealing the filibuster, an old Senate rule that allows the minority party to impose a supermajority requirement on any proposed legislation. This would leave Republican minority leader Mitch McConnell with a veto over Biden's agenda, though not an ironclad one.

As the essay notes, there were two parts to Reconstruction: the attempt to establish and protect the political rights for all regardless of race, and the attempts by some Radical

Republicans to create an interventionist government that would break the concentrated power of the wealthy planter class on behalf of white and black laborers.

Today's Democrats face their own titanic challenge, in that Senate malapportionment, the electoral college, and discriminatory voting restrictions have enabled the Republican Party to wield power without needing to win majorities, and the nation faces an economic crisis that exacerbates the already massive economic inequality of our new Gilded Age. The Democrats will need their own radicals to stiffen their spines against the inevitable opposition.

With the filibuster intact, Republicans will be able to block measures to address these and other problems—the reconciliation process, which allowed Democrats to pass desperately needed coronavirus aid with a simple majority, can only be used under narrow circumstances for particular forms of legislation. Already Republicans have proposed three times as many bills in 2021 as they did in 2020 to restrict voting access, with some state parties, such as the GOP of Arizona, proposing legislation that would allow state legislatures to overturn election results. Republican opposition to impeaching Trump for his incitement of a riot to overturn the 2020 election results was not mere partisanship; it was a reflection of Republican voters' turn against democracy, reflected in their chosen representatives.

In 1877, an economic crisis and ideological division within the multiracial constituencies of the Republican Party threatened their aspirations toward a more perfect union, whereas the unity and conviction of the Democrats, then the party of white identity, allowed them to overcome a larger political coalition. The American people gave the modern Democratic Party and its multiracial base the power to choose a different fate, but that doesn't mean the party will.

THE NEW
RECONSTRUCTION

AFTER GEORGE FLOYD WAS KILLED, DONALD TRUMP SENSED AN opportunity. Americans, anguished and angry over Floyd's death, had erupted in protest—some set fires, broke the windows of department stores, and stormed a police precinct. Commentators reached for historical analogies, circling in on 1968 and the twilight of the civil-rights era, when riots and rebellion engulfed one American city after another. Back then, Richard Nixon seized on a message of "law and order." He would restore normalcy by suppressing protest with the iron hand of the state. In return for his promise of pacification, Americans gave him the White House.

Surveying the protests, Trump saw a path to victory in Nixon's footsteps: The uprisings of 2020 could rescue him from his catastrophic mishandling of the coronavirus pandemic. The president leaned into his own "law and order" message. He lashed out against "thugs" and "terrorists," warning that "when the looting starts, the shooting starts."

Ahead of what was to be his comeback rally in Tulsa, Oklahoma, in June, Trump tweeted, "Any protesters, anarchists, agitators, looters or lowlifes who are going to Oklahoma please understand, you will not be treated like you have been in New York, Seattle, or Minneapolis"—making no distinction between those protesting peacefully and those who might engage in violence.

In this, Trump was returning to a familiar playbook. He was relying on the chaos of the protests to produce the kind of racist backlash that he had ridden to the presidency in 2016. Trump had blamed the 2014 protests in Ferguson, Missouri—a response to the shooting of Michael Brown by a police officer—on Barack Obama's indulgence of criminality. "With our weak leadership in Washington, you can expect Ferguson type riots and looting in other places," Trump predicted in 2014. As president, he saw such uprisings as deliverance.

Then something happened that Trump did not foresee. It didn't work.

Trump was elected president on a promise to restore an idealized past in which America's traditional aristocracy of race was unquestioned. But rather than restore that aristocracy, four years of catastrophe have—at least for the moment—discredited it. Instead of ushering in a golden age of prosperity and a return to the cultural conservatism of the 1950s, Trump's presidency has radicalized millions of white Americans who were previously inclined to dismiss systemic racism as a myth, the racial wealth gap as a product of black cultural pathology, and discriminatory policing as a matter of a few bad apples.

Those staples of the American racial discourse became hard to sustain this year, as the country was enveloped by overlapping national crises. The pandemic exposed the president. The nation needed an experienced policy maker; instead, it saw a professional hustler, playing to the cameras and claiming that the virus would disappear. As statistics emerged showing that Americans of color disproportionately filled the ranks of essential workers, the unemployed, and the dead, the White House and its allies in the conservative media downplayed the danger of the virus, urging Americans to return to work and resurrect the Trump economy, no matter the cost.

Meanwhile, the state's seeming indifference to an epidemic of racist killings continued unabated: On February 23, 2020, Ahmaud Arbery was fatally shot after being pursued by three men in Georgia who thought he looked suspicious; for months, the men walked free. On March 13, Breonna Taylor, an emergency-room technician, was killed by Louisville, Kentucky, police officers serving a no-knock warrant to find a cache of drugs that did not exist; months later, one of the officers was fired but no charges were filed. Then, on Memorial Day, the Minneapolis police officer Derek Chauvin kneeled on Floyd's neck and ignored his many pleas for help. The nation erupted. According to some polls, more than 23 million people participated in anti-police-brutality protests, potentially making this the largest protest movement in American history.

American history has produced a few similar awakenings. In 1955, the images of a mutilated Emmett Till helped spark the civil-rights movement. In 2013, the acquittal of Trayvon Martin's killer inspired Alicia Garza to declare that black lives matter, giving form to a movement dedicated to finishing the work begun by its predecessors. Just as today, the stories and images of shattered black lives inspired Americans to make the promises of the Declaration of Independence more than just a fable of the founding. But almost as quickly, the dream of remaking society faltered, when white Americans realized what they would have to sacrifice to deliver freedom. The urgent question now is whether this time is different.

The conditions in America today do not much resemble those of 1968. In fact, the best analogue to the current moment is the first and most consequential such awakening—in 1868. The story of that awakening offers a guide, and a warning. In the 1860s, the rise of a racist demagogue to the presidency, the valor of black soldiers and workers, and the stories of outrages against the emancipated in the South stunned white Northerners into writing the equality of man into the Constitution. The triumphs and failures of this anti-racist coalition led America to the present moment. It is now up to their successors to fulfill the promises of democracy, to make a more perfect union, to complete the work of Reconstruction.

THEY CAME FOR GEORGE RUBY in the middle of the night, as many as fifty of them, their faces blackened to conceal their identities. As the Confederate veterans dragged Ruby from his home, they mocked him for having believed that he would be safe in Jackson, Louisiana: "S'pose you thought the United States government would protect you, did you?" They dragged him at least a mile, to a creek, where they beat him with a paddle and left him, half dressed and bleeding, with a warning: Leave, and never return.

One of the few black agents of the Freedmen's Bureau, the federal agency established to facilitate the transition of the emancipated from slavery to freedom in the South, Ruby had come to Jackson in 1866 to open a school for the newly liberated. Although some of the men who attacked him were eventually tried, Ruby, under the guard of black Union soldiers, heeded his attackers' warning. But his choice of destination—Texas—would make him a frequent witness to the same violence he fled.

"Texas was very violent during the early years of Reconstruction," Merline Pitre, a historian and biographer of Ruby, told me. One observer at the time said that "there was so much violence in Texas that if he had to choose between hell and Texas, he would have chosen hell."

Ruby traveled through the state reviewing the work of the Freedmen's Bureau and sending dispatches to his superiors. As the historian Barry A. Crouch recounts in *The Dance of Freedom*, Ruby warned that the formerly enslaved were beset by the "fiendish lawlessness of the whites who murder and outrage the free people with the same indifference as displayed in the killing of snakes or other venomous reptiles," and that "terrorism engendered by the brutal and murderous acts of the inhabitants, mostly rebels," was preventing the freedmen from so much as building schools.

The post–Civil War years were a moment of great peril, but also great promise, for the emancipated. A stubborn coterie of Radical Republicans—longtime abolitionists and their allies—were not content to have simply saved the Union. They wanted to transform it: to make a nation where "all men are created equal" did not just mean white men.

But the country was exhausted by the ravages of war. The last thing most white Americans wanted was to be dragged through a bitter conflict over expanding the boundaries of American citizenship. They wanted to rebuild the country and get back to business. John Wilkes Booth had been moved to assassinate Abraham Lincoln not by the Confederate collapse but by the president's openness to extending the franchise to educated black men and those who had fought for the Union, an affront Booth described as "nigger citizenship."

Lincoln's successor, Andrew Johnson, viewed the Radical Republican project as an insult to the white men to whom the United States truly belonged. A Tennessee Democrat and self-styled champion of the white working class, the president believed that "Negroes have shown less capacity for government than any other race of people" and that allowing the formerly enslaved to vote would eventually lead to "such a tyranny as this continent has never yet witnessed." Encouraged by Johnson's words and actions, Southern elites worked to reduce the emancipated to conditions that resembled slavery in all but name.

Throughout the South, when freedmen signed contracts with their former masters, those contracts were broken; if they tried to seek work elsewhere, they were hunted down; if they reported their concerns to local authorities, they were told that the testimony of black people held no weight in court. When they tried to purchase land, they were denied; when they tried to borrow capital to establish businesses, they were rejected; when they demanded decent wages, they were met with violence.

In the midst of these terrors and denials, the emancipated organized as laborers, protesters, and voters, forming the Union Leagues and other Republican clubs that would become the basis of their political power. Southern whites insisted that the freedmen were unfit for the ballot, even as they witnessed their sophistication in protest and organization. In fact, what the former slave masters feared was not that black people were incapable of self-government, but the world that those emancipated people might create.

From 1868 to 1871, black people in the South faced a "wave of counter-revolutionary terror," the historian Eric Foner has written, one that "lacks a counterpart either in the American experience or in that of the other Western Hemisphere societies that abolished slavery in the nineteenth century." Texas courts, according to Foner, "indicted some 500 white men for the murder of blacks in 1865 and 1866, but not one was convicted." He cites one Northern observer who commented, "Murder is considered one of their inalienable state rights."

The system that emerged across the South was so racist and authoritarian that one Freedmen's Bureau agent wrote that the emancipated "would be just as well off with no law at all or no Government." Indeed, the police were often at the forefront of the violence. In 1866, in New Orleans, police joined an attack on Republicans organizing to amend the state constitution; dozens of the mostly black delegates were killed. General Philip Sheridan wrote in a letter to Ulysses S. Grant that the incident "was an absolute massacre by the police . . . perpetrated without the shadow of a necessity." The same year, in Memphis, white police officers started a fight with several black Union veterans, then used the conflict as a justification to begin firing at black people—civilians and soldiers alike—all over the city. The killing went on for days.

These stories began to reach the North in bureaucratic dispatches like Ruby's, in newspaper accounts, and in testimony to the congressional committee on Reconstruction. Northerners heard about Lucy Grimes of Texas, whose former owner demanded that she beat her own son, then had Grimes beaten to death when she refused. Her killers went unpunished because the court would not hear "negro testimony." Northerners also heard about Madison Newby, a former Union scout from Virginia driven by "rebel people" from land he had purchased, who testified that former slave masters were "taking the colored people and tying them up by the thumbs if they do not agree to work for six dollars a month." And they heard about Glasgow William, a Union veteran in Kentucky who was lynched in front of his wife by the Ku Klux Klan for declaring his intent to vote for "his old commander." (Newspapers sympathetic to the white South dismissed such stories; one called the KKK the "phantom of diseased imaginations.")

The South's intransigence in defeat and its campaign of terror against the emancipated was so heinous that even those inclined toward moderation began to reconsider. Carl Schurz, a German immigrant and Union general, was dispatched by the Johnson administration to investigate conditions in the South. Schurz sympathized with white Southerners who struggled to adjust to the new order. "It should not have surprised any fair-minded person that many Southern people should, for a time, have clung to the accustomed idea that the landowner must also own the black man tilling his land, and that any assertion of freedom of action on the part of that black man was insubordination equivalent to criminal revolt, and any dissent by the black man from the employer's opinion or taste, intolerable insolence," he wrote.

The horrors he witnessed, however, convinced him that the federal government had to intervene: "I saw in various hospitals negroes, women as well as men, whose ears had been cut off or whose bodies were slashed with knives or bruised with whips, or bludgeons, or punctured with shot wounds. Dead negroes were found in considerable number in the country roads or on the fields, shot to death, or strung upon the limbs of trees. In many districts the colored people were in a panic of fright, and the whites in a state of almost insane irritation against them."

When Schurz returned to Washington, Johnson refused to hear his findings. The president had already set his mind to maintaining the United States as a white man's government. He told Schurz that a report was unnecessary, then silently waited for Schurz to leave. "President Johnson evidently wished to suppress my testimony as to the condition of things in the South," Schurz wrote in his memoir. "I resolved not to let him do so."

The stories of Southern violence radicalized the white North. "The impression made by these things upon the minds of the Northern people can easily be imagined," Schurz wrote. "This popular temper could not fail to exercise influence upon Congress and stimulate radical tendencies among its members."

Still convinced that most of the country was on his side, Johnson sank into paranoia, grandeur, and self-pity. In his "Swing Around the Circle" tour, Johnson gave angry speeches before raucous crowds, comparing himself to Lincoln, calling for some Radical Republicans to be hanged as traitors, and blaming the New Orleans riot on those who had called for black suffrage in the first place, saying, "Every drop of blood that was shed is upon their skirts and they are responsible." He blocked the measures that Congress took up to protect the rights of the emancipated, describing them as racist against white people. He told black leaders that he was their "Moses," even as he denied their aspirations to full citizenship.

Johnson had reason to believe, in a country that had only just abolished slavery, that the Radicals' attempt to create a multiracial democracy would be rejected by the electorate. What he did not expect was that in his incompetence, coarseness, and vanity, he would end up discrediting his own racist crusade and would press the North into pursuing a program of racial justice that it had wanted to avoid.

Black leaders were conscious that Johnson's racism had, rather than weakening the cause of black suffrage, reaffirmed its necessity. *The Christian Recorder,* edited by the Reverend James Lynch, editorialized that "paradoxical as it may seem, President Johnson's opposition to our political interests will finally result in securing them to us." The Republicans swept the 1866 midterms, and Johnson was impeached in 1868—officially for violating the Tenure of Office Act, but this was mere pretext. The real reason was his obstruction of Congress's efforts to protect the emancipated. Johnson was acquitted, but his presidency never recovered.

The turmoil in the South, and Johnson's enabling of it, set Congress on the path to the Fourteenth and Fifteenth Amendments, ratified in 1868 and 1870, respectively. The amendments made everyone born or naturalized in the United States a citizen and made it unconstitutional to deprive Americans of the right to vote on the basis of race. Today, the principles underlying the Reconstruction amendments are largely taken for granted; few in the political mainstream openly oppose them, even as they might seek to undermine them. But these amendments are the foundation of true democracy in America, the North Star for every American liberation movement that has followed.

Congress also passed laws barring racial discrimination in public accommodations, which would be quickly ignored and then, almost a century later, revived by the civil-rights movement. State governments, though not without their flaws and struggles, massively expanded public education for black and white Southerners, funded public services, and built infrastructure. On the ashes of the planter oligarchy, the freedmen and their allies sought to build a new kind of democracy, one worthy of the name.

The Reconstruction agenda was not motivated by pure idealism. The Republican Party understood that without black votes it was not viable in the South and that its opposition would return to Congress stronger than it was before the war if black disenfranchisement succeeded. Still, a combination of partisan self-interest and egalitarian idealism established the conditions for multiracial democracy in the United States.

Swept up in the infinite possibilities of the moment, even the abolitionist Frederick Douglass, who before the war had excoriated America for the hollowness of its ideals, dared to imagine the nation as more than a white man's republic with black men as honored guests. "I want a home here not only for the Negro, the mulatto, and the Latin races; but I want the Asiatic to find a home here in the United States, and feel at home here, both for his sake and for ours," Douglass declared in 1869. "In whatever else other nations may have been great and grand, our greatness and grandeur will be found in the faithful application of the principle of perfect civil equality to the people of all races and of all creeds, and to men of no creeds."

BLACK AMERICANS TODAY DO NOT face the same wave of terror they did in the 1860s. Still, George Floyd, Breonna Taylor, and Ahmaud Arbery were only the most recent names Americans learned. There was Eric Garner, who was choked to death on a New York City sidewalk during an arrest as he rasped, "I can't breathe." There was Walter Scott in North

Charleston, South Carolina, who was shot in the back while fleeing an officer. There was Laquan McDonald in Chicago, who was shot sixteen times by an officer who kept firing even as McDonald lay motionless on the ground. There was Stephon Clark, who was gunned down while using a cellphone in his grandmother's backyard in Sacramento, California. There was Natasha McKenna, who died after being tased in a Virginia prison. There was Freddie Gray, who was seen being loaded into the back of a Baltimore police van in which his spinal cord was severed. There was Tamir Rice, a twelve-year-old with a toy gun in a Cleveland park, who was killed by police within moments of their arrival.

What these stories have in common is that they were all captured on video. Just as Southern dispatches and congressional testimony about the outrages against the emancipated radicalized the white North with a recognition of how the horrors of racism shaped black life in America, the proliferation of videos from cellphones and body cameras has provided a vivid picture of the casual and often fatal abuse of black Americans by police.

"There's a large swath of white people who I think thought black people were being hyperbolic about police humiliation and harassment," Patrisse Cullors, one of the co-founders of the Black Lives Matter movement, told me. "We started seeing more and more people share videos of white people calling the cops on black people and using the cops as their weapon against the black community. Those kinds of viral videos—that weren't just about black death but black people's everyday experience with policing—have shaped a new ideology. What are the police really here for? Who are they truly protecting?"

The continual accretion of gruesome evidence of police

violence has taken a toll on today's activists; some rarely watch the videos anymore. George Floyd was killed just a few blocks from the home of Miski Noor, an organizer in Minneapolis. But Noor could watch the video of his death for only a minute before turning away.

"I've seen enough," Noor told me. "I don't want to see any more." But the work of Cullors, Noor, and others ensured that these videos dramatically shifted public opinion about racism and American policing.

After the rise of Barack Obama, large numbers of white Americans became convinced not only that racism was a thing of the past but also that, to the extent racial prejudice remained a factor in American life, white people were its primary victims. "In 2008, in the battleground states, more white voters thought reverse discrimination was a bigger deal than classic racial discrimination," Cornell Belcher, a pollster who worked on both of Barack Obama's presidential campaigns, told me. The activism of Black Lives Matter, the Movement for Black Lives, and other groups, as well as the unceasing testimony of those lost to police violence, has reversed that trend. "In the past, white voters by and large didn't think that discrimination was a real big thing. Now they understand that it is."

A June 2020 Monmouth University poll found increases across all races in the belief that law enforcement discriminates against black people in the United States. The same poll found that 76 percent of Americans considered racism and discrimination a "big problem"—up from 51 percent in 2015. In a Pew Research Center poll the same month, fully 67 percent of Americans expressed some degree of support for Black Lives Matter.

These numbers are even more remarkable when

considered in historical context. In a 1964 poll taken nine months after the March on Washington, where Martin Luther King Jr. gave his "I Have a Dream" speech, 74 percent of Americans said such mass demonstrations were more likely to harm than to help the movement for racial equality. In 1965, after marchers in Selma, Alabama, were beaten by state troopers, less than half of Americans said they supported the marchers.

The shift that's occurred this time around "wasn't by happenstance," Brittany Packnett Cunningham, an activist and a writer, told me, nor is it only the product of video evidence. "It has been the work of generations of Black activists, Black thinkers, and Black scholars"—people like Angela Davis, Kimberlé Crenshaw, Michelle Alexander, and others—"that has gotten us here. Six years ago, people were not using the phrase 'systemic racism' beyond activist circles and academic circles. And now we are in a place where it is readily on people's lips, where folks from CEOs to grandmothers up the street are talking about it, reading about it, researching on it, listening to conversations about it."

All of that preparation met the moment: George Floyd's killing, the pandemic's unmistakable toll on black Americans, and Trump's callous and cynical response to both.

Still, like Andrew Johnson, Trump bet his political fortunes on his assumption that the majority of white Americans shared his fears and beliefs about black Americans. Like Johnson, Trump did not anticipate how his own behavior, and the behavior he enabled and encouraged, would discredit the cause he backed. He did not anticipate that the activists might succeed in convincing so many white Americans to see the protests as righteous and justified, that so many white Americans would understand police violence as an extension of his own cruelty, that the pandemic would open their eyes to deep-seated racial inequities.

"I think this country is at a turning point and has been for a little while. We went from celebrating the election of the first Black president in history to bemoaning a white nationalist in the White House," Alicia Garza told me. "People are grappling with the fact that we're not actually in a post-racial society."

How far will the possibilities of this moment extend? We could consider two potential outcomes: one focused on police and prisons, and a broader one, aimed at eliminating the deeply entrenched systems that keep black people from realizing full equality—a long-standing crisis Americans have tried to suppress with policing and prisons rather than attempting to resolve it.

A majority of Americans have accepted the diagnosis of Black Lives Matter activists, even if they have yet to embrace their more radical remedies, such as defunding the police. For the moment, the surge in public support for Black Lives Matter appears to be an expression of approval for the movement's most basic demand: that the police stop killing black people. This request is so reasonable that only those committed to white supremacy regard it as outrageous. Large majorities of Americans support reforms such as requiring the use of body cameras, banning choke holds, mandating a national police-misconduct database, and curtailing qualified immunity, which shields officers from liability for violating people's constitutional rights.

The urgency of addressing this crisis has been underscored by the ongoing behavior of police departments, whose officers have reacted much as the white South did after Appomattox: by brutalizing the people demanding change.

In New York City, officers drove two SUVs into a crowd of protesters. In Philadelphia, cops beat demonstrators with batons. In Louisville, police shot pepper balls at reporters. In Austin, Texas, police left a protester with a fractured skull and brain damage after firing beanbag rounds unprovoked. In Buffalo, New York, an elderly protester was shoved to the ground by police in full riot gear, sustained brain damage, and had to be hospitalized. The entire riot team resigned from the unit in protest—not because of their colleagues' behavior but because they faced sanction for it.

Yet the more the police sought to violently repress the protesters, the more people spilled into the streets in defiance, risking a solitary death in a hospital bed in order to assert their right to exist, to not have their lives stolen by armed agents of the state. "As the uprising went on, we saw the police really responding in ways that were retaliatory and vicious," Noor told me. "Kind of like, 'How dare you question me and my intentions and my power?'"

At the height of Reconstruction, racist horrors produced the political will to embrace measures once considered impossibly idealistic, such as black male suffrage. Many Black Lives Matter activists have a similarly radical vision. The calls to defund or abolish the police seem sudden to those who do not share their premises. But these activists see a line of continuity in American policing that stretches back to the New Orleans and Memphis killings that so outraged the postbellum white North, and back further still, to antebellum slave patrols. And although there is no firm consensus on how to put an end to this history, there is broad agreement that police should not be the solution to problems like poverty, addiction, and homelessness and that public resources should be used to meet the needs of communities.

In the face of implacable violence across generations, simply banning choke holds and mandating body cameras are not meaningful solutions. To these activists, centuries of liberal attempts at reform have only bureaucratized the role of the police as the armed guardians of a racist system, one that fractures black families, restricts black people's employment opportunities, and excludes them from the ballot box.

"I want to see the existing systems of policing and carceral punishment abolished and replaced with things that actually restore justice and keep people safe at home," Packnett Cunningham told me.

The problem is not simply that a chance encounter with police can lead to injury or death—but that once marked by the criminal-justice system, black people can be legally disenfranchised, denied public benefits, and discriminated against in employment, housing, and jury service. "People who have been convicted of felonies almost never truly reenter the society they inhabited prior to their conviction. Instead, they enter a separate society, a world hidden from public view, governed by a set of oppressive and discriminatory rules and laws that do not apply to everyone else," Michelle Alexander wrote in *The New Jim Crow* in 2010. "Because this new system is not explicitly based on race, it is easier to defend on seemingly neutral grounds."

In the aftermath of the Ferguson protests, it was fashionable to speak of a "new civil-rights movement." But it is perhaps more illuminating to see Black Lives Matter as a new banner raised on the same field of battle, stained by the blood of generations who came before. The fighters are new, but the conflict is the same one that Frederick Douglass and George Ruby fought, one that goes far beyond policing.

As Garza put it to me, American society has turned to

law enforcement to address the challenges Black communities face, but those challenges can't be solved with a badge and a gun. "You don't have schools that function well; you don't have teachers that get paid; you don't have hospitals in some communities," she said. "You don't have grocery stores in some communities. This creates the kinds of conditions that make people feel like police are necessary, but the solution is to actually reinvest in those things that give people a way to live a good life, where you have food, a roof over your head, where you can learn a craft or skill or just learn, period."

BELIEVING IN RACIAL EQUALITY IN the abstract and supporting policies that would make it a reality are two different things. Most white Americans have long professed the former and pointedly declined to do the latter. This paradox has shown up so many times in American history that social scientists have a name for it: the principle-implementation gap. This gap is what ultimately doomed the Reconstruction project.

One of the ways the principle-implementation gap manifests itself is in the distinction between civic equality and economic justice. After the Civil War, Representative Thaddeus Stevens, a Radical Republican, urged the federal government to seize the estates of wealthy former Confederates and use them in part to provide freedmen with some small compensation for centuries of forced labor. Stevens warned that without economic empowerment, freedmen would eventually find themselves at the mercy of their former masters.

"It is impossible that any practical equality of rights can exist where a few thousand men monopolize the whole landed property," Stevens wrote in 1865. "The whole fabric of Southern society must be changed, and never can it be done if this opportunity is lost. Without this, this government can never be, as it never has been, a true republic."

Even in his own party, Stevens's idea was viewed as extreme. Nineteenth-century Republicans believed in an ideology of "free labor," in which the interests of labor and capital were the same and all workers could elevate themselves into a life of plenty through diligence and entrepreneurship. By arming black men with the ballot, most Republicans believed they had set the stage for a free-labor society. They did not see what the emancipated saw: a world of state-sanctioned and informal coercion in which simply elevating oneself through hard work was impossible.

As the freedmen sought to secure their rights through state intervention—nondiscrimination laws in business and education, government jobs, and federal protection of voting rights—many Republicans recoiled. As the historian Heather Cox Richardson has written, these white Republicans began to see freedmen not as ideal free laborers but as a corrupt labor interest, committed to securing through government largesse what they could not earn through hard work. "When the majority of the Southern African-Americans could not overcome the overwhelming obstacles in their path to economic security," she wrote in *The Death of Reconstruction*, "Northerners saw their failure as a rejection of free-labor ideals, accused them of being deficient workers, and willingly read them out of American society."

Retreating from Reconstruction, these Republicans cast their objections to the project as advocacy for honest, limited government rather than as racism. But the results would ultimately be the same: an abandonment of the freedmen to their fate. Men like Carl Schurz, who had been briefly radicalized by the violence in the South and the extremism of

Andrew Johnson, began to see federal intervention on behalf of the freedmen as its own kind of tyranny.

"Schurz advocated political amnesty, an end to federal intervention, and a return to 'local self-government' by men of 'property and enterprise,'" Eric Foner writes. "Schurz sincerely believed blacks' rights would be more secure under such governments than under the Reconstruction regimes. But whether he quite appreciated it or not, his program had no other meaning than a return to white supremacy."

Local authority was ultimately restored by force of arms, as Democrats and their paramilitary allies overthrew the Reconstruction governments through intimidation, murder, and terrorism and used their restored power to disenfranchise the emancipated for almost a century. Many of the devices the Southern states used to do so—poll taxes, literacy tests—disenfranchised poor whites as well. (It was not the first or last time that the white elite would see the white poor as acceptable collateral damage in the fight for white supremacy.) At the national level, the economic collapse brought on by the Panic of 1873 wounded Republicans at the ballot box and further weakened support for the faltering Reconstruction project.

White Northerners deserted the cause as if they had never supported it. They understood that they were abandoning the emancipated to despotism, but most no longer considered the inalienable rights of black Americans their problem.

"For a brief period—for the seven mystic years that stretched between Johnson's 'Swing Around the Circle' to the Panic of 1873—the majority of thinking Americans of the North believed in the equal manhood of Negroes," W.E.B. Du Bois wrote in 1935. "While after long years the American world recovered in most matters, it has never yet quite understood why it could ever have thought that black men were altogether human." These Americans believed black lives mattered. But only for a moment.

Thaddeus Stevens knew that without sufficient economic power, civic equality becomes difficult to maintain. His insight has proved remarkably durable across American history. The question now is whether a new coalition, radicalized by racism, can defy that history.

The most dramatic advances for black Americans since Stevens's time have come in the form of civic equality, not economic justice. In 1932, Franklin D. Roosevelt broke the party of Lincoln's hold on Northern black voters with promises of a New Deal. But FDR's reliance on Southerners in Congress—the guardians of American apartheid—ensured that most black Americans were discriminated against by the policies that built the prosperous white middle class of the mid-twentieth century: the Social Security Act, the National Housing Act, the GI Bill, and others.

When President John F. Kennedy introduced, in June 1963, what would become the Civil Rights Act, he saw it as fulfilling the work of Reconstruction. "One hundred years of delay have passed since President Lincoln freed the slaves, yet their heirs, their grandsons, are not fully free. They are not yet freed from the bonds of injustice. They are not yet freed from social and economic oppression," Kennedy declared. "And this nation, for all its hopes and all its boasts, will not be fully free until all its citizens are free."

JFK's successor, Lyndon B. Johnson, sought to enact his vision with the passage of the Civil Rights Act, the Voting Rights Act, and the Fair Housing Act, in what is sometimes referred to as the Second Reconstruction. But just as the first Reconstruction had been obliterated by Jim Crow, the Great

Society's ambitions toward civic equality and economic justice were drowned by its crime-prevention programs. As the historian Elizabeth Hinton writes in *From the War on Poverty to the War on Crime,* those programs metastasized into a bipartisan policy of mass incarceration. Future administrations from both parties divested from the Great Society's social programs, while pouring funding into law enforcement. This, Hinton observes, left "law enforcement agencies, criminal justice institutions, and jails as the primary public programs in many low-income communities across the United States."

Americans remember the occasion of Martin Luther King's "I Have a Dream" speech as the March on Washington, but this is a shorthand: The 1963 event was actually called the March on Washington for Jobs and Freedom. King and others in the civil-rights movement did not see the goals of civic equality and economic justice as severable. Yet they, too, struggled to persuade white Americans to devote the necessary public resources to resolving the yawning economic disparities between black people and white people.

"White America, caught between the Negro upsurge and its own conscience, evolved a limited policy toward Negro freedom. It could not live with the intolerable brutality and bruising humiliation imposed upon the Negro by the society it cherished as democratic," King wrote in *The Nation* in 1966. "A hardening of opposition to the satisfaction of Negro needs must be anticipated as the movement presses against financial privilege."

King was right. The racial wealth gap remains as wide today as it was in 1968, when the Fair Housing Act was passed. The median net worth of the American family is about $100,000. But the median net worth of white families is more than $170,000—while that of black families is less than

$20,000. According to William Darity Jr., an economist and Duke public-policy professor, fully a quarter of white families have a net worth of more than $1 million, while only 4 percent of black families meet that threshold. These disparities in wealth persist among middle- and low-income families. In 2016, according to Pew, "lower-income white households had a net worth of $22,900, compared with only $5,000 for Black households and $7,900 for Hispanic households in this income tier." These disparities are not the product of hard work or cultural differences, as one conservative line of thinking would have it. They are the product of public policy, what Darity calls the "cumulative damages" of racial discrimination across generations.

What economic strides black Americans had made in the decades since 1968—largely through homeownership, the traditional cornerstone of wealth-building in the United States—were all but wiped out by the Great Recession of 2008. From 2005 to 2009, according to the Pew Research Center, the median net worth of black households dropped by 53 percent, while white-household net worth dropped by 16 percent.

Just as the Great Recession devastated the personal wealth of black Americans, the coronavirus recession now threatens to destroy black businesses, which are especially vulnerable to economic downturns, as they tend to lack corporate structures, easy access to credit, and large cash reserves. They are also less likely to be able to access government aid, because they may not have a preexisting relationship with the big banks that distribute the loans and because of outright discrimination. The National Community Reinvestment Coalition conducted an experiment in which white and black subjects requested information about loans to help keep their small businesses open during the pandemic. It found that white requesters received favorable treatment—were offered more loan products and were more likely to be encouraged to apply for them—compared with black requesters.

From February to April 2020, according to Robert Fairlie, an economist at UC Santa Cruz, 41 percent of black businesses stopped operations, compared with 22 percent of businesses overall. This loss will have a cascading effect, devastating not only the business owners themselves but the people who live in the cities and neighborhoods where they are located. "Black-owned businesses tend to hire a disproportionate number of Black employees," Fairlie told me.

In the aftermath of the coronavirus, the nation will have to be reconstructed. It will require a massive federal effort to keep Americans in their homes, provide them with employment, revive businesses that have not been able to function under pandemic conditions, protect workers' health and safety, sustain cash-strapped state governments, and ultimately restore American prosperity. It will take an even greater effort to do so in a manner that does not simply reproduce existing inequities. But the necessity of post-pandemic rebuilding also provides an opportunity for a truly sweeping New Reconstruction, one that could endeavor to resolve the unfinished work of the nation's past Reconstructions.

The obstacles facing such an effort are manifold. Too many Americans still view racism as largely a personal failing rather than a systemic force. In this view, one's soul can be purged of racism by wielding the correct jargon, denouncing the right villains, and posting heartfelt Instagram captions. Fulfilling the potential of the current moment will require white Americans to do more than just seek or advertise their personal salvation.

Then there is the question of whether the political vehicle of today's anti-racist coalition, the Democratic Party, is up to the task, should it prevail in the 2020 elections. Reversing the erosion of voting rights is an area of obvious partisan self-interest for Democrats and one likely to command broad support. The fight against racist policing and mass incarceration is largely a state and local one. Activists have yet to persuade a majority of voters to embrace their most radical proposals, but they have already achieved a great deal of success in stiffening the spines of politicians in their dealings with police unions, in electing progressive district attorneys over the objections of those unions and their allies, and in prompting officials to transfer certain law-enforcement responsibilities to other public servants. The greater challenge will be enacting the kind of sweeping reforms that would unwind what King called entrenched financial privilege.

"Efforts to remedy glaring racial inequality in the criminal-justice system, which whites have long denied but now acknowledge, tap into principles of equal treatment that have historically been easier to get whites on board for than the big structural changes that are needed to produce some semblance of actual equality," the political scientist Michael Tesler told me recently. "Whites have historically had little appetite for implementing the policies needed to achieve equality of outcomes."

As for the Democrats' presidential standard-bearer, Joe Biden has struck an ambitious note, invoking the legacy of Reconstructions past. "The history of this nation teaches us that in some of our darkest moments of despair, we've made some of our greatest progress," Biden declared amid the Floyd protests in June. "The Thirteenth, Fourteenth, Fifteenth Amendments followed the Civil War. The greatest economic growth in world history grew out of the Great Depression. The Civil Rights Act of 1964 and Voting Rights Act of '65 came on the tracks of Bull Connor's vicious dogs. . . . But it's going to take more than talk. We had talk before; we had protest before. We've got to now vow to make this at least an era of action and reverse the systemic racism with long-overdue concrete changes."

Such a call to action would be more promising if Biden himself were not an author of the system he now opposes. He became a U.S. senator in an era of racial backlash. He worked with segregationists to dismantle school-desegregation programs and was part of the bipartisan bloc that expanded mass incarceration. During the "tough on crime" era of the 1990s, he bragged on the Senate floor of the fondness for prisons and harsh punishment in the "liberal wing of the Democratic Party." Biden's selection of Kamala Harris as his running mate is historic, but Harris, a former prosecutor, is no radical on these matters.

Yet change is possible, even for an old hand like Biden. Ulysses S. Grant married into a slave-owning family and inherited an enslaved person from his father-in-law. Little in his past suggested that he would crush the slave empire of the Confederacy, smash the first Ku Klux Klan, and become the first American president to champion the full citizenship of black men. Before he signed the Civil Rights and Voting Rights acts as president, Senator Lyndon Johnson was a reliable segregationist. History has seen more-dramatic reversals than Joe Biden becoming a committed foe of systemic racism, though not many.

If Democrats seize the moment, it will be because the determination of a new generation of activists and the uniqueness of the party's current makeup have compelled them to do so. In the 1870s—and up through the 1960s—the American population was close to 90 percent white. Today it is 76 percent white. The growing diversity of the United States—and the Republican Party's embrace of white identity politics in response—has created a large constituency in the Democratic Party with a direct stake in the achievement of racial equality.

There has never been an anti-racist majority in American history; there may be one today in the racially and socioeconomically diverse coalition of voters radicalized by the abrupt transition from the hope of the Obama era to the cruelty of the Trump age. All political coalitions are eventually torn apart by their contradictions, but America has never seen a coalition quite like this.

History teaches that awakenings such as this one are rare. If a new president and a new Congress do not act before the American people's demand for justice gives way to complacency or is eclipsed by backlash, the next opportunity will be long in coming. But in these moments, great strides toward the unfulfilled promises of the founding are possible. It would be unexpected if a demagogue wielding the power of the presidency in the name of white man's government inspired Americans to recommit to defending the inalienable rights of their countrymen. But it would not be the first time.

THE SLOW FALL
OF AUTHORITARIAN
AMERICA

THE WEATHER WAS SO BEAUTIFUL THE DAY THAT WILLIAM McKinley was inaugurated as the twenty-fifth president of the United States that the *New York Times* correspondent covering the event wondered if it augured an administration "full of sunshine, good order, good humor, and general satisfaction."

McKinley was feeling quite sunny himself. A deep economic recession had discredited his Democratic predecessor Grover Cleveland's philosophy of limited government and laissez-faire economics, resulting in a resounding Republican victory in the 1896 election. McKinley even saw an easing of the tensions between North and South that had defined American politics since the Civil War. Columbia's wounds were bound; the nation was healing.

"I congratulate the country upon the fraternal spirit of the people and the manifestations of good will everywhere so apparent," McKinley told the inauguration crowd in Washington, D.C. "The North and the South no longer divide on the old lines, but upon principles and policies; and in this fact surely every lover of the country can find cause for true felicitation."

The twenty-fifth president had his reasons for being optimistic. Having abandoned their Reconstruction policy in 1877, the Republican Party was no longer weighed down by their role as the guardian of black rights. A Union veteran and abolitionist, McKinley was sympathetic to black Americans' plight, but his party would no longer take big risks on their behalf. It was time, as the historian Charles Calhoun documents, to "fold up the bloody shirt" for good and focus on the "full dinner pail." Even the *Times* found McKinley's optimism about national unity a bit presumptuous but noted that if his party followed his example of avoiding confrontation with white rule in the South, "sectionalism will indeed disappear."

The year after McKinley praised the "fraternal spirit of the people," the first successful coup d'état in American history would take place. The city of Wilmington, North Carolina, had been a bulwark against the tide of white supremacy in the South after Reconstruction. Wilmington was "the most integrated city in the South," wrote the historian Paula Giddings. "Nowhere was the black middle class, many of whom had attended one of the state's fifteen educational institutions available to them, more successful." Black men held public office and ran successful businesses, and black women "were active in Republican clubs and a wide range of voluntary associations."

That was precisely their offense. Where black poverty assured whites of their racial inferiority, black success was unforgivable insolence. As the historian David Zucchino writes, before helping lead a terrorist mob against the population of Wilmington and overthrowing its government,

Alfred Waddell, a former Confederate officer, read from the "White Declaration of Independence," which announced that "whites would no longer be ruled and will never again be ruled by men of African origin" or tolerate "the action of unscrupulous white men in affiliating with the Negroes." The black man had "demonstrated by antagonizing our interests in every way, and especially by his ballot, that he is incapable of realizing that his interests are and should be identical with those of the community." The preamble explained that the Founders "did not contemplate for their descendants subjection to an inferior race." The only acceptable outcome of elections was Democratic victory; by voting as they wished, black men had proven themselves unfit to participate.

Thousands of armed white paramilitaries then destroyed the black area of Wilmington, killing as many as three hundred people and overthrowing its government. Jeter C. Pritchard, the Republican senator from North Carolina, had written a letter to McKinley in October warning of "race war" in the state; McKinley had done nothing.

Nothing was also McKinley's response after the fact. A procession of black Republicans beseeched McKinley for intervention, but the president would offer nothing—not troops, not an investigation, not even so much as a sternly worded condemnation. McKinley "did not make a single public reference to the killings in Wilmington," Zucchino wrote. The black journalist Ida B. Wells would later observe that McKinley was "too much interested . . . in the national decoration of Confederate graves to pay any attention to the Negro's rights."

Wilmington showed Democrats across the South that the party of Lincoln would no longer stand in their way. And they took the lesson to heart. "The white supremacy campaign had demonstrated to the nation that the federal government would reproach whites for attacking and killing black citizens, but it would not punish them or even condemn them," Zucchino wrote. "Wilmington's leading white citizens had pioneered a formula that was soon duplicated across the South: deny black citizens the vote, first through terror and violence and then by legislation."

The reconciliation McKinley and the *Times* had hoped for in a policy of noninterference with the white South had come. All it cost the Republicans was the fundamental rights of the most vulnerable people in the country—whose votes they clearly no longer needed to prevail at the ballot box.

For the party of Lincoln, it must have seemed worth it—after all, their party dominated presidential politics for most of the next half century, until a Republican president's affinity for laissez-faire economics in the midst of catastrophe opened the door to a Democratic realignment and, later, the unraveling of the Southern despotism to which McKinley and his party had turned a blind eye.

FOUR DAYS AFTER ELECTION DAY, President-elect Joe Biden reached out his hand.

"I pledge to be a president who seeks not to divide, but to unify, who doesn't see red and blue states, but a United States," Biden said in his victory speech. "To those of you who voted for President Trump, I understand the disappointment tonight. I've lost a couple of elections myself. But now, let's give each other a chance."

Biden's appeal to unity was rejected. From November to January, Donald Trump executed one scheme after another in an attempt to overturn the election, blaming "massive voter fraud" for his loss. His attorneys made no secret of the source of this "fraud," demanding that courts toss out votes from mostly black jurisdictions. Trump himself declared that "Detroit and Philadelphia—known as two of the most corrupt political places anywhere in our country, easily—cannot be responsible for engineering the outcome of a presidential race." The fact that the president had made marginal gains in such places—improving on his abysmal showing among such voters in 2016—did not factor into his perception of their illegitimacy. Echoing the plotters in Wilmington, Trump argued that Biden's reliance on black votes for his victory rendered that victory illicit.

Through the lame-duck period, Trump tried one failed scheme after another. He attempted to strong-arm Republican state legislatures into overturning the election results. Trump demanded the U.S. Supreme Court—a third of which was now composed of his own appointees—decide the election by fiat. A majority of the Republican caucus in the House joined a lawsuit from Ken Paxton, the Texas attorney general, demanding the justices overturn the election. Trump urged his vice president, Mike Pence, to refuse to certify the election results—a bizarre gambit based on a fanciful interpretation of the Constitution that would grant Pence the unilateral power to choose the president.

Trump's efforts to overturn the election reached their tragic and absurd conclusion on January 6, 2021, when the president told a rally of supporters in Washington, D.C., that "when you catch somebody in a fraud, you are allowed to go by very different rules," and that they needed to "show strength" because "if Mike Pence does the right thing, we win the election." If they did not "fight like hell, you're not going to have a country anymore." Trump then urged the crowd to descend on the Capitol, telling them he would join them.

Instead, the president retired to the safety of the White House and watched on television as his supporters stormed the Capitol in an effort to force federal lawmakers to overturn the election results. It was a burlesque parody of Wilmington, an enraged rabble attempting to capture or kill federal lawmakers to force them to overturn an election in the name of democracy, a mob that had cheered police repression of Black Lives Matter protesters assaulting cops. Like much of the Trump era, the Capitol riot was a lethal farce, spun out of the darkest forces in American history, by a man entirely indifferent to the consequences for anyone but himself.

In his attempt to calm the tensions of the Trump era, Biden's advantage is that political violence remains much less common and much more unpopular than it was in the nineteenth century. He also had the grim "fortune" of that echo of Wilmington preceding his inauguration, as a warning of the forces arrayed against his message of unity. His inaugural offered a speech that was McKinley-like in tone but different in substance. Biden told the nation that to restore the soul and to secure the future of America requires more than words. It requires that most elusive of things in a democracy: "unity."

But unlike McKinley, Biden called for unity against the forces that led to Wilmington and to the Capitol riot. "A cry for racial justice some four hundred years in the making moves us. The dream of justice for all will be deferred no longer," Biden said. "A cry that can't be any more desperate or any more clear. And now, a rise in political extremism, white supremacy, domestic terrorism that we must confront and we will defeat." The distinctions between McKinley's call for unity and Biden's are the difference between a party that had already abandoned its multiracial coalition, and a party that remains reliant on one.

Even so, past national reconciliations, most notably that of 1877, have been contingent on the abandonment of aspirations toward multiracial democracy. This time may yet be different, but the path to a more perfect union remains an arduous one.

In that spirit, the politics of the post-Trump era may be more volatile than they seem. Perhaps the Democratic Party's new stalwarts in the suburbs temper its enthusiasm for interventionist government—or perhaps its long relationship with black voters suffers as older cohorts are replaced by younger generations with no living memory of the 1960s. Maybe the GOP's Trump-era success at expanding its share of the Latino vote in South Florida and the Rio Grande Valley leads to a more tolerant party—or perhaps those voters simply become more accepting of America's traditional racial hierarchy as white conservatives become more tolerant of them. Few would have predicted a Trump presidency watching Obama's second inauguration; the Biden era may offer more surprises than anticipated.

As Biden took office, the deaths from the coronavirus pandemic surged past 400,000. Nearly a million Americans had filed new unemployment claims the week before. The nation was not only divided; it faced the prospect of economic catastrophe even as an increased supply of vaccines offered hope that the pandemic might finally be contained. Without an aggressive, successful response to the intense suffering caused by both, the Democratic Party faces being shut out of power by an increasingly radicalized GOP with a fading commitment to liberal democracy, one in thrall to conspiratorial fantasies about its opposition.

The second impeachment of Donald Trump, as a result of his incitement of the Capitol riot, was a necessary deterrent to the ambitions of future chief executives who would consider seizing power by force. But it also fell short of conviction as all prior impeachments have, despite the fact that the former president had attempted to prolong his grip on power by force. Whether Republican Senators hinged their acquittal votes on flimsy constitutional pretexts, or on complete devotion to Trump, the message is the same: The Republican Party will not punish any efforts by its own supporters to subvert democracy, not even if their methods are lethal. Acquittal was nothing less than an invitation for Trump, or some future aspiring despot, to try again. Wilmington and its aftermath offer a warning of what can happen when political violence is sanctioned by indifference.

Those challenges would be daunting enough. But the structural factors that enabled Trump's victory also remained in place. Trump was the only president to lose the popular vote twice, because the electoral college—a compromise adopted in part to assuage the slave states at the time of the founding—allows presidents to win power without a majority of the vote. The Senate, a counter-majoritarian institution that enhances the power of sparsely populated states at the expense of more urban ones, was split down the middle, with little incentive for the Republican Party to do more than thwart Democratic ambitions in the hopes of seizing power again. The Gilded Age inequality of the early twenty-first century, and the political polarization that accompanies it, cannot be addressed without rebalancing the concentration of corporate power at the expense of labor—and all hopes of doing so legislatively run through a Senate incapacitated by the need to retain sixty votes to defeat a filibuster.

Those quandaries—political, racial, and economic—are all linked, but the ability of one president to address them before his administration is consumed by backlash is deeply constrained both by the narrow majorities of his party and the broad ideological disposition of his coalition.

The legacy of the Trump era, then, may linger with us for some time, even if the man himself does not. As much as he may have appeared to be the driver of the forces tearing the country apart, he was more a consequence of them, of our failure as a nation to live up to our founding promises. The cruelty was the point, but it was also always a part of us.

ACKNOWLEDGMENTS

I will forever be grateful to Alia Hanna Habib, my agent, for telling me that this book was a good idea and encouraging me to pursue it. I am also deeply thankful to my editors, Elizabeth Mendez Berry and Chris Jackson, for their creativity, patience and diligence in making this book the best it could be. Elizabeth, thank you for all your sage advice, all your careful edits, and all your other tireless efforts on my behalf. Thank you also to the rest of the One World team for all your efforts in trying to make this book a success.

This book would not have been possible without the hard work of my editors at *The Atlantic*, in particular Yoni Appelbaum, who brought me to *The Atlantic* and whose guidance has shaped so much of my writing over the past few years. I also want to thank Gillian White, Swati Sharma, Jeffrey Goldberg, Adrienne LaFrance, Don Peck, and John Swansburg for providing me with a platform, as well as the encouragement and feedback to make those pieces work. I also want to thank my colleagues Vann Newkirk and Hannah Giorgis for taking the time to read my work and offer suggestions, even though they had their own deadlines to meet.

I owe a great debt of gratitude to Ta-Nehisi Coates, Spencer Ackerman, Matt Bors, Gershom Gorenberg, Sara Yasin, Dara Lind, Rich Yeselson, and Wesley Lowery for taking the time to read early drafts of my pieces and for offering their generous and insightful feedback. This book is stronger because of your wisdom and judgement.

I also want to thank the historians and academics who have done so much work documenting the facts of the American present and past, so that those facts are there when our public memory fails us or when most of us find it too painful to look. Only by understanding the road we have taken can we be sure not to take the wrong path again, and without your work, we would have no maps to guide us.

I simply would not be here without my teachers, who gave shelter and focus to a troubled and angry teenager. I want to express my deepest appreciation to the educators at the Duke Ellington School of the Arts, in particular Donal Leace, who introduced me to Du Bois; Ken Johnson, who showed me how to tell a story; Cullen Swinson, who taught me to find wisdom in tradition; and Tracie Jade Jenkins, who showed me how thin the walls of the diaspora can be. I will also always be grateful to Kiese Laymon, who never told me explicitly when I was wrong but somehow still pointed me in the right direction.

Book writing is an anguished process, even when, as in this case, some of the material has already been published. I am so grateful to my family for supporting me through all of it, especially my courageous and brilliant wife, Alicia, and our little Honeybee; my ingenious brother Jared; and all of my sweet cousins, uncles, and aunts, whose weekly Zoom calls during the pandemic kept me tethered to a world of kindness and comfort.

Most of all I want to thank my parents, Jacquelyn and Daniel, who have loved me my entire life in a way I did not truly understand until I had a child of my own. Thank you for your patience, your sacrifices, and all the wounds that you had to endure to give me a chance at the life I have led.

NOTES

INTRODUCTION PROMISES MADE, PROMISES KEPT

xv   **"cannot be bought":** Robert Costa and Philip Rucker, "Trump Struggles to Turn Political Fling into Durable Campaign," *The Washington Post* (August 9, 2015), washingtonpost .com/politics/inside-trumps-orbit-growing-pains-for-a-sudden -front-runner/2015/08/09/7672a8be-3ec6-11e5-9443 -3ef23099398b_story.html.

xviii **the son of another president:** TPC Staff, "Distributional Analysis of the Conference Agreement for the Tax Cuts and Jobs Act" (Washington, D.C.: Tax Policy Center, 2017), taxpolicycenter.org/publications/distributional-analysis -conference-agreement-tax-cuts-and-jobs-act/full.

xviii **greatest victim:** Ashley Parker, Philip Rucker, and Josh Dawsey, "Trump the Victim: President Complains in Private About the Pandemic Hurting Him," *The Washington Post* (July 9, 2020). "Trump often launches into a monologue placing himself at the center of the nation's turmoil. The president has cast himself in the starring role of the blameless victim—of a deadly pandemic, of a stalled economy, of deep-seated racial unrest, all of which happened *to him* rather than the country" (emphasis in original). washingtonpost.com/politics/trump-the -victim-president-complains-in-private-about-the-pandemic -hurting-himself/2020/07/09/187142c6-c089-11ea-864a -0dd31b9d6917_story.html.

xviii **black and Latino voters:** Tara Bahrampour, "New Evidence Shows Contact Between Trump Official and Republican Redistricting Expert over Census Citizenship Question, Contradicting Earlier DOJ Claims," *The Washington Post* (November 12, 2019). The report notes that "a member of the president's transition team communicated directly about adding a citizenship question to the 2020 Census with a Republican redistricting strategist who determined the question would help Republicans and non-Hispanic whites."

xviii **crushed protests against brutality:** Robert Costa, Seung Min Kim, and Josh Dawsey, "Trump Calls Governors 'Weak,' Urges Them to Use Force Against Unruly Protests," *The Washington Post* (June 1, 2020). The headline makes a distinction the president himself does not make in urging governors to "dominate" protesters. In a July 2017 speech to police in Long Island, New York, Trump told his audience, "Please don't be too nice" to suspects, eliciting laughter and applause.

xviii **talk of systemic racism:** Haley Fuchs, "Trump Attack on Diversity Training Has a Quick and Chilling Effect," *The New York Times* (October 13, 2020). One of the few civil-rights investigations launched in the Trump era was into Princeton after the school's president announced efforts to "combat systemic racism at Princeton and beyond." Needless to say, if efforts toward inclusivity cannot even be discussed without incurring a federal investigation, they also cannot be addressed. nytimes.com/2020/10/13/us/politics/trump-diversity-training-race.html

xix **voting, employment, and education:** Rob Arthur, "Exclusive: Trump's Justice Department Is Investigating 60% Fewer Civil Rights Cases Than Obama's," *Vice News* (March 6, 2019), vice.com/en/article/bjq37m/exclusive-trumps-justice-department-is-investigating-60-fewer-civil-rights-cases-than-obamas.

THE CRUELTY OF BACKLASH

4 **Black voters were disenfranchised:** Jerrell H. Shoffner, "Custom, Law, and History: The Enduring Influence of Florida's Black Code," *Florida Historical Quarterly*, vol. 55, no. 3 (January 1977), 290.

4 **three hundred Americans would be lynched:** "Lynching in America," Equal Justice Initiative, lynchinginamerica.eji.org/.

IS THIS THE SECOND REDEMPTION?

7   **there were none:** "Black-American Members by Congress, 1870–Present," United States House of Representatives, history .house.gov/Exhibitions-and-Publications/BAIC/Historical-Data/ Black-American-Representatives-and-Senators-by-Congress/.

8   **"Many Northern Republicans":** Eric Foner, *Reconstruction: America's Unfinished Revolution 1863–1877* (New York: Harper & Row, 1988).

8   **were certainly not immune to those prejudices:** Emily Flitter and Chris Kahn, "Exclusive: Trump Supporters More Likely to View Blacks Negatively," Reuters (June 26, 2016), reuters.com/article/us-usa-election-race/exclusive-trump -supporters-more-likely-to-view-blacks-negatively-reuters-ipsos -poll-idUSKCN0ZE2SW.

8   **"more favorably than minority groups":** Michael Tesler, "A Newly Released Poll Shows the Populist Power of Donald Trump," *The Washington Post* (January 12, 2016), washingtonpost .com/news/monkey-cage/wp/2016/01/27/a-newly-released -poll-shows-the-populist-power-of-donald-trump/.

THE CRUELTY OF THE LOST CAUSE

18   **racial hierarchy in the late nineteenth:** Miles Parks, "Con-federate Statues Were Built to Further a 'White Supremacist Future,'" National Public Radio (August 20, 2017), npr.org/ 2017/08/20/544266880/confederate-statues-were-built-to -further-a-white-supremacist-future.

THE MYTH OF THE KINDLY GENERAL LEE

21   **"foundation on which Southerners built the Jim Crow system":** David Blight, "The Battle for Memorial Day in New Orleans," *The Atlantic* (May 29, 2017), theatlantic.com/politics/ archive/2017/05/the-battle-for-memorial-day-in-new-orleans/ 528423/.

22   **but goes on to explain that:** "Letter from Robert E. Lee to Mary Randolph Custis Lee (December 27, 1856)," *Encyclopedia Virginia* (07 Dec. 2020), encyclopediavirginia.org/Letter_from _Robert_E_Lee_to_Mary_Randolph_Custis_Lee_December _27_1856.

23   **"the worst man I ever see":** Elizabeth Brown Pryor, *Reading the Man* (New York: Viking Penguin, 2007), 264.

23   **"were reunited":** Eric Foner, *Reconstruction: America's Unfinished Revolution 1863–1877* (New York: Harper and Row, 1988).

24 **"His silence was permissive":** Richard Slotkin, *No Quarter: The Battle of the Crater, 1864* (New York: Random House Publishing Group, 2009).

25 **before Lee's surrender:** James McPherson, *Battle Cry of Freedom* (New York: Oxford University Press, 1988).

25 **"institution up to this time":** Thomas Cook, "The Views of General Robert E. Lee," *The New York Herald* (April 29, 1865), chroniclingamerica.loc.gov/lccn/sn83030313/1865-04-29/ed -1/seq-5/.

26 **"the widest possible difference":** Frederick Douglass, *Narrative of the Life of Frederick Douglass, An American Slave* (1845).

26 **"everything around him improving":** Robert Edward Lee, *The Recollections and Letters of Robert E. Lee* (New York: Doubleday, Page & Company, 1904), leefamilyarchive.org/papers/books/recollections/09.html.

26 **"naturally with the whites":** "Letter from Robert E. Lee to Robert E. Lee Jr. (March 12, 1868)," *Encyclopedia Virginia* (last modified: January 31, 2018), encyclopediavirginia.org/Letter _from_Robert_E_Lee_to_Robert_E_Lee_Jr_March_12_1868.

27 **shape their own fate:** "Robert E. Lee's Testimony Before Congress (February 17, 1866)," *Encyclopedia Virginia* (last modified: January 31, 2018).

28 **" 'liberty and dedicated to humanity' ":** Christopher Gwinn, "The Lee Controversy of 1803," The Blog of Gettysburg National Military Park (December 19, 2013), npsgnmp .wordpress.com/2013/12/19/the-lee-controversy-of-1903/.

THE CRUELTY OF THE LIES WE TELL OURSELVES

35 **Du Bois writes:** W.E.B. Du Bois, *Black Reconstruction in America* (New York: Oxford University Press, 2007).

THE NATIONALIST'S DELUSION

38 **"suffered through a long recession":** David Maraniss, "Duke Emerges from Loss Stronger Than Ever," *The Washington Post* (October 8, 1990).

38 **"not going to take it anymore":** Leon Daniel, "Duke's Run Shows Voters' Rage," United Press International (October 9, 1990).

39 **"just wanted to send a message to Washington":** Patrick Thomas, "The Persistent 'Gnat' That Louisiana Can't Get Out of Its Face," *Los Angeles Times* (October 14, 1990).

39 **"responsive to them":** Ibid.

39 **"overwhelming numbers":** Maraniss, "Duke Emerges."

40 **"it's not anti-this or anti-that":** David Dahl, "Duke Mixes Racism and Populism," *St. Petersburg Times* (October 5, 1990).

40 **"white middle class of Chicago or Queens":** Wayne King, "Bad Times on the Bayou," *The New York Times* (June 11, 1989), nytimes.com/1989/06/11/magazine/bad-times-on-the-bayou .html.

41 **"in deep trouble":** Glenn Kessler, "Donald Trump and David Duke: For the Record," *The Washington Post* (March 1, 2016), washingtonpost.com/news/fact-checker/wp/2016/03/01/ donald-trump-and-david-duke-for-the-record/.

41 **"in big trouble":** Eugene Kiely, "Trump's David Duke Amnesia," Factcheck.org (March 1, 2016), factcheck.org/2016/03/ trumps-david-duke-amnesia/.

50 **solve their problems:** Anne Case and Angus Deaton, "Rising Morbidity and Mortality in Midlife Among White Non-Hispanic Americans in the 21st Century," PNAS (December 8, 2015); Case and Deaton, "Mortality and Morbidity in the 21st Century," Brookings Institute (March 23, 2017).

52 **a nationalist one:** Edison Research National Exit Poll (2016). A subsequent survey by Pew Research provided to me in 2018 showed Clinton barely leading Trump, 44–43, among whites making less than $30,000, losing to him 37–58 among whites making $30,000 to 75,000, and losing to him 39–55 among whites making $75,000 or more.

52 **"the same or improved":** Daniel Cox, Rachel Lienesch, and Robert P. Jones, "Beyond Economics: Fears of Cultural Displacement Pushed the White Working Class to Trump," *Public Religion Research Institute/The Atlantic Report* (May 9, 2017), prri .org/research/white-working-class-attitudes-economy-trade -immigration-election-donald-trump/.

53 **even the educational divide disappears:** Michael Tesler, "The Education Gap Among Whites This Year Wasn't About Education. It Was About Race," *The Washington Post* (November 16, 2016), washingtonpost.com/news/monkey-cage/wp/ 2016/11/16/the-education-gap-among-whites-this-year-wasnt -about-education-it-was-about-race/.

53 **"was essentially unchanged":** Lisa J. Dettling, Joanne W. Hsu, Lindsay Jacobs, Kevin B. Moore, Jeffrey P. Thompson, and Elizabeth Llanes, "Recent Trends in Wealth-Holding by Race and Ethnicity: Evidence from the Survey of Consumer

Finances," Board of Governors of the Federal Reserve (September 27, 2017), federalreserve.gov/econres/notes/feds -notes/recent-trends-in-wealth-holding-by-race-and-ethnicity -evidence-from-the-survey-of-consumer-finances-20170927.htm.

54 **"similarities end":** Chuck Todd, *Meet the Press* (July 26, 2015), nbcnews.com/meet-the-press/meet-press-transcript-july-26 -2015-n400411.

55 **"It's just not where the country is":** Isaac Chotiner, "There's Been a Slightly Hysterical Tone About Race," *Slate* (August 25, 2017), slate.com/news-and-politics/2017/08/mark -lilla-thinks-identity-politics-are-destroying-the-democratic-party .html.

56 **"public and psychological wage":** W.E.B. Du Bois, *Black Reconstruction in America* (New York: Oxford University Press, 2007).

58 **"Ridiculous":** Jamelle Bouie, "There's No Such Thing as a Good Trump Voter," *Slate* (November 15, 2016), slate.com/news -and-politics/2016/11/there-is-no-such-thing-as-a-good-trump -voter.html.

59 **rapists and criminals:** Tim Dickinson (@7im), "Clinton is talking about trump supporters the way trump talks about Mexicans," Twitter (September 10, 2016).

59 **"definition of 'bigoted'":** Media Matters Staff, "Bloomberg's John Heilemann: Trump's Claim Clinton Is a 'Bigot' Is Justified by 'Basket of Deplorables' Comment," Media Matters (September 11, 2016), mediamatters.org/donald-trump/bloombergs -john-heilemann-trumps-claim-clinton-bigot-justified-basket -deplorables.

59 **"pond scum":** Alec MacGillis (@AlecMacGillis), "Yowza. @b_ehrenreich calls Hillary an 'elitist snob who writes off about a quarter of the American public as pond scum' #bas-ketofdeplorables," Twitter (September 10, 2016), twitter.com/ alecmacgillis/status/774681993846091784.

59 **"'deplorable' humans":** Jesse Singal (@jessesingal), "Not to be too cute but I have racist relatives. I'd like to think they aren't 'deplorable' humans," Twitter (September 13, 2016), twitter.com/jessesingal/status/775806963426922496 ?lang=en.

61 **"expected to adhere":** Zack Beauchamp, "A Conserva-tive Intellectual Explains Why the GOP Has Fallen to Donald Trump," *Vox* (September 22, 2016), vox.com/policy-and-politics/ 2016/9/22/12892682/donald-trump-samuel-goldman.

62 **"drive the vote":** Marisa Abrajano and Zoltan L. Hajnal,

White Backlash: Immigration, Race, and American Politics (Princeton, N.J.: Princeton University Press, 2015).

65 **during that time:** Michael Tesler, *Post-Racial or Most-Racial?* (Chicago: University of Chicago Press, 2016).

68 **like slavery at all:** Alexander H. Stephens, *Recollections of Alexander H. Stephens* (New York: Doubleday, Page & Company, 1910).

69 **"when they saw one":** James Baldwin, "The White Problem," in *The Cross of Redemption* (New York: Pantheon Books, 2010).

70 **Sokol writes:** Jason Sokol, *There Goes My Everything* (New York: Vintage, 2006).

71 **both the races:** *Eyes on the Prize*, directed by Henry Hampton, PBS (1987–1990).

THE CRUELTY OF RECONCILIATION

78 **to secure political advantage:** Michael Grunwald, *The New New Deal* (New York: Simon and Schuster, 2012).

78 **majority of the Democratic coalition:** Hannah Gilberstadt and Andrew Daniller, "Liberals Make Up the Largest Share of Democratic Voters, but Their Growth Has Slowed in Recent Years," Pew Research Center (January 17, 2020), pewresearch.org/fact-tank/2020/01/17/liberals-make-up-largest-share-of-democratic-voters/.

80 **calling him a radical Marxist:** Sam Brodey, "Loeffler Sinks to Last-Ditch 'Child Abuse' Accusations Against Warnock," *The Daily Beast* (January 2, 2021), thedailybeast.com/kelly-loeffler-sinks-to-last-ditch-child-abuse-accusation-against-raphael-warnock. Obviously, for much of the GOP, everyone to the left of Joe Manchin is a Marxist.

80 **Ossoff's nose:** Rick Rojas, "Georgia Senator Is Criticized for Ad Enlarging Jewish Opponent's Nose," *The New York Times* (July 27, 2020) nytimes.com/2020/07/27/us/politics/jon-ossoff-david-perdue-ad.html.

CIVILITY IS OVERRATED

85 **"prevent another from voting":** Richard Hofstadter and Michael Wallace, *American Violence* (New York: Alfred A. Knopf, Inc., 1970).

85 **"dead kidnappers":** Frederick Douglass, "The Fugitive Slave Law, Speech to the National Free Soil Convention at Pittsburgh, August 11, 1852," University of Rochester Frederick Douglass Project, rbscp.lib.rochester.edu/4385.

85   **lynched nationwide:** "Lynching in America," Equal Justice
     Initiative, lynchinginamerica.eji.org.

85   **a Senate investigation:** Bobby Allyn, "1969, a Year of Bomb-
     ings," *The New York Times* (August 27, 2009), cityroom.blogs
     .nytimes.com/2009/08/27/1969-a-year-of-bombings/.

87   **right to worry:** David Blight, *Race and Reunion* (Cambridge,
     Mass.: Belknap Press, 2001).

87   **"equality of man":** John W. Burgess, *Reconstruction and the
     Constitution 1866–1876* (New York: Scribner's, 1903).

87   **"a national ideology":** Manisha Sinha, *The Slave's Cause: A His-
     tory of Abolition* (New Haven, Conn.: Yale University Press, 2016).

88   **from the polity:** "Inaugural Address of William Howard
     Taft," Yale Law School Lillian Goldman Law Library, The Ava-
     lon Project, avalon.law.yale.edu/20th_century/taft.asp.

89   **"if not his interest":** W.E.B. Du Bois, "Editorial," *The Crisis*
     (October 1911).

89   **"civil rights":** David Levering Lewis, *W.E.B. Du Bois: Biography
     of a Race, 1868–1919* (New York: Henry Holt and Company,
     LLC, 1993).

89   **"out of Republican politics":** Ibid.

89   **"into the political process":** Nancy Weiss Malkiel, *Farewell
     to the Party of Lincoln* (Princeton, N.J.: Princeton University Press,
     1983).

90   **"mother-of-five":** James Jackson Kilpatrick, "Must We Repeal
     the Constitution to Give the Negro the Vote?" *National Review*
     (April 20, 1965).

90   **unmentioned by Kilpatrick:** William F. Buckley, "Why the
     South Must Prevail," *National Review* (August 24, 1957).

91   **" 'treated like animals' ":** Lilliana Mason, *Uncivil Agreement*
     (Chicago: University of Chicago Press, 2018).

92   **mending fences:** Antoine J. Banks, *Anger and Racial Politics*
     (Cambridge, U.K.: Cambridge University Press, 2014).

THE CRUELTY IS THE POINT

102 **through contempt:** Lili Loofbourow, "Brett Kavanaugh and
     the Cruelty of Male Bonding," *Slate* (September 25, 2018), slate
     .com/news-and-politics/2018/09/brett-kavanaugh-allegations
     -yearbook-male-bonding.html.

104 **not because of it:** David Barstow, Susanne Craig, and Russ
     Buettner, "Trump Engaged in Suspect Tax Schemes as He
     Reaped Riches from His Father," *The New York Times* (October 2,

2018), nytimes.com/interactive/2018/10/02/us/politics/
donald-trump-tax-schemes-fred-trump.html.

THE CRUELTY OF THE NATIVISTS

109 **"alien masters":** Paul Hanebrink, *A Specter Haunting Europe: The Myth of Judeo-Bolshevism* (Cambridge, Mass.: Belknap Press, 2018).

110 **"wanted footage":** Michael Brendan Dougherty, "The Fascists Were Using Antifa Against Conservatives," *National Review* (August 18, 2017), nationalreview.com/2017/08/antifa-fascist-strategy-against-conservatives/.

110 **banned from social-media services:** Thomas Beaumont, "Biden Motivated by Virginia Racial Violence, Trump Response," Associated Press (April 26, 2019), apnews.com/article/0da41bc7243c434b8d6522cc344c61bc.

WHITE NATIONALISM'S DEEP AMERICAN ROOTS

114 **"become offensive":** Trip Gabriel, "Before Trump, Steve King Set the Agenda for the Wall and Anti-Immigrant Politics," *The New York Times* (January 10, 2019), nytimes.com/2019/01/10/us/politics/steve-king-trump-immigration-wall.html?module=inline.

116 **"as our creed":** Jonathan Spiro, *Defending the Master Race: Conservation, Eugenics, and the Legacy of Madison Grant* (New Hampshire: University Press of New England, 2009).

117 **"Polish Jews":** Madison Grant, *The Passing of the Great Race, Or, The Racial Basis of European History* (New York: Charles Scribner's Sons, 1918).

117 **swarthy "Mediterraneans":** Nell Irvin Painter, *The History of White People* (New York: W. W. Norton, 2010).

118 **of white people:** Francis Walker, "Restriction of Immigration," *The Atlantic* (June 1896), theatlantic.com/magazine/archive/1896/06/restriction-of-immigration/306011/.

120 **"cannot be":** Warren G. Harding, "Address of the President of the United States at the Celebration of the Semicentennial Founding of the City of Birmingham, Alabama (26 October 1921)," Voices of Democracy, voicesofdemocracy.umd.edu/warren-g-harding-address-at-birmingham-speech-text/.

120 **"as immigration law":** Calvin Coolidge, "Whose Country Is This?" *Good Housekeeping* (February 1921), digital.library.cornell.edu/catalog/hearth6417403_1366_002.

122 **"cannot endure criticism":** Franz Boas, "Inventing a Great Race," *The New Republic* (January 13, 1917).

124 **"thus is made permanent":** David Reed, "America of the Melting Pot Comes to an End," *The New York Times* (April 27, 1924), nytimes.com/1924/04/27/archives/america-of-the -melting-pot-comes-to-end-effects-of-new-immigration.html.

124 **"has definitely ended":** Roger Daniels, *Guarding the Golden Door: American Immigration Policy and Immigrants Since 1882* (New York: Hill and Wang, 2004).

124 **January 1933:** Harold Callender, "The Nazi Mind: A Study in Nationalism," *The New York Times* (January 3, 1932). nytimes .com/1932/01/03/archives/the-nazi-mind-a-study-in -nationalism-what-is-happening-in-germany.html.

124 **"conception of the state":** James Q. Whitman, *Hitler's American Model* (Princeton, N.J.: Princeton University Press, 2018).

127 **national experiment:** John Higham, *Strangers in the Land: Patterns in American Nativism 1860–1925* (New Brunswick, N.J.: Rutgers University Press, 1955).

127 **nonwhites were not:** Ira Katznelson, *Fear Itself: The New Deal and the Origins of Our Time* (New York: W. W. Norton, 2013).

THE CRUELTY OF THE STEPHEN MILLERS

135 **of immigration detention:** Dara Lind, "The Disastrous, Forgotten 1996 Law That Created Today's Immigration Problem," *Vox* (April 28, 2016). "The '96 law essentially invented immigration enforcement as we know it today—where deportation is a constant and plausible threat to millions of immigrants." vox.com/2016/4/28/11515132/iirira-clinton -immigration.

135 **the "Dreamers," from deportation:** Muzaffar Chishti and Sarah Pierce, "Trump's Promise of Millions of Deportations Is Yet to Be Fulfilled," Migration Policy Institute, October 29, 2020. The authors note that "the Trump administration deported only slightly more than one-third as many unauthorized immigrants from the interior during its first four fiscal years than did the Obama administration during the same timeframe." Perhaps ironically, the Trump administration's fixation on deporting undocumented immigrants indiscriminately, rather than retaining the Obama-era prioritization of those with criminal records, appears to have slowed the process.

NOT THE RIGHT WAY

137 **colonial overseers:** Anthony Vaver, *Bound with an Iron Chain* (Westborough, Mass.: Pickpocket Publishing, 2011); Emily Jones Salmon, "Convict Labor During the Colonial Period," *Encyclopedia Virginia* (14 Dec. 2020). Web. 08 Mar. 2021. encyclopediavirginia.org/Convict_Labor_During_the_Colonial _Period.

138 **"useful citizens":** Alida C. Bowler and Edith Abbott, Wickersham Commission, "Report on Crime and the Foreign Born" (Washington, D.C.: U.S. Government Printing Office, 1931).

140 **"everybody's legal":** Mae Ngai, *Impossible Subjects: Illegal Aliens and the Making of Modern America* (Princeton, N.J.: Princeton University Press, 2004).

141 **considered to be nonwhite:** Michael Edison Hayden, "Stephen Miller's Affinity for White Nationalism Revealed in Leaked Emails," Southern Poverty Law Center (November 12, 2019), splcenter.org/hatewatch/2019/11/12/stephen-millers-affinity -white-nationalism-revealed-leaked-emails.

141 **told NPR in 2019:** "Former Breitbart Editor Katie McHugh on Stephen Miller and White Supremacy," National Public Radio (December 15, 2019), npr.org/2019/12/15/788195178/ former-breitbart-editor-katie-mchugh-on-stephen-miller-and -white-supremacy.

142 **published by the Southern Poverty Law Center:** Rosie Gray, "Get Out While You Can," BuzzFeed News (May 1, 2019), buzzfeednews.com/article/rosiegray/katie-mchugh.

142 **conceive of the national interest:** Muzaffar Chishti, Faye Hipsman, and Isabel Ball, "Fifty Years On, the 1965 Immigration and Nationality Act Continues to Reshape the United States," Migration Policy Institute (October 15, 2015), migrationpolicy.org/article/fifty-years-1965-immigration-and -nationality-act-continues-reshape-united-states.

143 **"named in the new rule":** Randy Capps, Julia Gelatt, and Mark Greenberg, "The Public-Charge Rule: Broad Impacts, but Few Will Be Denied Green Cards Based on Actual Benefits Use," Migration Policy Institute (March 2020), migrationpolicy .org/news/public-charge-denial-green-cards-benefits-use.

144 **"poor prospects":** David Roediger, *Working Toward Whiteness: How America's Immigrants Became White* (New York: Basic Books, 2005).

144 **"small wine village":** Kristine Phillips, "The Story of Donald Trump's Grandfather, Who Came to the U.S. as an

Unaccompanied Minor," *The Washington Post* (July 12, 2018), washingtonpost.com/news/retropolis/wp/2018/06/27/the -story-of-donald-trumps-grandfather-who-came-to-the-u-s-as-an -unaccompanied-minor/.

144 **poverty or persecution:** Ben Strauss, "How John Kelly's Boston Neighborhood Led Him to Trump's Side," *Politico Magazine* (April 10, 2018), politico.com/magazine/story/2018/04/10/ john-kelly-boston-neighborhood-donald-trump-217839/.

145 **maternal grandmother:** Ruth Glosser, *A Precious Legacy* (Pennsylvania: self-published, 1998). Provided to the author by David Glosser.

148 **ultimately barred from entering:** Ngai, *Impossible Subjects.*

149 **across the border:** Peter Schrag, *Not Fit for Our Society* (Berkeley: University of California Press, 2010). "The State Department, fearing Mexican retaliation against, among other targets, the growing number of U.S.-owned businesses south of the border, deterred Congress, substituting, among other things, stricter border inspections and tighter enforcement by consular officials of the long-standing restrictions on contract labor and on the entry of those likely to become public charges."

150 **near her home:** Kelly Lytle Hernández, *Migra! A History of the U.S. Border Patrol* (Berkeley: University of California Press, 2010).

151 **"humane deportation":** Yanan Wang, "Donald Trump's 'Humane' 1950s Model for Deportation, 'Operation Wetback,' Was Anything But," *The Washington Post* (November 11, 2015), washingtonpost.com/news/morning-mix/wp/2015/09/30/ donald-trumps-humane-1950s-model-for-deportation-operation -wetback-was-anything-but/.

151 **"civilized country":** Wickersham Commission, "Report on Enforcement of Deportation Laws of the United States" (Washington, D.C.: U.S. Government Printing Office, 1931).

152 **"with kids":** Michael D. Shear, Katie Benner, and Michael S. Schmidt, "'We Need to Take Away Children,' No Matter How Young, Justice Dept. Officials Said," *The New York Times* (October 6, 2020), nytimes.com/2020/10/06/us/politics/family -separation-border-immigration-jeff-sessions-rod-rosenstein .html.

153 **"in this country":** David S. Glosser, "Stephen Miller Is an Immigration Hypocrite. I Know Because I'm His Uncle," *Politico Magazine* (August 13, 2018), politico.com/magazine/story/ 2018/08/13/stephen-miller-is-an-immigration-hypocrite-i-know -because-im-his-uncle-219351.

153 **"owners of capital":** Nick Miroff and Josh Dawsey, "The

Advisor Who Scripts Trump's Immigration Policy," *The Washington Post* (August 17, 2019), washingtonpost.com/graphics/2019/politics/stephen-miller-trump-immigration/.

THE CRUELTY OF CONSPIRACY

157 **"no other god may exist"**: David Nirenberg, *Anti-Judaism: The Western Tradition* (New York: W. W. Norton, 2014).

159 **"devoid of men"**: Paul Hanebrink, *A Specter Haunting Europe: The Myth of Judeo-Bolshevism* (Cambridge, Mass.: Belknap Press, 2018).

161 **"the New World"**: David Brion Davis, "The Slave Trade and the Jews," *The New York Review of Books* (December 22, 1994), nybooks.com/articles/1994/12/22/the-slave-trade-and-the -jews/.

161 **"the slave trade"**: Seymour Drescher, "Jews and New Christians in the Atlantic Slave Trade," *Jews and the Civil War: A Reader*, edited by Jonathan D. Sarna and Adam Mendelsohn (New York: New York University Press, 2010).

162 **covert Jewish plots:** Nell Irvin Painter, *The History of White People* (New York: W. W. Norton, 2010).

WHY TAMIKA MALLORY WON'T CONDEMN FARRAKHAN

166 **the world's ills:** "Farrakhan Rails Against Jews, Israel and the U.S. Government in Wide-Ranging Saviours' Day Speech," Anti-Defamation League (February 26, 2018), adl.org/blog/farrakhan-rails-against-jews-israel-and-the-us-government-in -wide-ranging-saviours-day-speech.

167 **"last one you harm"**: "The Race for New York," *MacClean's* (April 18, 1988), archive.macleans.ca/article/1988/4/18/the -race-for-new-york.

168 **"hate me?"**: Louis Farrakhan (@LouisFarrakhan), "What have I done to make Jewish people hate me?" Twitter (March 6, 2018), twitter.com/LouisFarrakhan/status/971179634757914624.

169 **"doing it?"**: Amy Alexander, *The Farrakhan Factor: African-American Writers on Leadership, Nationhood, and Minister Louis Farrakhan* (New York: Grove Press, 1998).

170 **man himself:** Neil MacFarquhar, "Nation of Islam at a Crossroad as Leader Exits," *The New York Times* (February 26, 2007), nytimes.com/2007/02/26/us/26farrakhan.html.

THE CRUELTY OF EXCLUSION

182 **"regional" institution:** Andy Barr, "Rep. Davis: GOP a 'White, Rural, Regional Party,'" *Politico* (November 4, 2008), politico.com/story/2008/11/rep-davis-gop-a-white-rural -regional-party-015259; Perry Bacon, "Backlash Against Bush Apparent in RNC," *The Washington Post* (January 28, 2009): "'I think we're becoming a regional party,' said John Feehery, who was a top adviser to then-House Speaker J. Dennis Hastert (R-Ill.)." washingtonpost.com/wp-dyn/content/article/2009/ 01/27/AR2009012703127_pf.html.

182 **"lost Eden":** Matthew Continetti, "The Two Faces of the Tea Party," *The Weekly Standard* (June 28, 2010), washingtonexaminer .com/weekly-standard/the-two-faces-of-the-tea-party.

183 **someone like Obama:** Theda Skocpol and Vanessa Williamson, *The Tea Party and the Remaking of Republican Conservatism* (New York: Oxford University Press, 2013).

WHAT WE DO NOW WILL DEFINE US FOREVER

185 **Emma Green reported:** Emma Green, "The Nationalists Take Washington," *The Atlantic* (July 17, 2019), theatlantic.com/ politics/archive/2019/07/national-conservatism-conference/ 594202/.

186 **"why he's president":** Rich Lowry, "Why Donald Trump Is President," *National Review* (September 23, 2017), national review.com/corner/trump-nfl-protest-comments-example -why-hes-president/.

188 **"color against each other":** James Kirchick, "Leave Jews Out of It," *The Atlantic* (July 16, 2019), theatlantic.com/ideas/ archive/2019/07/pitting-jews-against-people-color-wont-work/ 594100/.

188 **of the perpetrators:** Of note is the fact that while I was referring to the Russian government's interference in the 2016 election here, Trump went on to cheer a violent attack on a second American election in the aftermath of 2020. In cheering attacks on the sovereignty of the United States, Trump leads Omar, 2–0.

THE CRUELTY OF PHILO-SEMITISM

200 **Jew-haters globally:** Katrin Bennhold, "Trump Emerges as Inspiration to Germany's Far Right," *The New York Times* (September 7, 2020), "In Germany, as in the United States, Mr. Trump has become an inspiration to these fringe groups. Among

them are not only long-established hard-right and neo-Nazi movements, but also now followers of QAnon, the internet conspiracy theory popular among some of Mr. Trump's supporters in the United States that hails him as a hero and liberator." nytimes.com/2020/09/07/world/europe/germany-trump-far -right.html.

THE JEWISH DIVIDE

202 **voting Democratic:** Elizabeth Podrebarac Sciupac and Gregory A. Smith, "How Religious Groups Voted in the Midterm Elections," Pew Research Center (November 7, 2018), pewresearch.org/fact-tank/2018/11/07/how-religious-groups -voted-in-the-midterm-elections/.

203 **"only in it for themselves":** Greg Miller, "Allegations of Racism Have Marked Trump's Presidency and Become Key Issue as Election Nears," *The Washington Post* (September 23, 2020), washingtonpost.com/national-security/trump-race-record/2020/ 09/23/332b0b68-f10f-11ea-b796-2dd09962649c_story.html.

206 **"despised people":** Louis Rouchames, "Abolitionists and the Jews," *Jews and the Civil War: A Reader,* edited by Jonathan D. Sarna and Adam Mendelsohn (New York: New York University Press, 2010).

207 **to secede:** Steven Weisman, *The Chosen Wars: How Judaism Became an American Religion* (New York: Simon and Schuster, 2018). Charleston had the largest Jewish population in the country prior to the pre–Civil War influx of German immigrants, which began in the years just before Fort Sumter.

207 **"oily Jew":** Adam Goodheart, "The Rabbi and the Rebellion," *The New York Times* (March 7, 2011), opinionator.blogs.nytimes .com/2011/03/07/the-rabbi-and-the-rebellion/.

207 **the Bible:** Raphall's sermon reprinted by *The New York Herald* (January 5, 1861), loc.gov/resource/sn83030313/1861-01-05/ ed-1/?sp=1&r=0.633,0.893,0.496,0.217,0.

209 **"great danger":** David Einhorn, "David Einhorn's Response to 'A Biblical View of Slavery,'" Jewish-American History Foundation, jewish-history.com/civilwar/einhorn.html.

210 **coalition today:** Eric Schickler, *Racial Realignment: The Transformation of American Liberalism 1932–1965* (Princeton, N.J.: Princeton University Press, 2016).

211 **"regional power status":** Raffaella A. Del Sarto, *Israel Under Siege: The Politics of Insecurity and the Rise of the Israeli Neo-Revisionist Right* (Washington, D.C.: Georgetown University Press, 2017).

212 **more intolerant:** Laura E. Adkins and Ben Sales, "The Kids Are All Right-Wing: How Israel's Younger Voters Have Grown More Conservative Over Time," Jewish Telegraphic Agency (April 10, 2019).

212 **Jewish Israelis:** "AJC 2019 Survey of American Jewish Opinion," American Jewish Committee (June 2, 2019), ajc.org/news/survey2019.

212 **more perfect union:** Americans may underestimate the level of formal discrimination against Palestinian citizens of Israel—for example, what Americans would recognize as restrictive housing covenants, outlawed in the U.S. in 1948, still exist in Israel. For a more comprehensive list, see the Israeli human rights organization B'Tselem's 2021 report, which argues that the current legal regime across Israel, the West Bank, and Gaza cumulatively represents a form of apartheid. btselem.org/sites/default/files/publications/202101_this_is_apartheid_eng.pdf

213 **they have made peace with abroad:** This tension has been explored at length in Peter Beinart's *The Crisis of Zionism* (New York: Henry Holt and Company, 2012).

213 **than they once were:** Israel remains very popular in the United States, at 75 percent favorability according to Gallup, although Palestinian favorability is also increasing. As long as Israel remains popular in the U.S. overall, pressure to resolve those contradictions will remain confined to more progressive and activist spaces. Of course, those are spaces in which American Jews often find themselves. See SLydia Saad, "Americans Still Favor Israel While Warming to Palestinians," Gallup, March 19, 2021, news.gallup.com/poll/340331/americans-favor-israel-warming-palestinians.aspx

214 **"full or partial jurisdiction":** Rashid Khalidi, *The Iron Cage: The Story of the Palestinian Struggle for Statehood* (Boston: Beacon Press, 2006).

216 **which they attacked:** Mehdi Hasan, "Six GOP House Members Who Need to Resign for Anti-Semitism Before Ilhan Omar," *The Intercept* (February 15, 2019), theintercept.com/2019/02/15/ilhan-omar-aipac-republicans-anti-semitism/.

217 **"your country":** Jason Hoffman, "Trump Turns Rosh Hashanah Call into Campaign Pitch and Tells Jewish Leaders 'We Love Your Country,'" CNN (September 16, 2020), cnn.com/2020/09/16/politics/trump-rosh-hashanah-campaign/index.html.

217 **prided himself on his close ties to Israel:** Robert Bowers, the gunman responsible for the Tree of Life synagogue

massacre, saw Trump as a puppet for Jewish interests. But his stated motive, the conspiracy theory that Jews were responsible for the 2018 migrant caravan, which he saw as some kind of existential threat, had been promoted in slightly different form by Trump allies blaming the caravan on George Soros and warning that the migrants sought "the destruction of American society and culture." See Pam Vogel, "Secret Democratic Plots, ISIS, Voter Fraud: The Worst Fox News Conspiracy Theories and Fearmongering About the Migrant Caravan (So Far)," *Media Matters,* October 25, 2018, mediamatters.org/fox -news/secret-democratic-plots-isis-voter-fraud-worst-fox-news -conspiracy-theories-and.

220 **white-nationalist forums:** Robert Evans, "How the MAGA-bomber and the Synagogue Shooter Were Likely Radicalized," Bellingcat (October 31, 2018), bellingcat.com/news/ americas/2018/10/31/magabomber-synagogue-shooter-likely -radicalized/.

222 **that existence:** Gershom Gorenberg, *The Unmaking of Israel* (New York: HarperCollins, 2011).

THE CRUELTY OF THE COVID CONTRACT

228 **the pandemic more seriously:** Ashley Parker and Philip Rucker, "One Question Still Dogs Trump: Why Not Try Harder to Solve the Coronavirus Crisis?" *The Washington Post* (July 26, 2020), washingtonpost.com/politics/trump-not-solve -coronavirus-crisis/2020/07/26/7fca9a92-cdb0-11ea-91f1 -28aca4d833a0_story.html#click=t.co/boU2NIQqYV.

228 **"not make sense politically":** Katherine Eban, "How Jared Kushner's Secret Testing Plan 'Went Poof into Thin Air,'" *Vanity Fair* (July 2020), vanityfair.com/news/2020/07/how-jared -kushners-secret-testing-plan-went-poof-into-thin-air.

228 **"as the enemy":** Ronald Brownstein, "Trump's War on Blue America," *The Atlantic* (September 19, 2019), theatlantic.com/ politics/archive/2019/09/trump-epa-california-car-emissions/ 598381/.

THE CORONAVIRUS WAS AN EMERGENCY UNTIL TRUMP FOUND OUT WHO WAS DYING

232 **across the political spectrum:** Richard Fausset, "Two Weapons, a Chase, a Killing and No Charges," *The New York Times* (April 26, 2020), nytimes.com/2020/04/26/us/ahmed -arbery-shooting-georgia.html.

232 **electronic voting machine:** Josie Duffy Rice (@jduffyrice),

"The DA that charged this black woman for felony voter fraud and took her to trial TWICE is the same DA that chose NOT to arrest the McMichaels for murdering Ahmaud Arbery, despite seeing the video of his death." Twitter (May 7, 2020). twitter .com/jduffyrice/status/1258414240450457606?lang=en.

233 **"with white personhood":** Charles Mills, *The Racial Contract* (Ithaca, N.Y.: Cornell University Press, 1997).

236 **deaths by August:** Matt Gertz, "Fox News' Dangerous Coronavirus 'Mission Accomplished' Moment," *Media Matters,* April 8, 2020, mediamatters.org/fox-news/fox-news-dangerous -coronavirus-mission-accomplished-moment.

236 *The Washington Post* **reported:** Kyle Swenson and Jenna Portnoy, "Nearly Seven Weeks into the Shutdown, Here's Why So Many Are Still Getting Sick," *The Washington Post,* (April 30, 2020). washingtonpost.com/local/new-coronavirus-cases -despite-shutdown/2020/04/30/a8e5685e-8566-11ea-878a -86477a724bdb_story.html.

237 **the essential, the unemployed, and the dead:** By February 2021, we had clearer data on these disparities, with Native Americans, black Americans, and Latinos all around twice as likely to die from the disease, and three to four times more likely to be hospitalized (cdc.gov/coronavirus/2019-ncov/covid-data/ investigations-discovery/hospitalization-death-by-race-ethnicity .html). Similarly, as of March 2021, according to the Bureau of Labor Statistics, the black unemployment rate was 9.9 percent and the Latino unemployment rate was 8.5 percent, compared to a white unemployment rate of 5.6 percent. In February 2020, black unemployment was 5.8 percent, Latino unemployment 4.4 percent, and white unemployment 3.1 percent.

238 **told local reporters in mid-April:** Angelina Mosher Salazar, "'Workers Are Scared,' Says Wisconsin Meatpacking Plant Worker Who Tested Positive for COVID-19," WUWM (April 22, 2020), wuwm.com/post/workers-are-scared-says -wisconsin-meatpacking-plant-worker-who-tested-positive-covid -19#stream/0.

239 **"large immigrant population":** Albert Samaha and Katie J. M. Baker, "Smithfield Foods Is Blaming 'Living Circumstances in Certain Cultures' for One of America's Largest COVID-19 Clusters," *BuzzFeed News* (April 20, 2020), buzzfeednews.com/ article/albertsamaha/smithfield-foods-coronavirus-outbreak.

239 **to the coronavirus had worked:** Mark Gordon, Pete Ricketts, Asa Hutchinson, Kim Reynolds, and Mike Parson, "Opinion: Five Republican Governors: Our States Stayed Open in the Covid-19

Pandemic. Here's Why Our Approach Worked," *The Washington Post* (May 5, 2020), washingtonpost.com/opinions/2020/05/05/republican-governors-our-states-stayed-open-covid-19-pandemic-heres-why-our-approach-worked/. Iowa had the seventeenth highest per capita COVID death rate in the country as of March 2021.

THE CRUELTY OF THE CODE OF SILENCE

245 **"big overgrown Negro":** James T. Patterson, *Brown v. Board of Education: A Civil Rights Milestone and Its Troubled Legacy* (New York: Oxford University Press, 2001).

249 **"Old Future New York":** Ezekiel Kweku, "To Donald Trump, the American City Will Always Be a Dystopic, 'Eighties Movies' New York," *MTV News* (March 3, 2017), mtv.com/news/2996373/to-donald-trump-the-american-city-will-always-be-a-dystopic-eighties-movies-new-york/.

ABOLISH POLICE UNIONS

250 **all he could:** David Dinkins, *A Mayor's Life* (New York: Public-Affairs, 2013).

250 **"expand the police force to record levels":** Sam Roberts, "Dinkins and the Police: A Campaign Issue," *The New York Times* (September 20, 1992), nytimes.com/1992/09/20/nyregion/dinkins-and-the-police-a-campaign-issue.html.

251 **"angry police demonstration in recent memory":** James C. McKinley Jr., "Officers Rally and Dinkins Is Their Target," *The New York Times* (September 17, 1992), nytimes.com/1992/09/17/nyregion/officers-rally-and-dinkins-is-their-target.html.

251 **submit to its authority:** Catherine S. Manegold, "Rally Puts Police Under New Scrutiny," *The New York Times* (September 27, 1992), nytimes.com/1992/09/27/nyregion/rally-puts-police-under-new-scrutiny.html.

252 **"How was I supposed to police them?":** Although this quote is from an interview, Corey Pegues goes into further detail about his experiences at the 1992 cop riot in his memoir, *Once a Cop: The Street, the Law, Two Worlds, One Man* (New York: Atria Books, 2016).

253 **turn a blind eye to abuse and corruption:** Quinn elaborates further in his book, *Walking with the Devil* (Minneapolis, Minn.: Quinn and Associates Publishing and Consulting, 2004).

254 **such as teachers:** Richard Trumka, the head of the AFL-CIO, told Jonathan Swan of *Axios* in February 2021, "Look, I came from a coal mine. My grandfather helped organize

that coal mine and we didn't have any protection. . . . The employer did all the disciplinary stuff. And I could tell you, it was never fair and it didn't help in policing." axios.com/trumka -police-unions-black-lives-matter-054cab8a-2340-417c-8bc2 -e1b84ae3a0cd.html.

255 **"With few watchmen on duty":** Samuel Walker, *The Police in America: An Introduction,* ninth edition (New York: McGraw Hill Education, 2018).

256 **known colloquially as "the third degree":** Wickersham Commission, "Report on Lawlessness in Law Enforcement" (Washington, D.C.: U.S. Government Printing Office, 1931).

257 **but by "disrespect for police":** William A. Westley, "Violence and the Police," *American Journal of Sociology,* vol. 59, no. 1 (1953), 34–41, jstor.org/stable/2771674.

258 **"exercise these virtues":** Egon Bittner, "The Functions of the Police in Modern Society," United States National Institute of Mental Health (1970).

260 **"protected from domestic violence":** Richard Nixon, "What Has Happened to America?" *Reader's Digest* (October 1967).

260 **run the country:** "Wallace: 'Liberal' Courts Hurt Police," *The Miami Herald* (August 30, 1967).

261 **"unlawful assembly" in Selma:** "Wallace on the Courts," reprinted in *The New York Times* (May 28, 1967).

261 **as Barry Goldwater never could:** Joseph E. Lowndes, *From the New Deal to the New Right: Race and the Southern Origins of Modern Conservatism* (New Haven, Conn.: Yale University Press, 2008).

261 **"rejected it":** Michael Flamm, *Law and Order: Street Crime, Civil Unrest, and the Crisis of Liberalism in the 1960s* (New York: Columbia University Press, 2005).

261 **strong support of their constituents:** James Forman Jr., *Locking Up Our Own* (New York: Farrar, Straus and Giroux, 2017).

263 **"who goes in front of it is found guilty":** Chris Hayes, "How the Police Benevolent Association Became a Political Force," The Gotham Center for New York City History (December 10, 2020). Hayes notes that "the PBA, William F. Buckley Jr.'s Conservative Party, and other allies launched immediate legal challenges and collected tens of thousands of signatures from New Yorkers to secure a ballot question in November on banning civilians from any oversight role of the police." gothamcenter.org/blog/how-the-police-benevolent-association -became-a-political-force.

263 **put them in danger:** Eric C. Schneider, *The Ecology of Homicide: Race, Place and Space in Postwar Philadelphia* (Philadelphia: University of Pennsylvania Press, 2020).

263 **result in an arrest:** Wesley Lowery, Kimbriel Kelly, Ted Mellnik, and Steven Rich, "Where Killings Go Unsolved," *The Washington Post* (June 6, 2018), washingtonpost.com/graphics/2018/investigations/where-murders-go-unsolved/.

264 **public safety rather than white supremacy:** "Buckley Praises Police of Selma," *The New York Times* (April 5, 1965), nytimes.com/1965/04/05/archives/buckley-praises-police-of-selma-hailed-by-5600-police-here-as-he.html. Buckley told the cheering police officers that the white civil-rights activist, Viola Liuzzo, who was gunned down by the Ku Klux Klan in Alabama while driving civil-rights activists, "might have expected to be shot," given that she was in a car with black men. It later turned out that one of the KKK members was an undercover FBI informant. In order to deflect attention from that fact, the FBI attempted to smear Liuzzo, a homemaker, as a promiscuous heroin addict who was engaging in infidelity with black men.

265 **erasing past misconduct records:** Reade Levinson, "Across the U.S., Police Contracts Shield Officers from Scrutiny and Discipline," Reuters (January 13, 2017), reuters.com/investigates/special-report/usa-police-unions/.

266 **reinstated by sympathetic arbitrators**: Stephen Rushin, "Police Arbitration," Vanderbilt Law Review (forthcoming, posted August 19, 2020), papers.ssrn.com/sol3/papers.cfm?abstract_id=3654483.

266 **requirements in union contracts:** Wesley Lowery, Kimbriel Kelly, and Steven Rich, "Fired/Rehired," *The Washington Post* (August 3, 2017), washingtonpost.com/graphics/2017/investigations/police-fired-rehired/.

266 **"substantial increase" in police killings:** Stacey Vanek Smith and Cardiff Garcia, "The Link Between Disproportionate Police Brutality and Police Unions," National Public Radio (June 12, 2020), npr.org/2020/06/12/876293261/the-link-between-disproportionate-police-brutality-and-police-unions.

267 **"by fellow officers":** United States National Institute of Justice, "Police Attitudes Toward Abuse of Authority" (May 2000), ojp.gov/pdffiles1/nij/181312.pdf.

269 **in the history of the United States:** Larry Buchanan, Quoctrung Bui, and Jugal K. Patel, "Black Lives Matter May Be the

Largest Movement in U.S. History," *The New York Times* (July 3, 2020), nytimes.com/interactive/2020/07/03/us/george-floyd -protests-crowd-size.html.

270 **"the black above represents citizens":** Jeff Sharlet, "A Flag for Trump's America," *Harper's*, July 2018, harpers.org/archive/ 2018/07/a-flag-for-trumps-america/.

271 **punishable by injury or death:** Sunil Dutta, "I'm a Cop. If You Don't Want to Get Hurt, Don't Challenge Me," *The Washington Post* (August 19, 2014), washingtonpost.com/ posteverything/wp/2014/08/19/im-a-cop-if-you-dont-want-to -get-hurt-dont-challenge-me/.

273 **"more dire by the day":** Radley Balko, *Rise of the Warrior Cop: The Militarization of America's Police Forces* (New York: PublicAffairs, 2013).

273 **the political scientist Michael Zoorob:** Michael Zoorob, "Blue Endorsements Matter: How the Fraternal Order of Police Contributed to Donald Trump's Victory," *PS: Political Science & Politics,* vol. 52, no. 2 (2019), 243–250.

273 **"most radical anti-police ticket in history":** Alexander Burns, "Joe Biden Had Close Ties with Police Leaders. Will They Help Him Now?" *The New York Times*, (October 24, 2020), nytimes.com/2020/10/24/us/politics/joe-biden-police.html.

277 **"shooting the patriots":** Andrew McCormick, "Madness on Capitol Hill," *The Nation* (January 7, 2021), thenation.com/ article/politics/capitol-trump-insurrection-explosions/.

277 **in honor of Brian Sicknick:** Initially, Sicknick's death was incorrectly reported as the result of blunt force trauma or an allergic reaction to bear spray used by the rioters. The medical examiner who ultimately ruled the strokes were responsible noted that "all that transpired played a role in his condition." Peter Hermann and Spencer Hsu, "Capitol Police Officer Brian Sicknick, Who Engaged Rioters, Suffered Two Strokes and Died of Natural Causes, Officials Say," *The Washington Post,* April 19, 2021, washingtonpost.com/local/public-safety/brian -sicknick-death-strokes/2021/04/19/36d2d310-617e-11eb-afbe -9a11a127d146_story.html.

277 **"I got called":** Pierre Thomas, Victor Ordonez, and Eliana Larramendia, "Capitol Police Officer Recounts Jan. 6 Attack: Exclusive," ABC News (February 22, 2021), abcnews.go.com/ Politics/capitol-police-officer-recounts-jan-attack-exclusive/story ?id=76036587.

278 **"problem with that":** Chip Mitchell, "Chicago Police Union President Defends Those Who Stormed the U.S. Capitol,"

WBEZ (January 7, 2021), wbez.org/stories/chicago-police
-union-president-defends-those-who-stormed-us-capitol/
6842fa80-3b83-4396-af05-a5f15f4ac740. For more on Catanzara's stewardship of the Chicago police union, see Eve Ewing,
"Blue Bloods: America's Brotherhood of Police Officers,"
Vanity Fair (August 25, 2020), vanityfair.com/culture/2020/08/
americas-brotherhood-of-police-officers.

THE CRUELTY OF THE PRESIDENT

285 **proposing legislation that would allow state legislatures:**
The Brennan Center, a civil-rights advocacy group, found that
"as of Feb. 19, 2021, legislators in 43 states have carried over,
prefiled, or introduced more than 250 bills that would make
it harder to vote—over seven times the number of restrictive
bills as compared to roughly this time last year." Those efforts
were particularly noticeable in Georgia, the site of Republicans'
loss of the Senate, where, *Mother Jones*'s Ari Berman reported,
Republican legislators engaged in "the most sustained effort to
roll back access to the ballot in Georgia since the Jim Crow era."
motherjones.com/politics/2021/03/georgia-republicans-pass
-the-most-restrictive-voting-laws-since-jim-crow.

THE NEW RECONSTRUCTION

290 **"have chosen hell":** For further reading on George Ruby from
Merline Pitre, see her essay "George T. Ruby: Galveston's First
Black Senator" in *Galveston Chronicles: The Queen City of the Gulf*
(Charleston, S.C.: The History Press, 2013).

290 **building schools:** Barry A. Crouch, *The Dance of Freedom: Texas
African Americans During Reconstruction* (Austin, Tex.: University of
Texas Press, 2007).

292 **"inalienable state rights":** Eric Foner, *Reconstruction: America's
Unfinished Revolution 1863–1877* (New York: Harper & Row,
1988).

293 **"six dollars a month":** "Report of the Joint Committee on
Reconstruction" (Washington, D.C.: U.S. Government Printing
Office), 1866.

293 **"his old commander":** "The Ku Klux Klan," *New-York Tribune*
(September 8, 1868). A particularly interesting edition: On the
front page, one can read about Confederate Colonel Nathan
Bedford Forrest defending the Klan; inside, one can read the
Tribune's rebuttal to General Robert E. Lee's insistence that black
men lack the intelligence to vote. loc.gov/resource/sn83030214/
1868-09-08/ed-1/?sp=1&r=0.008,0.447,0.866,0.348,0.

293 **"diseased imaginations":** "South Carolina," *The New York Times* (December 14, 1868). For more on Klan denial, see Elaine Frantz Parsons, "Klan Skepticism and Denial in Reconstruction-Era Public Discourse," *The Journal of Southern History*, vol. 77, no. 1 (2011), 53–90.

293 **"intolerable insolence," he wrote:** Carl Schurz, *The Reminiscences of Carl Schurz* (New York: The McClure Company, 1907–1908).

295 **never recovered:** "President Johnson," *Christian Recorder* (May 19, 1866).

296 **"men of no creeds":** Frederick Douglass, "Our Composite Nationality" (December 7, 1869), teachingamericanhistory.org/library/document/our-composite-nationality/.

299 **for racial equality:** R. J. Reinhart, "Protests Seen as Harming Civil Rights Movement in the '60s," Gallup (January 21, 2019). Shortly before the Reverend King's August 1963 March on Washington for Jobs and Freedom, Gallup again probed Americans' views of the civil-rights movement. This time, the question asked about the impact on the broader pursuit of racial equality. In that June 1963 survey, 60 percent of Americans said mass demonstrations hurt efforts to bring about racial equality, while 27 percent believed they helped. news.gallup.com/vault/246167/protests-seen-harming-civil-rights-movement-60s.aspx.

299 **supported the marchers:** Andrew Kohut, "From the Archives: 50 Years Ago: Mixed Views about Civil Rights but Support for Selma Demonstrators," Pew (January 16, 2020), pewresearch.org/fact-tank/2020/01/16/50-years-ago-mixed -views-about-civil-rights-but-support-for-selma-demonstrators/.

302 **"seemingly neutral grounds":** Michelle Alexander, *The New Jim Crow: Mass Incarceration in the Age of Colorblindness* (New York: The New Press, 2010).

304 **"out of American society":** Heather Cox Richardson, *The Death of Reconstruction: Race, Labor, and Politics in the Post–Civil War North, 1865–1901* (Cambridge, Mass.: Harvard University Press, 2001).

306 **only for a moment:** W.E.B. Du Bois, *Black Reconstruction in America* (New York: Oxford University Press, 2007).

307 **"across the United States":** Elizabeth Hinton, *From the War on Poverty to the War on Crime: The Making of Mass Incarceration in America* (Cambridge, Mass.: Harvard University Press, 2016).

308 **meet that threshold:** William Darity Jr., Fenaba R. Addo, and Imari Z. Smith, "A Subaltern Middle Class: The Case of the Missing 'Black Bourgeoisie' in America" (2020), onlinelibrary

.wiley.com/action/showCitFormats?doi=10.1111%2Fcoep
.12476.

308 **"income tier":** Rakesh Kochhar and Anthony Cilluffo, "How
Wealth Inequality Has Changed in the U.S. Since the Great
Recession, by Race, Ethnicity and Income," Pew (November 1,
2017), pewresearch.org/fact-tank/2017/11/01/how-wealth
-inequality-has-changed-in-the-u-s-since-the-great-recession-by
-race-ethnicity-and-income/.

309 **Fairlie told me:** Robert Fairlie, "The Impact of COVID-19
on Small Business Owners: Evidence of Early-Stage Losses from
the April 2020 Current Population Survey," National Bureau of
Economic Research (June 2020), nber.org/system/files/working
_papers/w27309/w27309.pdf.

CONCLUSION: THE SLOW FALL OF AUTHORITARIAN AMERICA

313 **"general satisfaction":** "The Inaugural Address," *The New
York Times* (March 5, 1897).

314 **"full dinner pail":** Charles Calhoun, *From Bloody Shirt to Full
Dinner Pail: The Transformation of Politics and Governance in the Gilded
Age* (New York: Farrar, Straus and Giroux, 2010). Calhoun writes
that "McKinley's administration marked the effective abandonment of blacks' rights by the GOP."

314 **"voluntary associations":** Paula Giddings, *Ida: A Sword
Among Lions* (New York: HarperCollins, 2008).

315 **unfit to participate:** David Zucchino, *Wilmington's Lie: The
Murderous Coup of 1898 and the Rise of White Supremacy* (New York:
Grove Atlantic, 2020).

BIBLIOGRAPHY

Abrajano, Marisa, and Zoltan L. Hajnal. *White Backlash: Immigration, Race, and American Politics*. Princeton, N.J.: Princeton University Press, 2015.

Alexander, Amy, ed. *The Farrakhan Factor: African-American Writers on Leadership, Nationhood, and Minister Louis Farrakhan*. New York: Grove Press, 1998.

Alexander, Michelle. *The New Jim Crow*. New York: The New Press, 2010.

Ali, Omar. *In the Lion's Mouth: Black Populism in the New South, 1886–1900*. Jackson: University Press of Mississippi, 2010.

Arendt, Hannah. *The Origins of Totalitarianism*. New York: Houghton Mifflin Harcourt, 1966.

———. *The Jewish Writings*. New York: Knopf Doubleday, 2009.

Baldwin, James. *The Cross of Redemption*. New York: Pantheon Books, 2010.

Balko, Radley. *Rise of the Warrior Cop: The Militarization of America's Police Forces*. New York: PublicAffairs, 2013.

Banks, Antoine J. *Anger and Racial Politics*. Cambridge, U.K.: Cambridge University Press, 2014.

Beinart, Peter. *The Crisis of Zionism*. New York: Henry Holt, 2012.

Blackmon, Douglas. *Slavery by Another Name*. New York: Random House, 2008.

Blight, David. *Race and Reunion*. Cambridge, Mass.: Belknap Press, 2001.

Calhoun, Charles. *From Bloody Shirt to Full Dinner Pail: The Transformation of Politics and Governance in the Gilded Age*. New York: Farrar, Straus and Giroux, 2010.

Coates, Ta-Nehisi. *We Were Eight Years in Power*. New York: One World, 2017.

Crouch, Barry A. *The Dance of Freedom: Texas African Americans During Reconstruction*. Austin: University of Texas Press, 2007.

Daniels, Roger. *Guarding the Golden Door: American Immigration Policy and Immigrants Since 1882*. New York: Hill and Wang, 2004.

Del Sarto, Raffaella. *Israel Under Siege: The Politics of Insecurity and the Rise of the Israeli Neo-Revisionist Right*. Washington, D.C.: Georgetown University Press, 2017.

Dinkins, David. *A Mayor's Life*. New York: PublicAffairs, 2013.

Douglass, Frederick. *Narrative of the Life of Frederick Douglass, An American Slave*. 1845.

Du Bois, W.E.B. *Black Reconstruction in America*. New York: Oxford University Press, 2007.

Flamm, Michael. *Law and Order: Street Crime, Civil Unrest, and the Crisis of Liberalism in the 1960s*. New York: Columbia University Press, 2005.

Foner, Eric. *Reconstruction: America's Unfinished Revolution 1863–1877*. New York: Harper & Row, 1988.

Forman, James Jr. *Locking Up Our Own*. New York: Farrar, Straus and Giroux, 2017.

Fortune, Timothy Thomas. *Black & White*. New York: Washington Square Press, 2007.

Franklin, John Hope, and Michael W. Fitzgerald. *Reconstruction After the Civil War, Third Edition*. Chicago: University of Chicago Press, 2013.

Frantz, Erica. *Authoritarianism*. New York: Oxford University Press, 2018.

Giddings, Paula. *Ida: A Sword Among Lions*. New York: HarperCollins, 2008.

Goldstone, Lawrence. *Inherently Unequal: The Betrayal of Equal Rights by the Supreme Court, 1865–1903*. New York: Walker & Co., 2011.

Gordon, Linda. *The Second Coming of the KKK*. New York: Liveright, 2017.

Gorenberg, Gershom. *The Unmaking of Israel.* New York: HarperCollins, 2011.

Hanebrink, Paul. *A Specter Haunting Europe: The Myth of Judeo-Bolshevism.* Cambridge, Mass.: Belknap Press, 2018.

Hernández, Kelly Lytle. *Migra! A History of the U.S. Border Patrol.* Berkeley: University of California Press, 2010.

Higham, John. *Strangers in the Land.* New Brunswick: Rutgers University Press, 1955.

Hinton, Elizabeth. *From the War on Poverty to the War on Crime: The Making of Mass Incarceration in America.* Cambridge, Mass.: Harvard University Press, 2016.

Hofstadter, Richard, and Michael Wallace. *American Violence.* New York: Alfred A. Knopf, 1970.

Joseph, Peniel. *Waiting 'Til the Midnight Hour.* New York: Henry Holt, 2006.

Katznelson, Ira. *Fear Itself: The New Deal and the Origins of Our Time.* New York: W. W. Norton, 2013.

Kendi, Ibram X. *Stamped from the Beginning.* New York: Nation Books, 2016.

Khalidi, Rashid. *The Iron Cage: The Story of the Palestinian Struggle for Statehood.* Boston: Beacon Press, 2006.

King, Martin Luther, Jr. *Where Do We Go from Here: Chaos or Community?* Boston: Beacon Press, 2010.

Lewis, David Levering. *W.E.B. Du Bois: Biography of a Race, 1868–1919.* New York: Henry Holt, 1993.

López, Ian Haney. *White by Law.* New York: New York University Press, 2006.

Lowndes, Joseph E. *From the New Deal to the New Right: Race and the Southern Origins of Modern Conservatism.* New Haven, Conn.: Yale University Press, 2008.

Malkiel, Nancy Weiss. *Farewell to the Party of Lincoln.* Princeton, N.J.: Princeton University Press, 1983.

Marable, Manning. *Race, Reform, and Rebellion: The Second Reconstruction and Beyond in Black America.* Jackson: University of Mississippi Press, 2007.

Mason, Lilliana. *Uncivil Agreement.* Chicago: University of Chicago Press, 2018.

McCarty, Nolan, Keith T. Poole, and Howard Rosenthal. *Polarized America*. Cambridge, Mass.: MIT Press, 2016.

McPherson, James. *Battle Cry of Freedom*. New York: Oxford University Press, 1988.

Mills, Charles. *The Racial Contract*. Ithaca, N.Y.: Cornell University Press, 1997.

Muhammad, Khalil Gibran. *The Condemnation of Blackness*. Cambridge, Mass.: Harvard University Press, 2010.

Ngai, Mae. *Impossible Subjects: Illegal Aliens and the Making of Modern America*. Princeton, N.J.: Princeton University Press, 2004.

Nirenberg, David. *Anti-Judaism: The Western Tradition*. New York: W. W. Norton, 2014.

Painter, Nell Irvin. *The History of White People*. New York: W. W. Norton, 2010.

———. *Standing at Armageddon: A Grassroots History of the Progressive Era*. New York: W. W. Norton, 1987.

Patterson, James T. *Brown v. Board of Education: A Civil Rights Milestone and Its Troubled Legacy*. New York: Oxford University Press, 2001.

Pegues, Corey. *Once a Cop: The Street, the Law, Two Worlds, One Man*. New York: Atria Books, 2016.

Perlstein, Rick. *Before the Storm*. New York: Nation Books, 2009.

———. *Nixonland*. New York: Scribner, 2008.

Pitzer, Andrea. *One Long Night*. New York: Little, Brown, 2017.

Pryor, Elizabeth Brown. *Reading the Man*. New York: Viking Penguin, 2007.

Quinn, Michael. *Walking with the Devil*. Minneapolis, Minn.: Quinn and Associates, 2004.

Richardson, Heather Cox. *The Death of Reconstruction: Race, Labor, and Politics in the Post–Civil War North, 1865–1901*. Cambridge, Mass.: Harvard University Press, 2001.

Rigueur, Leah Wright. *The Loneliness of the Black Republican*. Princeton, N.J.: Princeton University Press, 2015.

Roediger, David. *Working Toward Whiteness: How America's Immigrants Became White*. New York: Basic Books, 2005.

Rothstein, Richard. *The Color of Law*. New York: W. W. Norton, 2017.

Sarna, Jonathan D., and Adam Mendelsohn, eds. *Jews and the Civil War: A Reader.* New York: New York University Press, 2010.

Schama, Simon. *The Story of the Jews 1492–1900* (New York: Harper-Collins, 2017).

Schickler, Eric. *Racial Realignment: The Transformation of American Liberalism 1932–1965.* Princeton, N.J.: Princeton University Press, 2016.

Schneider, Eric C. *The Ecology of Homicide: Race, Place and Space in Postwar Philadelphia.* Philadelphia: University of Pennsylvania Press, 2020.

Schrag, Peter. *Not Fit for Our Society.* Berkeley: University of California Press, 2010.

Sinha, Manisha. *The Slave's Cause: A History of Abolition.* New Haven, Conn.: Yale University Press, 2016.

Sklansky, David. *Democracy and the Police.* Stanford, Calif.: Stanford University Press, 2008.

Skocpol, Theda, and Vanessa Williamson. *The Tea Party and the Remaking of Republican Conservatism.* New York: Oxford University Press, 2013.

Slotkin, Richard. *No Quarter: The Battle of the Crater, 1864.* New York: Random House Publishing Group, 2009.

Sokol, Jason. *There Goes My Everything.* New York: Vintage, 2006.

Spiro, Jonathan. *Defending the Master Race: Conservation, Eugenics, and the Legacy of Madison Grant.* New Hampshire: University Press of New England, 2009.

Svolik, Milan W. *The Politics of Authoritarian Rule.* Cambridge, U.K.: Cambridge University Press, 2012.

Tesler, Michael. *Post-Racial or Most-Racial?* Chicago: University of Chicago Press, 2016.

Vaver, Anthony. *Bound with an Iron Chain.* Westborough, Mass.: Pickpocket Publishing, 2011.

Walker, Samuel. *The Police in America: An Introduction.* New York: McGraw-Hill Higher Education, 2018.

Weisman, Steven. *The Chosen Wars: How Judaism Became an American Religion.* New York: Simon and Schuster, 2018.

Wells, Ida B. *Crusade for Justice.* Chicago: University of Chicago Press, 1970.

Whitman, James Q. *Hitler's American Model.* Princeton, N.J.: Princeton University Press, 2018.

Wilkerson, Isabel. *The Warmth of Other Suns.* New York: Random House, 2010.

Willett, Donald, ed. *Galveston Chronicles: The Queen City of the Gulf.* Charleston, S.C.: The History Press, 2013.

Williams, Heather Andrea. *Help Me to Find My People.* Chapel Hill: University of North Carolina Press, 2012.

Wineapple, Brenda. *The Impeachers.* New York: Random House, 2019.

Zucchino, David. *Wilmington's Lie: The Murderous Coup of 1898 and the Rise of White Supremacy.* New York: Grove Atlantic, 2020.